RICH

REAL ESTATE
Advantages

Tax and Legal Secrets
of Successful
Real Estate Investors

Other Bestselling Books by
Robert T. Kiyosaki & Sharon L. Lechter

Rich Dad Poor Dad
What the Rich Teach Their Kids About Money that the Poor and Middle Class Do Not

Rich Dad's CASHFLOW Quadrant
Rich Dad's Guide to Financial Freedom

Rich Dad's Guide to Investing
What the Rich Invest In that the Poor and Middle Class Do Not

Rich Dad's The Business School for People who Like Helping People
What the Rich Invest In that the Poor and Middle Class Do Not

Rich Dad's Rich Kid Smart Kid
Give Your Child a Financial Head Start

Rich Dad's Retire Young Retire Rich
How to Get Rich Quickly and Stay Rich Forever

Rich Dad's Prophecy
Why the Biggest Stock Market Crash in History is Still Coming...
And How You Can Prepare Yourself and Profit From it!

Rich Dad's Sucess Stories
Real-Life Success Stories from Real-Life People Who Followed the Rich Dad Lessons

Rich Dad's Guide to Becoming Rich *Without Cutting Up Your Credit Cards*
Turn "Bad Debt" into "Good Debt"

Rich Dad's Who Took My Money?
Why Slow Investors Lose and Fast Money Wins!

Rich Dad Poor Dad for Teens
The Secrets About Money — That You Don't Learn In School!

Rich Dad's Escape from the Rat Race
How to Become a Rich Kid by Following Rich Dad's Advice

Rich Dad's Before You Quit Your Job
Ten Real-Life Lessons Every Entrepreneur Should Know About Building a Multi-Million Dollar Business

Rich Dad's Teach To Be Rich
Because the best way to learn is to teach and the best way to get rich is to help others become rich.

Rich Dad's Advisors® Books by
Garrett Sutton, Esq.

Own Your Own Corporation
Why the rich own their own companies and everyone else works for them

How to Buy & Sell a Business
How You Can Win in the Business Quadrant

The ABC's of Getting Out of Debt
Turn Bad Debt into Good Debt and Bad Credit into Good Credit

The ABC's of Writing Winning Business Plans
How to prepare a business plan that others will want to read – and invest in

REAL ESTATE
Advantages

Tax and Legal Secrets of Successful Real Estate Investors

SHARON LECHTER, C.P.A.
Co-author of the #1 *New York Times* Bestseller *Rich Dad Poor Dad*
AND GARRETT SUTTON, ESQ.

WARNER
BUSINESS
BOOKS™

NEW YORK   BOSTON

This publication is designed to educate and provide general information regarding the subject matter covered. However, laws and practices often vary from state to state and are subject to change. Because each factual situation is different, specific advice should be tailored to the particular circumstances. For this reason, the reader is advised to consult with his or her own advisor regarding that individual's specific situation.

The authors have taken reasonable precautions in the preparation of this book and believe the facts presented in the book are accurate as of the date it was written. However, neither the authors nor the publisher assume any responsibility for any errors or omissions. The authors and publisher specifically disclaim any liability resulting from the use or application of the information contained in this book, and the information is not intended to serve as legal advice related to individual situations.

CASHFLOW, Rich Dad, Rich Dad's Advisors, Rich Dad's Seminars, ESBI, B-I Triangle are registered trademarks of CASHFLOW® Technologies, Inc.

E B   E|B
S I   S|I

Visit Rich Dad's Web site at www.richdad.com

Warner Business Books
Hachette Book Group USA
1271 Avenue of the Americas
New York, NY 10020

Visit our Web site at: www.HachetteBookGroupUSA.com

Printed in the United States of America

First Edition: November 2006
10   9   8   7   6   5   4   3   2   1

Warner Business Books is an imprint of Warner Books, Inc. Warner Business Books is a trademark of Time Warner Inc. or an affiliated company. Used under license by Hachette Book Group USA, which is not affiliated with Time Warner Inc.

Library of Congress Cataloging-in-Publication Data

Lechter, Sharon L.
   Rich dad's real estate advantages : tax and legal secrets of successful real estate investors / Sharon L. Lechter and Garrett Sutton.
       p.   cm.
   ISBN-13: 978-0-446-69411-7
   ISBN-10: 0-446-69411-8
       1. Real estate investment—United States.   2. Real estate investment—Law and legislation—United States.   3. Real estate investment—Taxation—Law and legislation—United States.
   I. Sutton, Garrett.   II. Title.

HD255.L39   2006
332.63'240973—dc22

2006015024

Acknowledgments

We would like to thank the following individuals for their encouragement and their support in making this book a reality: Kathy Spitzer, Esq., Michael Lechter, Esq., Robert Kiyosaki, Ken McElroy, and Mona Gambetta of the Rich Dad team and Gary Gorman, and Michael Sion for their contributions and expertise.

Most of all, we would like to thank our families for their patience and support as this book was being written.

SHARON LECHTER
GARRETT SUTTON

Contents

Part Four   Legal Strategies

Part Five   Selection Strategies

Foreword by Robert T. Kiyosaki

Before I began my business career, my rich dad insisted that I learn to be a real estate investor. At first, I thought he wanted me to invest in real estate simply for real estate itself. As the years went on and my base of education grew, I came to better understand the bigger picture of the world of investing. Rich dad said, "If you want to be a sophisticated investor, you must see what your eyes cannot see." What my eyes could not see were the legal and tax advantages that real estate investing offers the more informed investor. In other words, there is far more to real estate than dirt, sticks, and bricks. This book, written by Sharon Lechter, my partner and my coauthor for *Rich Dad Poor Dad* and the *Rich Dad* series of books, and Garrett Sutton, one of our Rich Dad's Advisors, goes into the real reasons why the rich invest in real estate. *Real Estate Advantages* will take you into the world of real estate investing that the average investor rarely sees.

Today I make my money from all three asset classes: businesses, real estate, and paper assets. But I hold the bulk of my wealth in real estate. Yet more than storing my wealth in real estate, I am able to magnify my wealth using the advantages that real estate offers the sophisticated investor.

Like all asset classes, real estate has its trends. As we write this book, there is much talk about the real estate bubble bursting. Many people are afraid of such a burst. Sophisticated real estate investors, and I, can't wait for it to happen. For that is when we can swoop into the market and ride the wave back up.

If you learn the ins and outs of real estate investing, you can make money in real estate whether the market is going up, down, or sideways. That is why my rich dad preferred investing for cash flow instead of capital gains. As long as your property is cash flow positive, you can ride out a downturn in the real estate market. The flippers and capital gains buyers who are left holding properties for resale in a plummeting market are the ones who will be hurt the most.

You also need to surround yourself with good advisors. As a real estate investor you must seek tax advice from a tax accountant and legal advice from an attorney, which is why both Sharon and Garrett wrote this book. I do not know the details of the tax and legal advantages they describe—but I make sure my tax and legal advisors do.

If you are ready to become a sophisticated investor and find out how to use tax, legal, and other little-known advantages that investing in real estate offers, and how to find your own team of advisors, this book is for you.

Preface

Why two authors?

As rich dad said, "It's not *what* you know, it's *who* you know, that is really important to your financial success."

In all of our Rich Dad books, Robert and I stress the importance of having good advisors. Our success at The Rich Dad Company has been in large part due to the advisors Robert, Kim, and I have surrounded ourselves with and consulted with as the company has grown. Our Rich Dad's Advisor's Series of books are written by those very same advisors. We have many people asking us to publish their books as part of the Advisor's series, but we have continued to publish books written by only those Advisors who have truly advised us along the way.

Real Estate Advantages reveals the tax and legal strategies used by successful real estate investors. These strategies are available to anyone who wants to start investing in real estate. Since we have included both tax and legal strategies in the book it was important to have the right authors to explain each of these strategies.

As Garrett and I have said from stage many times, you don't want an accountant to advise you on legal issues, and you don't want an attorney to advise you on tax and accounting issues. For this reason, both Garrett and I have contributed to *Real Estate Advantages*.

Many accountants may advise you to operate your real estate investments as a sole proprietorship. When you tell them you have read in Rich Dad books that you need asset protection by setting up the right corporate structure, they may disagree and tell you that all you need is additional insurance. What should you do? Find a different accountant.

Many lawyers have begun tax services as another way to bring revenue into their firms. Unless they have tax specialists and CPAs on their staff you may not want to use these services.

Let the lawyers create your asset protection strategy through the use of the appropriate entities for your investments and for where you live. And let the accountants create the best strategy for utilizing all elements of the tax law to your advantage.

Garrett has advised thousands of people in asset protection and entity selection. His advice in this book could at the least save you thousands of dollars or in the extreme, prevent you from losing everything due to improper planning!

This book will also share what you can do to find your own team of advisors. Finding great advisors is one of the first and most important steps you need to take in becoming a successful real estate investor.

Garrett and I wish you the greatest success in your real estate investing!

SHARON LECHTER

Part One

Real Estate Advantages

Does the government care if you own real estate?

Not really.

Does the government offer significant advantages if you do own real estate?

Absolutely.

But aren't there risks that limit the benefits of owning real estate?

Perhaps.

Have the rich figured out ways to minimize that risk to their advantage?

Of course.

And so can you.

Real estate offers huge financial advantages to those who will learn the system. And, as this book will illustrate, any risks can efficiently be managed through insurance, legal structures, and other common strategies that are neither difficult nor expensive. There are great advantages to investing in real estate both as a moneymaking business and as a wealth builder. And the financial benefits flow from several sources, including the appreciation of your land and property values and the monthly cash flow you can earn by renting out residential, office, or commercial space in a structure on your land. In addition, you stand to benefit greatly through tax reduction from depreciation on those structures and through options to roll over profits, as allowed in the tax code. You can even benefit from writing off business expenses associated with your investment. And because of these advantages, it is easier to raise capital for real estate ventures.

Real estate investors can accelerate their wealth building much faster than with other assets, such as stocks, bonds, and tax-deferred retirement funds. Our financial, tax, and legal systems are set up to reward property owners who are educated enough to seize the available advantages. And best of all for starting investors, they don't need an enormous cash reserve to buy real estate. They can start small.

Like first-time home buyers, real estate investors can secure bank loans and make monthly payments as owners of rental property. And as they watch their equity grow, they can parlay their initial investment property's increased value into garnering a new loan to purchase a second property. Pulling this cash out has a second benefit in that they do not have to pay taxes on the money they receive because it is from their equity. And so on. They can learn as they go, perhaps making some mistakes and increasing their knowledge through experience, as their holdings expand.

The financial, tax, and legal advantages—as spelled out in this book—of owning real estate are enormous. And the question you, the reader, may ask is: Why don't more investors follow this route to success?

The answer is twofold and simple: lack of knowledge and fear.

Begin Your Education Now

Many investors who avoid real estate are afraid of the anticipated difficulties of being landlords. They hear horror stories. They think to themselves, "I don't want to fix toilets," and "I don't want to get calls from tenants in the middle of the night." But know that there are strategies for intelligently managing a property that any capable person can implement. As well, many people fear the threat of a lawsuit. And rightly so. We are a litigious society.

Attorneys are rewarded for bringing claims against wealthy individuals. But know that there are asset protection strategies we'll discuss that can reduce your exposure and limit your liability. In all, the rewards of owning real estate far outweigh the drawbacks for most prudent investors.

When it comes to lack of knowledge, most people are unaware of the advantages to be gained from investing in real estate. This is understandable. Most of us in our society aren't raised to consider investing in real estate. It's certainly not taught in schools. The standard pattern is to go to school, get a job, climb up the corporate ladder of a career, put earnings in a bank, maybe buy stocks, mutual funds, and bonds, and save for a rainy day, including retirement. Most of us don't realize that real estate investments allow our money to accelerate at a greater pace than typical paper investments. In fact, real estate has historically trended up in value and yielded higher returns than the securities markets.

There are really three types of income:

• *Earned Income:* This is what you bring home from work in the form of a paycheck. You go to the office from eight to five. If you stopped going to work, your earned income ends.

• *Passive Income:* This is what comes to you from an investment such as real estate. If you get sick and can't earn a paycheck from your job, your real estate is still working for you. (Even better, this income may not be subject to Social Security and Medicare withholdings, and in some cases incurs no tax at all because of your ability to depreciate a property's value, or to defer claimed gains by rolling over a sale to another property.)

• *Portfolio Income:* This is what comes from the dividends and increases in value in paper assets such as stocks, bonds, and mutual funds. It's the most popular form of investment income for the masses, because it's easier to manage than real estate and other investments.

The point of this book isn't to encourage readers to invest only in real estate.The Rich Dad philosophy is to diversify, (although in a different sense than the word as used by financial planners) to put your savings and earnings into three different areas: businesses, real estate, and paper assets. This is because each sector is subject to market fluctuations and corrections, and your investment risk must be spread out. The point of this book is to explain the financial, tax, and legal advantages of investing in real estate as a passive-income earner and to encourage you to utilize these investment advantages.

If this is the first Rich Dad book you are reading, please know that Rich Dad's philosophy is that your primary residence should not be considered an asset, because it is not generating regular income for you. (Rich Dad has a simple definition for "asset": something that puts money in your pocket. A "liability," conversely, is something that takes money *from* your pocket.) With your primary residence, you're paying the mortgage, and therefore the cash flow is going *from* you (to the bank), not *toward* you. Your home mortgage is an example of "bad debt." Still, the tax code offers some advantages for homeowners, which we'll discuss in later chapters.

Real estate becomes an asset when it brings you cash flow. By following the advice in this book, as a real estate investor you will be putting other people's money—the lender bank's and your tenants'—to work for you. If your monthly mortgage on a rental property is $5,000, but your tenants are paying you $6,000, then you're earning $1,000 in cash. Your bank loan is "good debt."

Rich Dad Tip

Good debt is debt that is used to purchase an asset that puts money in your pocket. Bad debt is debt that is used to purchase a toy or doo-dad that takes money out of your pocket. A real estate investment makes use of good debt.

How This Book Will Help You

This book is divided into five parts:

1. "Real Estate Advantages" explains the theories and facts behind the benefits of real estate investing.
2. "Get in the Game" instructs how to create an investment plan, assemble a team of advisors, and choose investments.

3. "Tax Strategies" teaches how to crunch the numbers of potential investments, make full use of tax advantages, and manage your investments.
4. "Legal Strategies" covers methods for protecting your investments and yourself.
5. "Selection Strategies" reveals how to research and choose profitable properties.

This book is not intended to make you a tax expert or legal expert on real estate. Nor is this book offering a get-rich-quick scheme (there are enough of those pipe dreams being sold all the time in books and brochures, seminars and infomercials). *Real Estate Advantages* is for readers who are serious about educating themselves about investing in real estate. It's for readers who want to learn about these advantages that the rich already know about, because these advantages are available to all of us.

This book will help you know what questions to ask the advisors who will constitute your investment team. In *Rich Dad Poor Dad*, Robert T. Kiyosaki has famously cited the advice his "rich dad" gave him: "Business and investing are team sports." While most successful real estate investors learn by doing, as you forge ahead in real estate, you won't be on your own. You will assemble a team of advisors—from real estate agents to lenders, lawyers, accountants, property managers, and even repair and cleaning people—as explained in Chapter 5. You'll know whom you need and when.

Also know that you need not absorb the contents of this book like a sponge. As you progress in your real estate investing career, you can return time and again to the book. And since your education will be ongoing, we strongly urge you to explore the other titles listed in our resource section found in Appendix A.

Your Opportunity Awaits

Becoming a successful real estate investor is within most investors' reach. The authors of this book—Sharon Lechter and Garrett Sutton—are living examples of this. Both Sharon and Garrett are building their personal wealth through real estate. Sharon, a founder of The Rich Dad Company and co-author of many Rich Dad books, is an accountant by trade; Garrett is an attorney, Rich Dad's Advisor, and author. Neither enjoyed previous careers as real estate professionals. But each has practiced the principles in this book and reaped the rewards. So can you.

As with other investment options, the world of real estate is vast and no one can become an expert in every area. Nor should anyone try. You are wise to specialize in one type of market—such as small single-family homes, or apartment complexes with a certain number of units, and in a geographic area familiar to you.

If you're a small investor, successfully investing in real estate will allow you to move out of the great mass of fellow investors who put their paycheck savings into modest paper investments. Real estate investing will power up your earning potential and put you into a different class of investor entirely. For there are two kinds of investors, as pointed out by *Rich Dad*'s CASH-FLOW Quadrant . . .

Chapter 1

Understanding the "Why" of Real Estate

The CASHFLOW Quadrant above appeared in the second book in the *Rich Dad* series, *Rich Dad's CASHFLOW Quadrant: Rich Dad's Guide to Financial Freedom*. The "E-S" on the left side of the Quadrant stands for employees and self-employed. These two types of income earners manage personal finances the way almost all of us have been trained to do by our parents and society in general: to forge a career in an income-producing occupation and plow paycheck savings into (1) paying off bills, loans, and mortgages, (2) buying a home, and (3) investing in stocks, bonds, and retirement funds.

This financial pattern is the status quo. Our educational system doesn't teach us how to handle money. Our culture teaches us to go to school, go to work, save for retirement. So that's what most of us do. We "park" our money.

If you're like most people, you remain on the left side of the Quadrant, working for your money. Other people's money isn't working for *you*. Your earned income—what you bring in from your job—is paying off bills and debt; what's left over goes into investments to generate portfolio income. You're not doing what those on the right side of the Quadrant do: enjoy the benefits of passive income, as described in the introduction to Part One.

Your goal, if you want to grow your wealth as quickly as possible, is to move to the right side of the Quadrant. "B-I" stands for business owners and investors. These income earners have their money working for *them*. Their assets are diversified among businesses, real estate, and paper (stocks and bonds). The businesses and properties in these investors' portfolios are generating passive income—meaning that other people's money, time, and energy are working for these investors, as is their own money.

This chart illustrates why the rich are getting richer. It delineates the different mentality between the two groups of investors. The employees and self-employed on the left side rely on their jobs to slowly build their estates. The business owners and investors on the right-hand side rely on their dynamic assets to accelerate their wealth. This doesn't mean that your goal in moving to the right side is to give up your primary career as an employee or self-employee. Rather, the goal is to begin putting your income into assets on the right side that will transform your earning ability and pull you out of the rat race.

Real Estate Is a Pillar of Your Investments

The three asset classes on the right-hand side of the "Why the Rich Get Richer" chart are Business, Real Estate, and Paper. Robert T. Kiyosaki's rich dad's formula for getting wealthy was to start a business, use the cash flow from that business (primarily after-tax monies) to invest in real estate, and

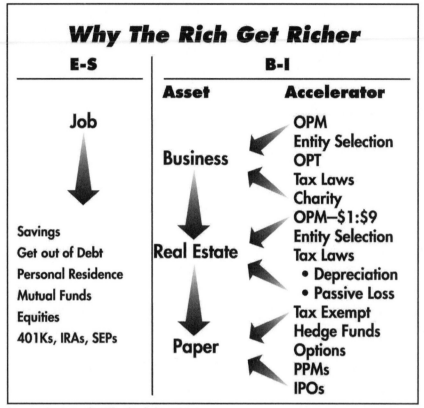

Why The Rich Get Richer

E-S	B-I	
	Asset	**Accelerator**
Job		OPM
		Entity Selection
	Business	OPT
		Tax Laws
		Charity
		OPM–$1:$9
Savings		Entity Selection
Get out of Debt	**Real Estate**	Tax Laws
Personal Residence		• Depreciation
Mutual Funds		• Passive Loss
Equities		Tax Exempt
401Ks, IRAs, SEPs		Hedge Funds
	Paper	Options
		PPMs
		IPOs

Source: Rich Dad's Who Took My Money

hold that wealth in real estate and paper assets, where it will increase. All three asset classes worked for Kiyosaki's rich dad. (For those of you who don't know, Robert's "rich dad" was the father of Robert's best friend, and became Robert's financial mentor and a very rich man. Robert's father, "poor dad," was a salary earner who believed in education and company or government pensions and invested only in long-term, low-appreciating paper assets; he died poor.)

In the Accelerator column are the different methods by which you can accelerate your wealth within each asset class. An explanation of chart abbreviations: OPM is "other people's money"—that is, money from lenders, such as banks or investment partners. OPT is "other people's time." (In a business, you have employees working for you, benefiting your bottom line.) "OPM–$1:$9" refers to a real estate investor's ability to borrow from a bank or other lender nine-tenths of the cost of an investment, while using the investor's own money to cover the remaining one-tenth—an example of leveraging "good debt." PPM is "private placement memorandum," which young companies use to attract investment capital, and which can pay off handsomely. IPO is "initial public offering," which includes an attractive opening price for stock that a company issues for the first time for purchase by investors outside the company.

This book deals with the accelerators that specifically relate to real estate. You may wonder, from reading *Rich Dad's Who Took My Money?*, if you must start a business before investing in real estate. The answer is no. You can funnel after-tax earnings from your job (on the left side of the Quadrant) into real estate. Some people eventually make real estate investing itself their business.

As was noted in the introduction to this part, real estate as an asset can accelerate income much faster than other assets, such as paper. Real estate also affords special tax benefits. Note that Depreciation and Passive Loss are shown as accelerators in the Real Estate asset class in the chart. Passive loss—when passive income is negative—allows the property owner to write off a deduction (accountants call it a paper loss) every year based on business expenses plus the calculated cost (depreciation) of repairing a structural component or piece of personal property used in the building on your land, since these items deteriorate over time. (Depreciation and passive loss will be discussed in depth in Chapter 8.)

In sum, investing in real estate can be the key to moving you from the left side of the Quadrant to the right side. It can be the key to building your estate. But it requires educating yourself.

The easiest method of investing, albeit not usually the most successful, to build an estate is through portfolio income—simply putting your earnings into stocks, bonds, and mutual funds, either on your own or by using a tax-deferred retirement plan or by entrusting your earnings to a financial planner. That's what investors on the left side of the Quadrant do.

The most difficult method of investing is running your own business (such as a franchise, store, restaurant, or personal services company) with employees. This requires education and a time commitment, but offers a potentially far greater rate of return than portfolio (or even real estate) income. Yet running a business also entails a much greater risk. (Nine out of ten businesses fail within their first five years.)

Investing in real estate requires a bit more education than investing for portfolio income, but much less education than running a business. Also, as we'll discuss, real estate income typically provides a much greater return (as well as tax savings) than portfolio income.

To succeed in real estate, you must be prepared to wade into the water and learn from your mistakes. And you need to consider building a team of experts in order to minimize your mistakes.

When you are ready to do so, you can start realizing the benefits of leverage to amass wealth in real estate. Let's take a look at that right now in our first case.

Case No. 1
Jerry and Justin

Jerry and Justin were twin brothers. While they looked alike, had the exact same mannerisms, and could fool not only their teachers in school but their girlfriends as well, they differed in one big respect.

Justin wanted security in all things. And when it came to investing, Justin would put his money only in funds indexed to the Standard & Poor's 500, a compilation of large companies representing the U.S. stock market known as the S&P 500.

This strategy worked well for Justin because he was not forced to ever worry about extraneous issues. Yes, if the U.S. and/or global economy went into recession, his investment would be affected. But so would everyone else's investment. That was a risk we all took. Nevertheless, Justin felt safe because he was not subject to the investment risks that Jerry took.

Jerry believed in real estate. He liked the fact that he could put $10,000 down on a house and the bank would loan him another $90,000 to buy a $100,000 house. He appreciated that there were additional risks to owning real estate. He knew that while he could be sued by tenants, neighbors, and vendors, brother Justin would never be sued for owning his paper assets. But Jerry understood that asset protection strategies could limit his liability and reduce his exposure. And Jerry felt confident that the leverage of real estate would exceed his brother's return. Through the leverage offered by real estate, Jerry could own a $100,000 house asset compared to Justin's $10,000 S&P 500 fund account.

The chart below chronicles how well the brothers did from 1992 to 2002, a ten-year period.

While Justin's $10,000 grew to $17,397, albeit with no extraneous risk, Jerry's $10,000 investment (with the $90,000 loan) was valued at $158,673. Clearly, the benefits of leverage are worthy of further exploration . . .

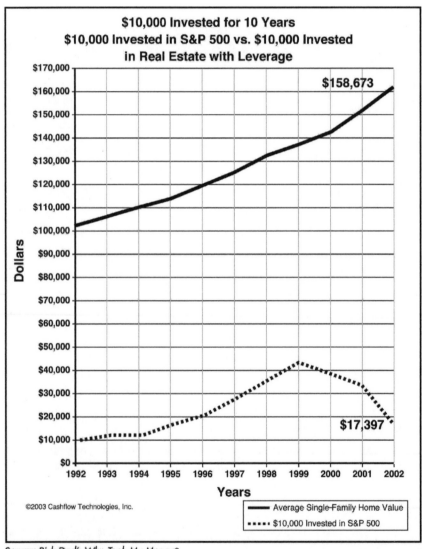

Source: Rich Dad's Who Took My Money?

Chapter 2

The Benefits of Leverage

In the "Why the Rich Get Richer" chart in Chapter 1, you will note the "OPM—$1:$9" accelerator for the Real Estate asset category. To reiterate, this accelerator exemplifies leveraging "good debt"—that which brings income flowing toward you that exceeds your payment on the debt. This accelerator refers to an investor's ability to borrow from a bank (or other lender) 90 percent of the cost of an investment, while using the investor's own money to cover the remaining 10 percent. It's a 9:1 leverage.

What this accelerator does is allow you to use other people's money to cover 90 percent of your investment, while you enjoy 100 percent of the investment advantages in building up equity in your property, and you also enjoy 100 percent of the tax advantages that further increase the value of your investment. What's more, the accelerator gives you the ability to use the combined equity you build up in each property to buy more properties at 10 percent down and increase your wealth exponentially. That's the power of leverage!

We'll discuss the tax advantages of depreciation a little later. For now, let's consider an example of how the OPM—$1:$9 accelerator can increase the velocity of your money far more than two other common investment strategies. Suppose you have $20,000 to invest. Here are three choices:

- *Choice 1:* Invest $20,000 in a mutual fund that earns 5 percent a year. (This is what most E-S investors do: put their savings into paper.)

After seven years, your $20,000 should have grown to $28,142, assuming no market fluctuations.

- *Choice 2:* Invest $20,000 and borrow $180,000 from the bank for a $200,000 rental property, and let your equity compound. (This is using the OPM—$1:$9 accelerator, but only initially.) Assume rental income only breaks even with expenses and the property appreciates at a rate of 5 percent a year.

After seven years, the property will be worth $281,000, and your equity (the $281,000 minus what you still owe the bank) is $101,420, assuming no market fluctuations.

- *Choice 3:* Invest $20,000 and borrow $180,000 from the bank for a $200,000 rental property. Rather than letting the equity compound, you borrow out the appreciation every two years and invest it in a new property at 10 percent down. (See, you're repeating your use of the OPM—$1:$9 accelerator!)

After seven years, your *four* properties will be worth $2,022,218, and your net equity will be $273,198, assuming no market fluctuations.

To summarize the hypothetical $20,000 investment:

Net Equity After Seven Years	Average Annual Return
Choice 1: $28,142	5.8%
Choice 2: $101,420	58.2%
Choice 3: $273,198	180.9%

Choices 1 and 2 are examples of parking your money. Choice 3 is an example of increasing the velocity of your money. While borrowing out your appreciation may not be right for everyone, it is the right choice for the investor who wishes to significantly increase wealth through the magic of leverage in real estate.

This is the formula for using Choice 3:

1. Invest money into an asset.
2. Get the original investment money back.

3. Keep control of the original asset.
4. Move the money into a new asset.
5. Get the investment money back.
6. Repeat the process.

What Choice 3 actually does is allow you, the personal investor, to invest much like a bank does. The strategy allows you to expand your money supply to increase your earning power. Like a bank or other financial institution, you can make your money move. The more times a dollar moves (being reinvested in a new moneymaking property), the greater the money supply you tap (since the dollar leverages other dollars), and the greater that dollar's earning power.

Now can you see the value of using other people's money to build your wealth? Of course, the ability to work this magic doesn't come at once. It requires an initial investment in your financial education. That education can begin by reading this book. But it also will involve implementing the directions in this book and (to repeat from Chapter 1) learning by doing. (And it will involve ongoing learning—which should continue throughout your life.)

This brings us to a cautionary note: You must always make intelligent investment decisions based soundly on your education and experience, for if you don't, you may end up overleveraged. If you own multiple investment properties and one of them proves to be a bad investment—not providing sufficient returns or even losing money—it can cause your whole house of cards to collapse. You may find yourself robbing Peter to pay Paul. You must be prudent and ensure that if, say, one of your properties goes vacant, you can survive the downturn in your anticipated income. This can be accomplished by keeping a "reserve," which is an account where you hold enough cash or liquid assets to help you pay your real estate expenses in case you have a vacancy. People usually keep from three months up to a year of expenses in their reserve account.

Again, that ability to plan your investments and continually assess their performance will come with education and knowledge gained from experience and from building your team of advisors (to be discussed in Chapter 5).

The Advantage of Depreciation with Leverage

An advantage of investing in real estate, in addition to its ability to appreciate in value and allow the continual leverage of equity, is the tax savings real estate affords. When you borrow 90 percent of a payment on a property, it doesn't mean you own only 10 percent of that property. You own 100 percent of it. Therefore, you are entitled to *100 percent* of the tax deductions.

There are two categories of deductions for real estate: depreciation and passive loss. We'll discuss these a bit further on in this chapter and explain the applicable federal tax laws more fully in Chapter 8. For now, let's look at the following chart to see how using the OPM—$1:$9 accelerator can benefit you beyond the appreciation:

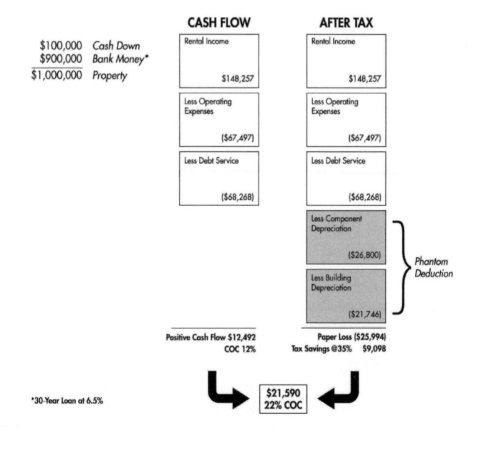

In this chart's example, you put $100,000 of your own cash down on a $1-million rental property and borrow the remaining $900,000 from a bank at a 30-year loan rate of roughly 6.5 percent. Note the Cash Flow column on the chart. Your rental income for the first year is $148,257. Your operating expense is $67,497, and your debt service (the interest on the bank loan plus other principal payments you've made on the loan) is $68,268. Subtract these amounts from your income and you arrive at $12,492. That positive cash flow represents the cash-on-cash (COC) return on your cash investment of $100,000. This return is better than 12 percent.

But that double-digit return isn't the only benefit accruing to you from your rental property. Look at the After Tax column on the chart. Your reportable income on your tax return will be your rental income minus your operating expense and only the interest you've paid on your debt service (not the principal payments)—plus two other deductions, what we term *phantom deductions.* One phantom deduction is "component depreciation" (also known as cost segregation depreciation), which means the annual decline in the various components of a building, such as its shell and walls, roofing and flooring, carpets and furniture, electrical, heating, and plumbing systems. Each of these has a "useful life," or life expectancy, of more than one year, and will need replacement at some point. Their costs can be capitalized and prorated over the years you own the property. The other phantom deduction is "building depreciation," which means the annual decline in the useful life of a building's structure.

In all, your "paper loss" recognized by the Internal Revenue Service is $25,994. If you are in a tax-effective rate of 35 percent (which is higher than most income earners' rate), you can claim 35 percent of your paper loss ($9,098 in this example) to offset other income. Add that savings of $9,098 to your $12,492 in positive cash flow, and you have actually realized a $21,590 cash-on-cash return for the year on your $100,000 investment—roughly 22 percent. That's an extremely impressive return!

The Government Respects Real Estate

We've mentioned the tax write-offs for the phantom deductions—component and building depreciations. There is another write-off to consider: passive loss.

After you've taken your rental income and deducted your operating expenses, interest on debt service, and phantom deductions, the resulting income or loss is considered your *passive income* or *passive loss*. The tax laws allow you to offset your earned income by up to $25,000 in passive losses from real estate, as long as your adjusted gross income is below $100,000. (Above the $100,000 level to $149,999, there is a sliding scale for what you can deduct from real estate losses. Those with $150,000 or more of adjusted gross income can't claim this deduction. Unless, that is, you utilize the real estate professional strategy we'll discuss in Chapter 9.)

Why are there such great tax advantages for owning and investing in real estate? Our nation's tax laws are written to support those people—business owners and investors—who create jobs and housing. The laws benefit the risk-takers, the doers, who spur the economy. Therefore, if you invest capital into your community by buying real estate, you are rewarded with tax breaks so that you can maintain and continue investing while at the same time, you provide a valuable social service. As well, the government learned its lesson a generation ago that it does a very poor job of providing low-cost housing. It is more efficient to encourage the private sector through tax advantages to perform this service than for the government to muddle its way through the important community need of housing.

The government also allows special tax and legal protections for property owners in the form of legal entities. How you hold your property becomes very important as your investments increase. You don't want a legal problem arising at one—such as a tenant tripping on stairs at one of your apartment buildings—to put your other holdings and personal assets at risk of a lawsuit settlement or judgment. These legal entity strategies will be discussed in depth in Part Four, "Legal Strategies."

Summary of Leverage Advantages

Using the OPM—$1:$9 accelerator, your cash investment of 10 percent into a property is rewarded with income potential, full ownership, appreciation of equity, and tax deductions. The lender, which invests 90 percent of the purchase price, realizes only one benefit while being repaid its capital: interest payments. As long as you pay the debt service to the bank, you enjoy the

leverages of ownership, appreciation, and depreciation. It's almost too good
to be true and looks like this:

	You	*Your Lender*
Money	10%	90%
Ownership	100%	0%
Appreciation	100%	0%
Deductions	100%	0%

The returns from leveraging equity, and the tax advantages of ownership, make real estate the quickest way to wealth for many people. Even
people who are struggling out of financial straits can invest in real estate to
their advantage.

And when real estate is treated as a *business*, the income potential
increases . . .

Chapter 3

Capital Gain
vs. Cash Flow

As we saw in the CASHFLOW Quadrant in Chapter 1, the business owners and investors on the right-hand side of the Quadrant benefit from the work, time, and money of other people. When it comes to investing in real estate, you want to increase your wealth not only from the property's apprecia- tion—its "capital gain"—over time but also from the cash flow the property can generate.

When you invest in real estate, you are pursuing two different goals. One goal is that the value of your property will appreciate over time above the price you paid for it so you'll be able to sell it for more than you bought it. Those are the two crucial points in time for your property: when you buy it and when you sell it. This is *capital gains investing*.

The other goal is that your property will generate a positive income for you each and every month. You're aiming for the revenue from rental income to exceed the operating costs and mortgage payment. This is *cash flow in- vesting*. And having your money generating passive income for you—income that comes to you whether you get out of bed in the morning or not—is a

Rich Dad investment principle. An income-generating property is like an employee working for you. This passive income from a property would end if you sell that property. You may enjoy a capital gain from the sale, but you no longer have that money actively working for you to earn you even more money. To replace it, you may need to reinvest that money into another investment that yields positive cash flow.

A person who is solely a capital gain investor looks at the optimal time to buy a property (i.e., when its market price is relatively low) and the optimal time to sell (when it appears the market value has peaked or risks plummeting). A cash flow investor looks at the income history and potential of a property and usually considers selling only when indicators (such as a decrease in an area's population) point to a drop in cash flow; or when money from capital gains can be parlayed into a more lucrative income-generating investment, such as a larger property; or when the property has fully depreciated over time and this tax advantage can no longer be enjoyed.

Rich Dad's philosophy is that once you have your dollar in your asset column, you want to keep it working for you, generating even more dollars that, in turn, will work for you, too. And so on. You may not want to do what most small investors do, which is to park your money and hope that it will increase in value (appreciation) over time.

When it comes to real estate, you want to enjoy its appreciation *and* its generation of income. You want capital gains *and* cash flow.

In Real Estate, Time Is Your Ally

The good news about real estate is that its value historically goes up. As we said in the introduction to this part, land is a finite resource. There's only so much of it. As the human population increases, the value of real estate increases.

Of course, there are market cycles that can lift or lower values, including market corrections, downward trends, and artificially inflated price bubbles that burst. There are other factors, including natural disasters, such as hurricanes, flooding, and drought, and man-made disasters, such as crime waves and pollution, that can diminish property values. The fluctuations of the financial markets and interest rates, and the vacillating fortunes of area industries that employ people and create wealth, have a bearing on real estate markets, too. But in general, over the long term, real estate goes up. In the United States, overall appreciation over the past four decades has been above 6 percent annualized. If you buy property, it stands to appreciate over time, but there are no guarantees.

What's more, there's always a good deal to be found. If prices seem too high in a certain market, it may scare off competitors and leave an opening for the savvy buyer who looks a little harder. Or if it seems like a particular market or segment has tanked, it offers opportunity to the aggressive investor to buy at a reduced rate.

Here's an example. Robert Kiyosaki moved to Phoenix in 1991 because of a plunge in real estate values in that city. Nationwide, the default of savings and loans, along with overvaluation in real estate and overleveraged debt among investors, led to crashes in many markets. Robert purchased two apartment complexes in Phoenix for dimes on the dollar. By 1994, these investments had proved profitable enough to make him financially free. He had enough passive cash flow from those two properties alone to cover his monthly living expenses, hence financial freedom.

The key with earning a capital gain is to hold on to a property for a minimum of one year. This is because you'll get a capital gains tax rate (at this writing, 15 percent at the federal level for the United States), which is lower than the rate on ordinary income, if you've held a property for at least one year.

Some investors pursue a strategy of "flipping" properties—buying low and selling high as soon as possible, often without holding a property for at least a year. These "fix-and-flippers" who sell before owning a property for a year get hit with the higher tax rate. That defeats the purpose of banking on a capital gain. In addition, if they do it too often, the IRS could categorize them as "dealers," and the capital gains income could be considered earned income and subject not only to the higher rates but also to employment taxes. But, with their money accelerated, even at a higher capital gains rate, the strategy works for some people. Some people use the flipping strategy to help them build up cash more quickly in order to move into larger properties.

One more word of caution: When real estate is at its highest and the bubble is about to burst, the flippers may be caught holding properties with no cash flow, and with declining values due to the real estate bubble bursting. This is another reason why *Rich Dad* prefers cash flow investing over flipping.

Case No. 2
Tony and Terri

Tony and Terri had once dated but found it was easier and less complicated to simply be friends. Their friendship was strengthened by their mutual interest in investing in real estate. But as they had found in their prior closer relationship, each had their own way of doing things.

Tony was impatient. He wanted to get in, do his work, and move on. He liked turning his assets over as quickly as possible. Terri was just the opposite. She wanted to get to know her property and liked the benefits of long-term ownership, monthly cash flow, and appreciation over time. It was clear that their investing strategies mirrored their romantic predilections, and never the twain would meet.

Tony's desire for accelerated action came with a greater financial burden. By flipping properties every few months, he was subject to short-term capital gains at his ordinary income rate. Of greater consequence, by doing these turns on a regular basis, it became his trade or business. As such, a salary was properly paid along with payroll taxes. Accordingly, Tom paid a 35 percent ordinary income tax, payroll taxes of 15.3 percent on the first $90,000 or so of income, and state taxes on top of that. Over 50 percent of Tony's short-term profits were eaten up in taxes.

Terri, on the other hand, did not jump from property to property. When she found one she liked, she held on to it for a year or longer. As such, she enjoyed the benefit of a 15 percent capital gains tax when she sold a property. So, for example, on a $100,000 gain, she paid a long-term rate of only $15,000, whereas Tony had to pay over $50,000 on the same (but faster) gain.

And like so many others, both Tony and Terri liked the idea of trading up for a better property. But Tony, due to his accelerated activities, wasn't allowed to do so on a tax-free basis. Terri, on the other hand, by being patient and holding on for over a year, was able to use a 1031 transaction (discussed more fully in Chapter 10). She could trade up tax-free for a newer and better property every year or so. All in all, Terri greatly appreciated the slow satisfaction of real estate wealth building.

Like Terri, the Rich Dad philosophy is to keep a property as long as its value continues to appreciate and its cash flow is sufficient to at least cover the costs of owning the property. Again, everyone has a different style and agenda, but it bears remembering that when renters cover your mortgage payment and operating costs, they're in effect paying you to have your equity grow. That's why Rich Dad's preference is for cash flow over parking your money in paper. And "parking" is the operative word here. When you park your car, how much acceleration do you get? The same thing happens (or, really, doesn't happen) when you park your money in paper assets.

What you can charge and receive for rent is determined by what the market will bear, just as with any other good or service in the economy. Therefore, your cash flow and profit from a property are really determined by how much you paid for the property (and the rate of interest on your loan). As the old real estate adage holds: "You make your profits when you buy." Acquire the right property at the right price with the right financing, and cash flow and profit will follow.

Building up your capital gain—your growth in equity—and securing cash flow are both important to growing your wealth through real estate. As we previously stated, the U.S. tax code is set up to reward property holders. The government knows that it can't properly or efficiently perform the service of housing, which is why there are government-sanctioned tax advantages to investing in real estate. And financial institutions such as banks are eager to lend money to investors who can prove themselves good risks by being capable of generating cash flow from the properties in which they invest. This allows the knowledgeable investor to accelerate income with the OPM—$1:$9 accelerator.

As a knowledgeable investor, you can put your money to work to build wealth fairly quickly. Time is our most precious resource. For you as a real estate investor, time is an ally.

Now it's time for you to put together your plan on investing in real estate. Chapter 4 explains how this is done.

Part Two

Get in the Game

Chapter 4

Creating Your Real Estate Plan

"Those who fail to plan, plan to fail" is a wise saying. As with any other worthy endeavor, to succeed in real estate requires putting together a workable plan and implementing it. If you already have a plan and a team and are investing, you may want to skip ahead to Part Three, where we get into the meaty tax issues.

But if you're starting out, the question is where to begin. And the answer is, by getting a clear and complete picture of your current financial standing. To do so, it is imperative you take a hard, brutally honest look at your financial affairs.

Get Your Financial Report Card in Order

Before you can determine where you want to go, you must determine where you are right now. But not nearly enough investors take this initial, crucial step.

To assemble your financial report card, start with the *income statement* part of your *financial statement*. This lists your income and expenses on a monthly basis. If you're like most adults in our society, you're living out of your checkbook. Each month it's money in, money out . . . and hopefully at the end of the month you have enough money to pay all your bills. When you determine your income statement, you'll see what your financial activity is each month.

After you've produced your income statement, you need to put together your *balance sheet*. This lists your assets and liabilities. It's a snapshot of your wealth at this point in time. It shows what's in your asset column, generating income for you. These assets usually include your investments, such as savings accounts, stocks, 401(k) plans, mutual funds, real estate investments, and any business you own. Your balance sheet also shows what's in your liability column, sending your money elsewhere, such as the balance left on your mortgage, the balance left on your car payments, and your credit card debt.

Our goal at *Rich Dad* is to provide the information and tools for people who want to reduce their reliance on earned income and increase their passive and portfolio income through the creation or acquisition of assets. There are a couple of tools available at richdad.com that may help you produce your financial statement and balance sheet. One is a "personal financial calculator" sheet you can download, for free, to determine your financial statement and balance sheet. (Click on "Creating Your Plan." You will need Adobe Acrobat Reader to use the calculator.) Another tool is the CASHFLOW® 101 Board Game, which you can order online. Each player fills out a financial statement and a balance sheet. A player sheet from the CASHFLOW® 101 Board Game is found on page 31.

When you put together your financial statements—your income statement and your balance sheet—you'll see where you'll want to make improvements. You'll want to add to your assets and reduce your liabilities. You'll want to increase your income and decrease expenses. For most adults who have an income, from 95 percent to 100 percent of their income is earned income—what they work for either as an employee or self-employed (as described in Part One's introduction). It's what's in the paycheck after getting out of bed in the morning, commuting to the job, putting in the workday toil, over and over again.

Profession

Player

Goal: To get out of the Rat Race and onto the Fast Track by building up your Passive Income to be greater than your Total Expenses

Income Statement

Income

Description	Cash Flow
Salary:	
Interest:	
Dividends:	
Real Estate:	
Businesses:	

Auditor

Person on your right

Passive Income= _____
(Cash Flows from Interest +
Dividends + Real Estate + Businesses)

**Total
Income:** _____

Expenses

Taxes:	
Home Mortgage:	
School Loan Payment:	
Car Payment:	
Credit Card Payment:	
Retail Payment:	
Other Expenses:	
Child Expenses:	
Bank Loan Payment:	

Number of
Children: _____
(Begin game with 0 Children)
Per Child
Expense: _____

**Total
Expenses:** _____

**Monthly
Cash Flow:** _____
(Paycheck)

Balance Sheet

Assets

Savings:		
Stocks/Mutual's/CDs	No. of Shares:	Cost/Share:
Real Estate:	Down Pay:	Cost:
Business:	Down Pay:	Cost:

Liabilities

Home Mortgage:
School Loans:
Car Loans:
Credit Cards:
Retail Debt:
RE Mortgage:
Liability: (Business)
Bank Loan:

Source: CASHFLOW® 101 Board Game

After you've produced your income statement and balance sheet, you may find you're not getting ahead at all. Maybe you're spending as much as you're making. Maybe you're spending *more* than you're making. If you are currently struggling with debt consider reading *Rich Dad's ABCs of Getting Out of Debt*, by Garrett Sutton, Esq. Also, you may see that you have *no* passive or portfolio income.

That's okay. Accept it. Acknowledge it. And ask yourself a very important question: Are you satisfied with remaining on the left side of the CASHFLOW Quadrant, or do you truly aspire to move to the right side?

If your answer is that you're content to remain a paycheck earner with no outside income or assets apart from what you park in paper, then you don't need a financial plan for accelerating your wealth. But if your answer is that you truly *do* wish to move to the right side, and will take the necessary steps to do so, then now is the time for you to create a financial plan to see what you can begin doing—right now—to generate passive and portfolio income and grow your wealth.

Key to that plan may be investing in real estate. And guess what? You've already taken an important first step in recording information on your income statement and balance sheet. If you want to become a business owner and investor—including in real estate—your banker or other lender will need to see your financial statements. (He'll give you a similar form to fill out.)

Your financial statements—your income statement and your balance sheet—are your report card on your life. The report cards you got in school determined whether you advanced to the next grade or classes. Your financial report card determines whether a lender will loan you money for the investments that will advance your wealth.

Setting Goals for Your Real Estate Investment Plan

After producing your financial report card, a plan for investing will begin to snap into focus. Your financial statements will help you set goals. You may recognize that your debt is too high overall, or in certain areas, and you need to start paying it down. You may identify areas you definitely want to bolster in your asset column. Cutting expenses and liabilities is one tack. Another is boosting your income.

Unless you want and are able to increase your earned income through working more hours or securing a raise or higher-paying job, you'll need to increase your passive or portfolio income. Passive income is almost always the quickest source of increasing wealth. And, again, it's the method advised by *Rich Dad*. After all, passive income—to reiterate—means other people's time, energy, and money *working for you*.

Your financial report card will tell you what percent of your income is currently passive income. If you're like most people, the answer is zero. When you set a goal for making passive income, you must decide what percent of your income you aim to make passive. You may set a goal to reach in one year, and a different (larger) goal to reach after a longer period, such as five years. You will decide what a reasonable figure for the monthly passive income will be: $1,000? $5,000? $10,000? $100,000?

Your individual goals will depend upon what you're willing to do to make them happen. And know that you can modify or change your goals as you get into the real estate game and learn what works and what doesn't.

Once you take a hard look at your assets and liabilities, your eyes will be open to new possibilities. You will likely have gained a very different perspective about finances and possibilities. Some people have been known to downsize their homes in order to put equity to work in investments. Some have even rented their large homes and moved to smaller accommodations to, again, generate cash flow.

Your investment style, of course, depends on *your* wants and needs.

Setting a Goal for Buying Your First Property

When setting a goal to buy that first cash-generating property, some people decide to jump right in, because they are, by nature, people who learn best by doing. They are willing to learn quickly from their mistakes. Others decide they need to educate themselves better first, consult with experienced investors, and find advisors (which will be discussed in Chapter 5). Each of us is different. You should do what feels comfortable for *you*.

Let's say, for example, that you've decided to reduce spending and increase earned income with a preliminary goal of saving $10,000 to invest in real estate. You've resolved to accomplish this in the next six months and to purchase your first rental property within six months after that. In other words, you want to buy your first property within a year.

A worthy goal. And as you gain experience, you'll continue setting new goals (such as, say, owning five properties within the next ten years). But you must also decide—from the outset—what type of real estate interests you. Even this choice could very well change as you gain experience, but here are some of the many options:

Single-family homes
Condominiums
Duplexes
Fourplexes
Trailer parks
Motels
Hotels
Apartments
Storage units
Commercial office
Commercial industrial
Storefront retail

Within each of these very different categories is a wide range of possibilities: small apartment complexes, complexes with one hundred units or more, starter-market family homes, homes in gated communities, strip-mall retail space, high-rise office buildings, and so on.

Within this range of possibilities are geographic distinctions: properties in your city (or another), in your county (or another), rural, suburban, inner city, waterfront, and so on.

What's more, with all of the above, there are these very different strategies:

- Foreclosures: a way to buy properties cheaply, without intention of earning cash flow from them
- Fix and flip: also a way to buy cheaply, with the intent of selling quickly for a profit
- Buy and hold: meant to earn appreciation

- Buy, hold, and rent: also meant to earn appreciation, but also to earn cash flow. This is Rich Dad's strategy.

The Wisdom of Mastering One Investment Area

One thing to keep in mind is that the real estate world is vast. Therefore, it is often best to master one process—to become an expert, say, in buying, holding, and renting single-family residences in middle-class neighborhoods in your city; or in doing the same with four-to-twelve-unit apartment complexes patronized by single workers. As you learn the process of investing in real estate in a certain sector of the market, it becomes easier. You get better at it all the time. Since different neighborhoods have different dynamics, it's also smart to specialize in a certain geographic area. And it's not a bad idea to begin in your own neighborhood, since you know the market and you're right there to observe trends.

Familiarity with a product from personal experience may also be what drives you to invest in a certain type of property. For example, you may have been a tenant in small apartment complexes for many years, and know what works and what doesn't in a well-run complex. As well, you may want to start at the lower end of properties, because, if possible, you won't want to make beginner's mistakes on larger, expensive properties.

Case No. 3
Omar, Ashleigh, and Zook

Omar was itching to get into real estate. He had read ten books and had bought—and later regretted buying—one $5,000 system from a get-rich-quick real estate promoter who he later learned had never actually owned real estate. Recovering from that lesson, Omar had talked to over a dozen real estate brokers in his local area.

Omar had come to appreciate that real estate was not a get-rich-quick enterprise but rather a slow process of growth and incremental success. Still, he was impatient to begin the process. He had saved $20,000, and it was definitely not appreciating in his savings account, which paid a measly 1 percent annual return. When inflation was factored in, he knew he was actually losing money.

So he was intrigued when Ashleigh was introduced to him by a local broker. Ashleigh was an attractive woman in her early forties who had put together a number of real estate syndications. Her typical deal was for five to ten investors to put up $20,000 to $50,000 toward the purchase of a large apartment complex. Ashleigh received a commission on the purchase of the real estate, a monthly management fee, and 20 percent of the equity in the deal. When all the numbers were added up, Ashleigh was quite well compensated. But, as she freely admitted, many of her investors simply didn't have the time or inclination to be actively involved. And they were willing to pay for her assistance.

Omar was intrigued by Ashleigh's proposal. He could put his $20,000 into her investment and perhaps in five years, or whenever he and the other partners decided to sell, could receive $35,000 to $40,000. At least, that's what the projections said.

Omar was seriously considering the investment until he spoke to Zook, another real estate broker who had taken an interest in Omar and his investment path. Zook questioned whether Omar really wanted to be a limited partner in a real estate syndication. While it was an excellent investment for some people, Zook thought that it didn't seem to be a good fit for Omar. In the syndication as a limited partner, Omar would have no say in how the property was managed. He would have no control and no voice in the project. As such, Omar wouldn't really learn anything about real estate management and acquisition. He would be a passive investor instead of an active and involved real estate entrepreneur.

Omar appreciated Zook's comments. He refocused on his goals, which were to learn about real estate by starting small and then grow into larger properties as his experience and confidence expanded. He realized it was possible that a few mistakes might be made on his first investments and acknowledged that he would prefer to make them early on smaller properties where the consequences would not be so dramatic.

Omar politely declined Ashleigh's opportunity to invest. He explained to her that as a passive investor he couldn't learn real estate the way he wanted to learn it. Instead, Zook found Omar a $100,000 duplex to buy with $15,000 down. Omar's remaining $5,000 was held in a reserve account in the event of any emergencies or vacancies.

Omar used this first opportunity to learn about what it took to manage real estate and to increase its value. This knowledge was extremely useful when Omar bought his next duplex, a fourplex, and, eventually, larger properties.

And here is why it gets easier for Omar, and other investors like him. A system becomes a blueprint for investing. And the chances for making mistakes decreases as experience increases. There's yet another plus of repeating a successful formula: Once you get established in an area of investing—after you've become known as someone who buys a certain type of property— you gain momentum. For example, brokers will seek you out when good deals arise. You'll hear about these deals before the mob of other would-be buyers do.

A final point about sticking to the same game plan when investing in real estate: When you assemble your team of advisors, your real estate agent will be an expert in the sector you're investing in, but most likely will not be an expert in other sectors. For example, your agent may be used to handling duplexes, but not strip malls.

By sticking with one game, you won't have to seek out new team members. It's best to find your team, understand what it's good at, and use it as your investment vehicle. By doing so—by sticking to one formula—you leverage your experience. Of course, when you are ready to broaden your investment criteria, you can always seek out new team members.

Now let's talk about creating your team of advisors . . .

Chapter 5

Creating Your Team of Advisors

Rich Dad Tip

"Business and investing are team sports."—Rich Dad

We mentioned toward the end of the previous chapter that specializing in a certain area of property investing gives you *momentum*. You become known as an investor looking for certain types of property. And so, when such a property—say, a fixer-upper residence in a lower-middle-class neighborhood—comes up for sale, real estate professionals, such as agents, appraisers, or loan officers, who keep close tabs on the market, and who may have worked with you on other deals, are prone to tip you off. They want to make money as badly as you do. They want to maximize their time by working with serious buyers. And they want to cultivate their relationship with you with an eye toward future business collaborations. These people are valuable connections for you and are the very type of members you want on your investment team. The better you do, the better they do, and vice versa.

Case No. 4
Charles and Wilson

Charles was an experienced real estate investor who never seemed to get in on the best deals. Yes, he had a number of duplexes and fourplexes around town. But he never could seem to break into the larger properties—the ten-to-forty-unit buildings he really wanted to own. Those larger properties were highly sought after in his area, and Charles wasn't privy to the early information about their availability.

Wilson, on the other hand, always knew about the best deals. In fact, he had his choice of them. And by knowing which properties were for sale before they hit the market, Wilson had been able to dramatically improve his real estate portfolio in the last few years.

Charles was determined to know how Wilson succeeded. After considering numerous ways to best approach him, Charles finally decided to buy Wilson dinner on the pretense of discussing "the market." Wilson readily agreed, and one week later they sat down to break bread and discuss real estate.

One good bottle of wine was followed by a superior bottle. Wilson was enjoying the discussion and grew more forthcoming as the night continued.

Charles then asked Wilson the question he had been holding: how did he learn about the best deals?

Wilson smiled as he gave his answer. The brokers were his friends, he said. It was that simple. And as friends he respected the amount of work they put in to become successful. Many of them starved for the first five or so years of their career as they learned the local market and got to know the buyers and sellers.

Wilson also said he never challenged a broker's right to a commission. He never went around a broker directly to the seller in hopes of negotiating a better deal. And he never tried to talk a broker into taking a reduced commission in order to make a deal work.

The commission reduction comment stung Charles. Four years earlier he had talked a local broker into forgoing $10,000 of a $25,000 commission in order for a deal to fly. While pleased with himself at the time, he knew later the $10,000 was not that material to the transaction. And now he realized that that $10,000 had cost him a great deal of early market intelligence.

Wilson knew that his comment had registered with Charles. He went on to say that the brokers all spoke to each other. If one investor didn't appreciate their efforts and pressured for commission reductions, the word got around. And the result was that the best deals did not reach such people.

Charles acknowledged his past transgressions and asked what could be done. Wilson said he needed to do some fence mending. He needed to acknowledge the mistake and let them know it wouldn't happen again. Above all, he needed to respect the brokers' efforts and be willing to compensate them for their time. And he needed to be clear with the brokers that he was a serious buyer of ten-to-forty-unit apartment buildings. The brokers, of course, want to deal with investors who can quickly purchase the property without a lot of issues and complications. Wilson indicated that reminding them you were that person went a long way toward getting the first call of availability.

Charles thanked Wilson for his insight and resolved to better utilize the investor network.

The ability to network is crucial to the career of a successful real estate investor. Successful people know that it's not only *what* you know, but *whom* you know. As you embark on your career as a real estate investor, you must begin building your network of advisors, support groups, and friends who become conduits of information and potential allies on deals, and allow you to grow quicker.

This may lead you to a fundamental change in thinking. Most of us, growing up in school, were trained to work alone. Relying on others was called cheating. But learning the real estate business—and succeeding at it—requires expertise in a number of areas, and it's impractical and probably impossible to master every one of them. What you want to do is assemble a team of experts from each area and leverage their expertise. You don't have to know everything; you just need to know whom to call.

This approach is connected to another principle: To be successful, you must surround yourself with people who help you create your success. We're referring to mentors. Before we talk about the kinds of people you want on your investment team as advisors and associates, let's examine the role of mentors.

Mentors on the Right Side

In the book *Rich Dad's CASHFLOW Quadrant: Rich Dad's Guide to Financial Freedom* is an exercise for the reader to write down the six people he or she spends the most time with. The reader then figures out which quadrant each of these six people is on: the left side or the right side. The side for employees and the self-employed or the side with business owners and investors? The reader also must ask which side he or she is on and which side he or she *wants* to be on. If the reader is on the left side and wishes to move to the right side, he or she should begin surrounding himself or herself with people on the right side, for these right-siders will encourage and help the reader along that path.

Part of human nature is to resist change. To effect change in, say, recovery from addiction, a person must aggressively pull away from an unhealthful environment that perpetuates addictive behavior, and situate himself or herself among nonaddicts and recovering addicts. For you to move from the left side of the CASHFLOW Quadrant to the right side, you should, similarly, situate yourself among people already on the right side or who are moving toward the right side. The motivation and support these like-minded people can provide will spur a positive development in your financial and investing habits. They will be mentors, sustaining your momentum as you undertake this major life change. For there will be obstacles, including friends, associates, and possibly family members, who will be naysayers, thinking you're perhaps losing your mind by pursuing radically new goals.

Let's get back to listing people in your life. If one of them is on the right side of the Quadrant, doing the real estate investing you want to do, start there. This person will know more at the moment than you do about this sort of business. This person can be a mentor. And remember, this person is already connected to advisors and mentors who helped make this person successful. So this person can be a tremendous resource.

Outside of your current circle, here are some other circles to immediately explore that can yield mentors:

• *Free real estate seminars:* Most communities have these. Scan calendars in your local newspaper. Read advertisements in the business section.

Real estate agencies and mortgage brokers often hold seminars for the public. Scan their Web sites or call and ask about upcoming events.

• *Local real estate clubs:* Many communities have these, just as they have stock investing clubs. These clubs are groups of people who want to learn more about investing and even form their own investment groups. Some attendees will be beginners, like you. Others will be much more experienced, and candidates to be mentors.

• *Community colleges and community education programs through cities or counties:* These offer classes in real estate investing. And through them you can meet other potential investors. In fact, there is a Rich Dad's CASHFLOW Personal Finance course as well as a Rich Dad's Real Estate course offered through many community colleges across the United States as well as in other countries. Please contact The Rich Dad Company through richdad.com for further information.

• *CASHFLOW game clubs:* These clubs have formed around the nation and overseas. Go to richdad.com to find a CASHFLOW club near you.

Get yourself involved with these groups and start asking questions. Your learning curve will accelerate. You'll begin learning the terminology and vocabulary of money. You may not want to jump into the first deal presented, but your mind will begin recognizing opportunities all around you that were there all along although you weren't interested in focusing on them at the time. On your morning walk or jog, or on a bicycle ride, or simply driving around town, you'll start paying attention to real estate signs, which are signposts to the market. You'll become more aware, seeing what others don't see. (A big advantage of experienced real estate investors is that they see opportunities others are blind to, simply because these investors have experience and knowledge.)

You can also start reading magazine and newspaper articles and trade publications on real estate. For example, the trade journal for people who own apartment complexes is *Multi-Housing News*. If you're interested in this area of real estate, subscribe to this magazine. You should also surf the Internet for free sites full of information.

Read the Rich Dad's Advisors book *The ABC's of Real Estate Investing*, by Ken McElroy, another Rich Dad's Advisor who specializes in real estate investing and property management.

Remember, the most valuable piece of real estate is the six inches between your ears. The act of educating yourself is essential to forging your real estate investing career. Pushing yourself to get an education serves four essential purposes:

1. It begins the *demystification* of real estate for you. The biggest cause of inaction is fear. Fear of the unknown. Fear of making a mistake. Fear of being wrong, of looking stupid.

2. By wading into the real estate game, you'll quickly see that it doesn't take special genius or unhealthy greed or tremendous cash reserves to get started. Ordinary people are pursuing their goals with ordinary resources and reasonable motives.

3. Stepping out into the world of real estate by educating yourself will help lead you to find out what sort of real estate investing is right for you— what kind of property and market suits your nature and goals. If you find you're interested in single-family homes, you need to gravitate toward investors and professionals with similar interests, and not, say, people interested in storage units or office buildings. You need to be among people from whom you'll absorb pertinent information. (And when you pay attention to real estate signs around town, you'll see which Realtor or other agent has signs most often in the areas in which you're interested. This agent could prove to be a tremendous mentor for you and could possibly become a member of your team of advisors.)

4. Getting out into the real estate world and educating yourself will yield you mentors. These people can guide you on your way.

Why should a mentor give you his or her time? Typically, someone who has been successful is happy to share his or her success. Those who aren't willing to share may consider you a potential competitor and therefore wouldn't be good mentors to you anyway. There are more people in the world who are willing to help you than those who aren't. But a couple cautionary points about mentor-student relationships:

1. The power of exchange is very important. Make sure you're not abusing the mentor's time. Make sure you do something to compensate the men-

tor for his or her advice. Maybe it's just taking the person to lunch. Maybe it's cutting the person's lawn. Whatever it is, keep the exchange even and also let the person know you appreciate the advice.

2. Realize that offering to go into a business partnership with a mentor may not serve the mentor well (nor would it serve *you* well after you've gained experience and someone approaches *you* to be a mentor). This is because if you are using the mentor's knowledge and network, you better be contributing something else that is equally valuable to the partnership, such as the majority of the money or the majority of "sweat equity" (time and energy). If you're only willing to put in the same effort and money, or less than half, while asking the mentor to put in money *and* experience, the mentor will decline the partnership. This is because the mentor will also end up cleaning up your mistakes caused by your lack of knowledge. And, of course, the mentor could most likely do the deal without you.

Your mentor could prove especially valuable as you take the next step in real estate investing after getting your initial education: putting together your investment team.

Building Your Team of Advisors

Through talking to people who do what you want to do in real estate investing, you'll immerse yourself in a new environment and start establishing your investment network. These people may not be the ones you end up with on your team, but it's a start.

Every investor will need advisors specific to his or her investment project. Let's say, for example, you want to invest in single-family fixer-uppers. People interested in these properties, or who are already investing in them, are the ones you'll gravitate toward.

One way to speed the formation of your team is to find a mentor who is successful in the investing you want to do. Ask this person for referrals of whom this person uses for loans, appraisals, accounting, and so on (a thorough list of team members is below). Another way is to get on the *Rich Dad* forums at richdad.com, announce your geographic area, and say you're looking for advisors in that area. Put together your list of potential advisors and begin interviewing these people. For example, if you are looking for a lawyer specializing in real estate contracts and law, ask the mentor whom he or she uses. Same with finding an accountant, mortgage broker, or loan officer. Word of mouth is a useful referral tool.

When you approach a potential professional you're considering for your team, interview the person. Ask about the person's experience in the field, whether the person is taking on new business, if you're the sort of client the person is interested in, if the person has clients investing in the kind of projects you have in mind, and whether the person would invest in those projects himself or herself. Ask the person's policy on getting back to you—does it typically take twenty-four or forty-eight hours to return a phone call? Will the person handle your account or pass it on to a colleague or junior in the office? If so, does the junior have experience? What's the billing practice—charging per hour or per transaction? Also ask for client references. Then call those clients and ask if they're happy with the professional.

It is very important that your advisors are familiar with your area of investing. You want to pay for their advice (from their prior experience personally or with clients). You do not want them learning or "researching" on your dime. When the advisor is a neighbor or relative, be particularly careful that he or she can be a qualified and competent advisor. Remember the old saying "You get what you pay for!"

If the person seems to know what he or she is doing, and you feel comfortable with him or her, those are positive signs. Once you do put someone on your team, you're anticipating nurturing a long-term relationship. This is especially true of real estate attorneys, accountants, and lenders. They are intimately familiar with your personal situation, and therefore you want them to be invested in your benefit. The better you do, the more business you bring them. There must be a high level of trust. There must be mutual respect.

Here is a typical list of advisors and associates on your investment team:

- *Real Estate Brokers:* These Realtors or other agents know the market, recognize trends, have access to key information, can tip you off to deals, and can help you make deals. They are your eyes and ears to the market.
- *Other Real Estate Investors:* Like agents, other real estate investors can tip you off to deals or bring you into deals.

- *Real Estate Lenders* (mortgage brokers or loan officers): These professionals may be at banks or other lending institutions. Or they may be private individuals. Some lenders specialize in single-family home loans, others in commercial loans. When you're first starting out, the benefit of finding a lender is to help you know what you're qualified to invest in. Hopefully, this lender will be prepared to support you in your purchase. But when you're actually ready to proceed, get quotes from several lenders and find out who is best for you in the market at this point in time.

(As a special note, you can find other sources of investment capital, such as family members or friends. But if you do, the relationship must be clearly spelled out, such as whether it's a loan that must be repaid in full or a loan seeking a percentage of potential profits. Everything must be properly, legally documented. Remember, it's a business deal. Personal relationships can be ruined by volatile business relationships. When two good friends decide to invest in real estate, someone needs to tell them they must "plan the divorce before they get married." They need to prepare an exit strategy to the investment—how they would sell the property or buy the other partner out—before they even get into it. This is because emotions can easily heat up during an investment, and sanity can go out the door.)

- *Escrow Officer*
- *Appraiser*
- *Home Inspector*
- *Real Estate Attorney:* This lawyer must be a specialist in real estate, practice in your legal jurisdiction (laws vary from state to state, and even county to county and city to city), and be experienced in your specific type of real estate (e.g., single-family residences). You don't want to hire an attorney who is new to your area, for you'd be paying for the attorney's learning curve.

- *Bookkeeper:* There are differences among bookkeepers, real estate accountants, and tax accountants. Bookkeepers typically cost less per hour than accountants. Bookkeepers keep your day-to-day records orderly and up-to-date. (When you start out with your first property, you may handle these tasks yourself. It's a good learning experience, but, unfortunately, also an opportunity to make mistakes. As your investments grow more complicated, a bookkeeper is highly recommended. Do you want to spend your time keeping your books or looking for properties?)

• *Real Estate Accountant:* This professional analyzes the records your bookkeeper prepares and manages, and makes sure your financial statements are correct.

• *Tax Accountant:* This professional, usually a certified public accountant, helps you strategize your spending with an eye toward minimizing your taxes. The advice could include, for example, investing in more property to offset reportable income from a current property. The tax accountant also lets you know what you should be doing today to plan for the future. Another role for the tax accountant: to represent you in the event of an IRS audit. In fact, you are wise not to show up yourself at the audit meeting (unless you're required to), since you may volunteer more information than needed and hurt your cause. The accountant understands what the IRS is looking for and typically can resolve the issues more quickly and efficiently. (Your tax accountant and real estate accountant may be the same person, if that person is qualified in both areas. And when you start out in real estate investing, you may have only a tax accountant, not a real estate accountant, too.)

• *Insurance Agent.* You'll need insurance on your property to cover property risk and liability risk. You'll need an agent specializing in real estate.

• *Property Manager:* When you first start out with a rental property, you'll likely manage it yourself. But as your investments grow in size and quantity, a property manager could well be a wise investment to save you time and energy.

The following five team members may be permanent members or not. You may want to get quotes from several parties on each project as needed (especially when you first start investing) to ensure you're paying a reasonable price. Once you find a capable contractor who is reliable and works for a fair price, you may stick with that person from then on. A key trait of such a person is personality: a pleasant working relationship. If you end up with a property manager on your team, the property manager may hire the following people:

• Handyman
• Cleaning service
• Landscaper

- Roofer
- Plumber

As you advance through the world of investing, your team members will change. As you gain experience and become more successful, you may need a larger mortgage company.

If you become the biggest client an attorney or accountant has, you may part ways and find the next level of advisor in such a category, to draw on even greater knowledge. For an advisor at a higher level will have larger clients and therefore will have developed knowledge on larger projects. You'll be paying for that knowledge base.

Now let's take action . . .

Chapter 6

Taking Action

There is no teacher like experience. When you set out on your first real estate investment, you must not let the fear of making mistakes stop you. Everyone makes mistakes, but you can learn from them. And you can't really learn the business without learning by *doing*. If you think for a moment, you made plenty of mistakes along the way to each goal you've conquered in life. This goes back to your earliest years. You learned to crawl before you walked, and stumbled and tumbled a great deal before you were able to stay upright. Later you fell off your bicycle more than once. You learned to float before you swam. And so on.

Our school system drums into us that we must avoid making mistakes, and strive for perfection. Well, no investment you'll ever make will be perfect. There will be challenges, and there will be mistakes. As you gain experience, you'll make fewer mistakes. But you'll get absolutely nowhere if you stay on the sidelines and don't get yourself into the game!

You don't have to start out with a big project, and you should not start out recklessly. Once you've begun diligently educating yourself about real estate (and remember the resource section in Appendix A), you should get out and start looking at properties.

If you're the typical beginner, you will find some tempting prospects and write a few offers with appropriate contingencies. By so doing, you will begin learning the game in earnest. You shouldn't tender offers frivolously just as a learning experience and waste people's time. But you should ask a lot of questions while you're searching for properties on which to make offers. From the moment an agent arrives when you're looking at a property, ask about the "comps"—the prices on comparable homes in the neighborhood. Ask about the neighborhood, the crime rate, what the crack in the wall signifies, and so on. Look at the roof. Look at the yard. How old is the furnace? The air conditioner? Is there deferred maintenance—repairs that should have been done but haven't yet? Is there a lien on the property? Is there an easement? Any news of new roads coming in? Is the property within the city's borders? Is it near a bus line? Near schools? How is the school district? (Remember, you'll want to rent out the place and will need information to make your own pitch to prospective tenants.)

The agent may not have answers for every question, but if you're a serious buyer, the agent will surely get those answers. Professionals like to answer questions because it shows they know what they're talking about. The best question to ask the agent is: What questions should I have asked about this place that I haven't? You should ask that same question of brokers, lenders, appraisers, and others. That's how you learn.

As you gather increasing information, ask yourself if a particular prospect is a good investment. Is it within your risk tolerance? Are you taking the steps to learn about it so you truly understand what you're doing? When you have a contract drawn up, does it contain the necessary contingencies, such as having a home inspector look over the place? (And if you know you want to invest, you can begin the process of forming an appropriate entity such as a limited liability company, to hold the asset, which will be discussed in Part Four, "Legal Strategies.")

Putting together a real estate deal takes time and energy. It's work. But if you have the right temperament—meaning you're dogged enough to keep searching until you find a good prospect, and disciplined enough to do due diligence on that prospect—the work is rewarding. In fact, you'll happily discover that it's *fun*. When you finally find something, and do the financials, and see that you can leverage your money and make a good return, it's very exciting. It's also a good self-esteem builder. Many of us have spent years in the same occupation. When you branch out into something new, like buying a piece of real estate, and make it work, it's invigorating. When you're getting a check each month, it gives you a great sense of accomplishment. The accomplishment is paying you. And it whets your appetite for more accomplishments—more real estate deals.

Rich Dad's philosophy is that we should enjoy lifelong learning. Any type of investing, whether in paper assets, a business, or real estate, means employing your intellectual faculties in a vigorous way. It's good for you. And when you've made a good real estate investment, it's financially rewarding, too.

But, again, before you can make any money in real estate, you have to get out there and start trying.

Learning From Mistakes

Case No. 5
The Leed Family

Early in their real estate investing career, the Leed family bought property in the White Mountains of Arizona. They wanted to build a corporate-retreat center on the rural land. It was a "back of a napkin" deal, with the area sketched out, but it looked very clean-cut. The property lines were clearly marked on a survey drawing provided by the seller. The property was described in detail and at length (the legal "meets and bounds" description) in the complete title document. But after the Leeds bought the property, they performed a survey and discovered that slivers of the property along a lakefront were not owned by them—the slivers were not included in the legal description of the property in the deed. The property had been through a fair number of ownerships, and these slivers had not been conveyed to the Leeds. The lesson they learned was to make sure to get their own property survey before buying. The long description in a title does not always cover what you think it does. Fortunately, the Leeds weren't hurt by the deal. They ended up selling the property for a tidy profit.

Another Leed family lesson has to do with their son Scott. The lesson he learned on his first investment property can be called "the $3,000 driveway." He and his best friend, each then twenty-five, formed a limited liability company and bought a fourplex in a low-income area. The property produced a positive cash flow. But investments often include surprises, and the young men's fourplex delivered one within a short time after they'd completed their purchase: City officials sent them, the owners of record, a notice that the entire back driveway had to be repaved.

The partners came up with the money, but it wasn't the last unexpected expense for their fourplex. The costs began adding up. It was almost comical. An air conditioner went out in one unit, and they had to pay for their tenant to stay in a motel until the problem was fixed in the sweltering Arizona summer. Another tenant had a dog with fleas, and the whole building became infested. The harried landlords had to have the fourplex completely fumigated. Meanwhile, personality conflicts emerged between the two, and they realized they shouldn't be in business together. All in all—it was a learning experience.

Fortunately, the real estate market was trending up, and the two now former best friends were able to sell the fourplex after eighteen months. Scott put his experience from that first property to use when he bought his next fourplex, which was a higher-level building. He now knew much more about what to look for in a building and in tenants (flea-infested pets were excluded). He also stashed away some cash reserves to meet whatever unexpected problems arose.

None of these lessons would have come without having made mistakes. Don't let mistakes get you down. You become a good real estate investor through earnest study, networking, effort—and trial and error. And you'll continue learning new lessons with each investment.

Chapter 7

Setting Up Your Books

Keep a Separate Account

As soon as you buy an investment property, it's wise to set up a separate bank checking account to handle the income and expenses. That way you can clearly track the investment instead of mingling money with your other accounts. Remember, before you buy a property, you will determine your expectations for it, including what your positive cash flow must be to make it a viable investment. Maintaining a separate account specific to the investment makes it easier to pay attention to money coming in and going out.

Even if you have to add money to the account from other sources, it's important to keep a separate account for your investment. Each real estate investment you make is really a separate business. And, as we'll discuss ahead, you will want to put the investment property into its own legal entity, such as a limited liability company. As well, a segregated account will prove helpful to your tax accountant, your bookkeeper, and heaven forbid, the IRS if you're ever audited.

Case No. 6
Pam

Pam owned a beauty salon and a fourplex. Against the advice of her CPA and attorney, she held both her business and her rental real estate in her own name as a sole proprietor. Her attorney was concerned for asset protection reasons. A claim against the beauty salon (for even a bad hair day) could expose the fourplex to a creditor's judgment, and vice versa. Pam's CPA was concerned that the books were not being handled properly. All activities of the beauty salon business and the real estate business were mixed into the same bank account. It was a recipe for confusion, or worse.

One day Pam's supplier for hair products came into her store and demanded he be paid $4,000 for back invoices before any beauty supplies were delivered. Pam was taken aback by this request. Her records indicated the supplier had been paid. The supplier argued otherwise. Pam knew she needed the popular and expensive shampoos and rinses and colors to keep people coming into the store. So she reluctantly paid the supplier, with the agreement that she had a credit on future purchases if she overpaid. The $4,000 payment left Pam's account with a $12 balance.

That afternoon two tenants at the fourplex called to say they were moving back to Guatemala. Pam was incredulous. Why was it only her tenants who moved? The tenants properly requested the repayment of their $500 deposits. Pam was struck by this coincidence of events. She didn't have the money in her account to pay back the deposits. While she may have a credit on hair supplies, she didn't dare offer the tenants a repayment in shampoos and conditioners. She knew that the state required that the deposits be repaid within three days. Pam told the tenants she would get them the money in due time.

Pam was in a panic. She knew that her business and real estate were profitable. But the books now indicated otherwise. And, worse yet, under state law she now owed the deposit money in seventy-two hours. Failure to make these payments could result in fines, penalties, and interest.

Rather than run into trouble, Pam went to the bank and obtained an unsecured loan for $5,000. With the new money, she paid the tenants their deposits back and immediately retained a bookkeeper to keep track of her activities through separate bank accounts.

Having a Bookkeeper

When it comes to tracking cash flow in a property, your bookkeeper really is your eyes and ears. If the bookkeeper sees something amiss—such as a glaringly large monthly telephone bill, or unpaid rent—he or she should notify you.

While you're ultimately responsible for assuring a property's positive cash flow, your bookkeeper is not only there to process tenants' checks for deposit and prepare vendor invoices for payment. A good bookkeeper also reviews the inflow and outflow of money. (Some investors may choose, instead, to have a property manager collect tenants' checks and pay the bills by writing checks. There also is inexpensive bookkeeping software you can buy. The role of your bookkeeper depends on your needs.)

Whatever your system of keeping books, you should check your books every month to gauge your investment's performance. This will help you decide whether, and where, you need to cut expenses or boost income to make the property meet its goals. (Maybe you find, by scrutinizing bills paid out, that you're paying too much for landscaping and need to rebid the service. Maybe your water bills have increased because you unknowingly have a broken water pipe.)

Too often, investors don't keep an eye on their property, and they end up in trouble. If you find the need to boost a property's income, your advisors may have suggestions. If you own an apartment complex, maybe you can put in vending machines or a laundry room to boost income. Maybe you need to cut your utility expenses by having apartments separately metered. And as a landlord you need to watch not only your books but the market itself. Has the rent gone up in comparable properties? Should you be raising your rates, too?

Having a Tax Accountant or CPA

Your CPA not only helps you prepare your tax return at the end of the year but during the course of the year should ensure that you're taking all possible deductions and also help you plan your investment strategy for the future.

Your tax accountant helps you see the big picture. Can you reduce your estimated quarterly payments? Should you increase them? How will a new investment property impact your overall financial position? Should you even get into the property? In terms of key members of your advisory team, your CPA will be one of the most important. Remember, the right tax and financial advice can save you tens of thousands of dollars. And know that the wrong advice (or a lack of advice altogether) can cost you even more, and sometimes all that you own.

There is a big difference between a bookkeeper and a tax accountant or CPA. You don't want to pay a tax accountant or CPA for what a bookkeeper can do for you at much lower rates. But do not expect your bookkeeper to see the big picture. You want your bookkeeper keeping an eye on the details and cash balances, and you want your tax accountant and/or CPA to be keeping an eye on the big picture and your overall wealth strategy and plan.

Set Up Your Books from the Start

An investment property is time-intensive and serious business. So set up your separate account and get your bookkeeper and accountant on board from the very start, so that you can manage your investment in a businesslike manner.

Your finances can become tangled up very quickly if you neglect this preparatory work. And since these systems must be set in place anyway, you might as well get them in order from the start. Especially since once your books are properly set up, the tax savings can begin . . .

Part Three

Tax Strategies

Mention the word "taxes" and most people cringe and frown. By becoming a sophisticated real estate investor, you can transform yourself so that the next time you hear the word "taxes," you can smile and say, "What taxes?"

There are several provisions in the tax code that were written to encourage real estate investing. As mentioned before, the government wants to reward investors who provide housing for those who need it. As investors continue to build new buildings, they also provide employment for thousands of people. In short, real estate investors are favored by the tax code because their efforts help the economy in general.

In analyzing a property, many people first look at the cash-on-cash return from the operations of the real estate before including the tax impact in order to qualify the property for further review. If the property works well economically before taxes, it will most certainly be much better when the tax impact is included. This was shown in the example for leverage in Chapter 2 where the cash-on-cash return went from over 12 percent to over 22 percent just by adding the impact from tax savings in the calculation.

The same can be true for any property you analyze. But first you need a basic understanding of analyzing the numbers and the tax strategies. In this section of the book, we will review the tax strategies used by sophisticated real estate investors. We do not expect you to become your own tax accountant or to become an expert from reading this book, but hopefully you will have new questions to ask of your tax accountant and/or CPA that can accelerate your own wealth through the application of these tax strategies.

Chapter 8

Understand the Numbers

Now it is time to take tax advantage of your real estate. But to do so, it is important to know what you have. And that starts before you buy the property.

Analyze the Numbers of the Property

When you're looking at a real estate property, the financial information given to you by the current owner and the real estate agent is called the pro forma. In Latin, the term means "as if." For real estate cynics, it means "as if you expect me to believe those numbers."

The pro forma contains the property's sales price and operating costs, such as utilities and taxes, insurance, repairs, and business expenses; and it projects the property's value and income based on such market factors as a full occupancy rate. The pro forma may well represent, as our cynic comment illustrates, a pipe dream. The pro forma may not reflect at all the reality of the property's worth and income potential. Instead, it may only represent what the seller and the seller's real estate agent think a buyer will want to see, or what is needed to justify the asking price. As such, you use the pro forma as a skeptical starting point—to decide whether you're interested in even considering buying the property.

If you sign a contract to buy the property, you'll include a purchase contingency allowing you to obtain actual financial figures, commonly called the financials, on the property. The contingency will read something like this: "This offer shall be contingent upon Buyer's complete review and acceptance of the financial records associated with the subject property." If it's a rental property, you'll take a close look at what the rental income is. You'll also review rental prices at comparable properties ("comps") in the neighborhood to make sure the pro forma figures are in the ballpark. You'll determine how many rental properties are in the area, which can be done by having your agent pull up local rental listings. You'll consider whether the rental market is saturated in the area, or if there is even a market for rental properties in that area and in the price range you're intending to charge.

You'll examine the property's operating expenses for utilities, property tax, and the like by asking the seller to show you the actual bills from the utility company and the tax collector. You'll determine what extra expenses you may incur, especially when you have your building inspector examine the place as part of your due diligence. Was the seller personally doing maintenance on the property? Is this work you'll have to contract out in the future? Are there needed repairs you'll have to make? How great a cash reserve will you have to factor in for onetime expenses? For example, if the roof looks like it may need replacing, how much should you set aside?

In this way, you'll know if you need to ask the seller for a price allowance or a "haircut" (both of which mean a dollar reduction) to make the deal a go.

You also must consider what your actual debt service (the principal and interest payments) will be on the loan you obtain. And you must consider how much of a cushion you'll need if the property is vacant of renters for a significant period. What sort of financial reserve will you require to weather a protracted lack of cash flow?

In this way, you'll figure out yourself, separate and apart from the seller's pro forma, if the property will yield a positive cash flow—bringing net monthly income after deducting the operating expenses and debt service. And you'll decide how risky the investment is.

Analyze the Numbers' Impact on Your Personal Financials

If the property you're looking to buy seems a good investment risk and one that will yield a positive cash flow, you must next analyze the property's impact on your overall financial situation.

The property's positive cash flow will only be part of your cash-on-cash return. We previously used a cash flow chart example in Chapter 2. We're going to use a new one here, which involves the purchase of a five-unit apartment building for $450,000 with 20 percent down.

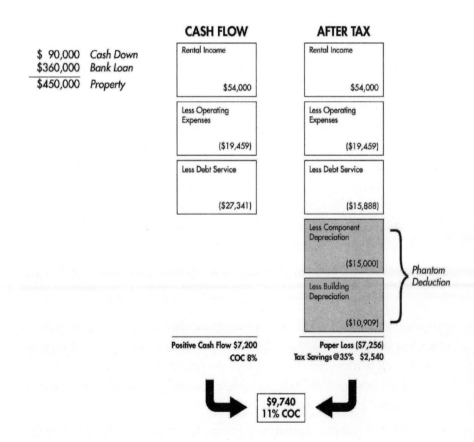

The IRS considers your rental property as a business and gives you several deductions. One is the payments you make on the interest (but not the principal) of your debt service. In addition, there are the "phantom deductions"—the "passive loss" from component depreciation and from building depreciation, which are computed at an annual rate (discussed later in this chapter). So after you take your rental income (five units at $900 each per month, or $54,000 per year) and subtract operating expenses ($19,459), you also subtract the interest payments ($15,888) on debt service, and you subtract the component and building depreciation ($15,000 and $10,909, respectively). You multiply this "paper loss" ($7,256) by your tax rate (35 percent), and determine your tax savings ($2,540).

You add the tax savings ($2,540) to your net cash flow from the property before taxes ($7,200) and come up with your true cash-on-cash return: $9,740, or 11 percent. Your true cash-on-cash return will show you how good (or not so good) a particular real estate investment will be for you.

In this case, the investor put down 20 percent of the $450,000 purchase price of the property. So the $90,000 investment yielded a cash-on-cash return of nearly 11 percent.

Obviously, real estate enjoys a distinct tax advantage over the stock market. If your projected paper loss in a rental property is $7,256, you can claim $2,540 in tax savings. But if you lost the same $7,256 in the stock market (and it would be a true drop in value, not a paper loss), you would only be able to claim the maximum for a capital loss—$3,000—on your annual tax return. To claim the entire loss would take you three years.

This example illustrates how real estate can be a far better investment than stock. And the big advantage of passive income from real estate over portfolio income (from stock)—and especially over earned income (from your job), which the IRS taxes at the highest rate of the three types of income (potentially over 50 percent when payroll taxes are included)—is that the income from real estate can come to you tax-free due to the write-offs for depreciation.

In our example, the $7,200 in positive cash flow was not taxed! The depreciation wiped out that profit—on paper!

Determining what your depreciation will be on a property is a crucial step in assessing a property's benefit to you and deciding whether to invest in the property.

Allocating Costs for Depreciation

In a real estate investment, there are four types of property: land, land improvements, personal property, and the structures or buildings (which should be further broken down into the structure and its component parts). The value of the land cannot be depreciated. Assets included in land improvements (e.g., sidewalks) and personal property have relatively short useful lives and thus are subject to accelerated depreciation methods. A tremendous tax savings can be achieved through dividing the dollar amount attributed to the building into the components and the structure itself. The tax law allows you to depreciate the components of the building (for example, wall and floor tiles, certain lighting, certain partitions, and certain electrical systems). It is recommended that you have a cost segregation study performed by an independent party to determine what portion of your building can be categorized as components. Your CPA or tax accountant should be able to recommend a company qualified to perform this study for you.

With the U.S. Master Tax Guide as our source for category examples, let's look at the personal property and building categories separately:

• Personal property items include those that can be removed without damage or disablement to the structure or its operation and maintenance. These include furniture, and electronic appliances such as washers, dryers, computers, televisions, and telephones. These items fall into different recovery periods for depreciation, per the federal tax code, which assigns a "class life" to each item. In general, personal property in residential rental properties falls into either five-year or seven-year schedules for depreciation. (For example, furniture, appliances, computers, and carpeting are in the five-year category, while desks and fax machines are considered seven-year property.) Your tax accountant can allocate these costs, and determine the rate of depreciation, which generally is an accelerated rate (and better than the building depreciation) for the first few years.

• Building items include the structure and the components such as those that relate to the operation and maintenance of a building, such as ceilings and roofs, walls and windows, electrical and plumbing, central air conditioning and heating systems, chimneys and bathtubs, sinks and lighting fixtures, walls and windows, fire escapes and stairs, floors and doors, landscaping and paving. Without a cost segregation, the value of these items is depreciated over 27-and-a-half years in a residential rental property, and over 39 years in a nonresidential, or commercial real property. (How Congress came up with 27½ and 39 years is something only a lobbyist would know.) However, this is where the component depreciation can be a great benefit. To demonstrate the effect of this rule, the tax court permitted the use of cost segregation technique for the following building improvements in *Hospital Corporation of America v. Commissioner:*

Item	5-yr life	39-yr life
Primary and secondary electrical distribution systems	x	
Branch electrical wiring and communications special equipment		x
Wiring and related property items in the laboratory and maintenance shop	x	
Other wiring and related property	x	
Wiring to television equipment	x	
Conduit, floor boxes and power boxes	x	
Electrical wiring relating to internal communications	x	
Carpeting	x	
Vinyl wall and floor coverings	x	
Kitchen wall pipings and steam lines	x	
Patient corridor handrails	x	
Overhead lights		x
Accordion doors and partitions	x	
Bathroom accessories and mirrors		x
Acoustical tile ceilings		x
Steam boilers		x

In this example the company was allowed to depreciate the components over a 5 year life and the rest of the building over a 39 year life since it was a commercial property. Without a component study, or cost segregation, the total cost attributed to the building and its component would be subject to "straight line depreciation"—meaning you divide the value of the building or structure by the depreciation term (e.g., 27.5 for a residential property, or 39 for commercial) to come up with your annual depreciation, a rate that remains constant for the 27-and-a-half year or 39 year period.

As a general rule, here is how you will determine the value of the personal property and of the building or structure:

1. Determine the value of the land. Land is not depreciable. One way to figure out the land's value is to begin with the purchase price of the property. Next, obtain the local tax assessor's statement of value for the land and building. Note the assessor's ratio of the land value to building value. Apply that ratio to the purchase price, and you will see how much the land is worth. Some accountants use the 20-80 rule, where 20% is allocated to the land and 80% is allocated to the structure. It is recommended that you use a more verifiable approach where it is available.

2. List and assign values to each item of personal property. (The appraiser on your team of advisors can help you with this.) A note of caution: It's usually difficult to substantiate on a tax return that personal property accounts for more than 30 to 40 percent of a building's value.

3. Subtract the value of the land and of personal property from the purchase price, and you will have the value of the building/structure. This is where the cost segregation study divides the costs between the structure costs and its components. In our chart, the component (personal property) depreciation was $15,000, and the building depreciation was $10,909. That "phantom deduction" of $25,909 proved a substantial role in yielding the paper loss of $7,256 and the tax savings of $2,540 against your other income which helped make the real estate investment a lucrative one.

In this example we showed an increase from a cash return from 8 percent to 11 percent when you factor in component and building depreciation. This rate of return could have been increased even more if the debt had been spread over a longer period of time. For instance the debt used in the example was a mortgage of $360,000 at an interest rate of 6 percent, amortized over 15 years.

If instead, you had an interest only loan in this example, your entire debt service payments would be deductible interest, and your cash on cash return would increase to over 15 percent. Also your rate of return could be increased if you could reduce your down-payment from 20 percent of the purchase price to 10 percent. Maybe you could convince the seller to carry 10% of the purchase price with a 5 year balloon payment. This would double your cash on cash rate of return.

These examples are just to show you how you can analyze the numbers including the tax impact to achieve the best cash on cash return on your investment. It is all right if you do not understand them all now, but through experience and review with your tax accountant and/or CPA you will begin to understand the relationships between the various strategies and your desired rate of return.

Passive Loss Rule

Investing in rental real estate offers a wonderful safety net to offset your income from nonpassive sources (such as wages or dividends) on your tax return. If your adjusted gross income is under $100,000, you can offset up to $25,000 of your ordinary income from losses in real estate (which would be "passive losses," since real estate gives you passive income). This is true for both single taxpayers and married individuals who file jointly. In order to take up to the $25,000 deduction, you (or you and your spouse if you file a joint return) have to have "actively participated" in the passive real estate rental activity. What does that mean? Active participation is not a stringent standard (and should not be confused with "material participation"). For example, you may be treated as actively participating if you make management decisions such as approving new tenants, deciding on rental terms, approving expenditures, and the like. So be careful: If you have a property management company taking care of your rental, be sure that you are still involved at some level.

There are some exceptions to the $25,000. One exception has to do with your tax marital status. If you are married, filing a separate return, and have lived apart from your spouse for the entire tax year, your special allowance cannot be more than $12,500. If you lived with your spouse at any time during the year and are filing a separate return, you cannot use the deduction at all. So you must be single or married and filing jointly to take full advantage of the rule.

Another important exception to the rule relates directly to your income level. The full $25,000 offset is only available to individuals or to couples filing jointly whose income does not exceed $100,000. Once your income exceeds $100,000, the deduction begins to be phased out, and at $150,000 it is lost altogether. So if your income is over $150,000, you can't use passive losses from real estate to offset ordinary income.

How, then, can you enjoy the full benefit of passive losses? By reading the next chapter . . .

Chapter 9

Make Real Estate Your Business

So you would like to enjoy the full benefit of passive losses on your real estate. Have you thought about becoming a real estate professional? While creating a job for yourself may contradict the notion that self-employment is not the path to passive wealth, the tax benefits are hard to ignore.

Claiming Passive Loss

If you as a real estate investor can qualify as a real estate professional under Section 2064 of the U.S. Tax Code, the tax savings can be significant.

A bit of background. The 1986 Tax Reform Act limited the amount of losses an individual party can claim on an annual tax return from real estate investments. Lawmakers found that there were too many tax shelters for wealthy (and even middle-class) property owners. People were investing for tax savings instead of for economic benefit. When that happens, the efficiency of the market is constrained. So the law was changed so that people whose annual adjusted gross income was below $100,000 were limited to claiming no more than $25,000 in passive loss, and those with $100,000 to $150,000 in income were limited to a sliding scale of losses below $25,000. And those with an income above $150,000 were prevented from using any passive losses at all from real estate investments to offset ordinary income.

As we saw in the previous chapter, passive loss—including the paper losses created by depreciation—can provide a significant tax deduction.

Imagine if you could claim the entire amount of depreciation, along with all the other business expenses discussed ahead, against your household's combined earned income. That's the advantage of being a real estate professional.

Case No. 7
John and Marsha

John and Marsha were a successful couple. The IRS loved seeing their tax return every year.

Marsha was a well-compensated dermatologist. In the last three years, she had established her own medical practice. Not only did Marsha see regular rash and fungi patients, but she also performed various lucrative elective procedures ranging from Botox injections to laser hair removals. The better her clients looked, the more Marsha was paid.

John was a mortgage broker who had left the lending business to manage Marsha's practice. There was such a demand for Marsha's services that John found his business savvy quite useful in administering the multimillion-dollar practice. Going into their fourth year of business, John had streamlined systems and put a good team in place. He now had more time to deal with the couple's real estate portfolio.

As a mortgage broker John appreciated the leverage and financial power of real estate. Over the last four years, he and Marsha had used some of their after-tax dollars to invest in four-to-twenty-unit apartment buildings around town. They had also purchased a three-unit commercial strip center, with a convenience store, dry cleaner, and video rental store as tenants.

But John didn't like the fact that the passive losses on their real estate investments weren't able to offset Marsha's high annual income. Because Marsha's W-2 income from employment was over the threshold of $150,000 per year, their real estate losses, which were $200,000 a year or more, were suspended. That is, when the first and second notes against the properties were paid off and the properties themselves showed a profit, or if there was a profit on the sale of the property, the losses could be used to shelter those future profits. But until that day of real estate profits arrived, the losses that were accumulating were of no benefit.

John and Marsha met with their CPA to discuss the situation. When John complained about the suspended real estate losses, the CPA smiled and said three words: "Real estate professional."

John was puzzled. As a mortgage broker he *was* a real estate professional. He asked what the importance of the term was.

The CPA replied by explaining that if John spent over half his time on real estate and that real estate time was over 750 hours per year, he would be considered a real estate professional. As a real estate professional John could write off 100 percent of the couple's real estate losses against Marsha's ordinary income, the money she earned as a dermatologist. The CPA further noted that Marsha's salary was $500,000 per year and their passive real estate losses were $200,000 per year. By having John as a real estate professional, the CPA explained, Marsha's taxable income would be reduced to $300,000. That $200,000 reduction (at a 35 percent federal income tax rate) meant a $70,000 tax savings.

John and Marsha liked those numbers. For the upcoming year, and in years to come, John would be a real estate professional.

Qualifying as a Real Estate Professional

The tax code has two conditions that must be met for a person to treat rental real estate activities as nonpassive:

1. The person must perform at least half of all worked hours in the tax year in real property trades or businesses. In other words, if the person has another job, or part-time job, outside of real estate, then the person must work at least the same number of hours in activities directly connected to real estate.

2. The person must perform at least 750 hours of work during the tax year in real property trades or businesses. (That number of hours translates

roughly to fourteen and a half hours per week.) It is important to note that the real estate activities that qualify you as a professional don't necessarily involve having professional licenses. According to the tax code, these "personal services" in which the person "materially participates" cover the gamut of investment activity in which real property "is developed or redeveloped, constructed or reconstructed, acquired, converted, rented or leased, operated or managed, or brokered."

Let's review each service involved.

DEVELOPING OR REDEVELOPING
Development or redevelopment includes all time spent on the improvement of a piece of real estate. You do not have to perform the actual work yourself (although you certainly may). All time spent hiring, meeting, reviewing, discussing, and supervising the work of the various engineers, planners, county and city officials, architects, contractors, and other professionals, such as attorneys and accountants, counts toward your 750-hour requirement. Developing or redeveloping a piece of property includes any activity where you are improving real estate, either by dividing it, subdividing it, erecting actual structures on it, adding amenities such as roads to it, or knocking down old or unwanted structures.

CONSTRUCTING OR RECONSTRUCTING
Construction or reconstruction is a narrower category included within the scope of development or redevelopment. Thus, you may include in your hours any hiring, firing, meetings, supervising, inspecting, reviewing of plans and work, or any actual work performed by you in the process of building.

ACQUIRING
If you are a diligent buyer, and depending upon the property, the process of acquiring a piece of real estate can take some time. Whether you use a Realtor or not, you will likely need to meet with sales agents. If you do use a Realtor, you will spend a significant amount of time with him or her; if you don't use a Realtor, you will spend a significant amount of time looking through local papers and driving around the area you are interested in. Either way, you will spend time looking at actual properties, offering, counteroffering, setting up

financing, speaking with insurance agents, dealing with inspectors, inspecting yourself, traveling to and from the property, and hopefully actually closing on the property. But remember, if you don't close, you can still count all the hours spent attempting to acquire.

CONVERTING

Converting a piece of property is a similar activity to redeveloping or reconstructing real estate discussed above. As an example, converting could involve the zoning changes and architectural and construction work necessary to change an old Victorian family home into a four-unit rental.

RENTING AND LEASING

Renting and leasing includes any activity where your end goal is to find someone, be it a company or individual, to occupy a piece of real estate that you own and to compensate you for the privilege. These activities include advertising, drafting leases (whether you do it yourself or spend time with your attorney), showing the property, interviewing renters, checking on the property, or any other management activity. If you hire a property management company, this would include any time you spend with the company reviewing leases and approving tenants.

OPERATING OR MANAGING

This is similar to renting or leasing in that it includes time spent with your management company, or, if you do not have a management company, it would include what would probably be a much greater amount of time spent actually managing the property yourself. It includes time spent writing checks, paying bills, meeting with your accountant and attorney, inspecting the property, hiring repairmen or fixing problems yourself, all the issues included under renting or leasing, as well as the flip side of being a landlord—evicting unwanted tenants.

BROKERING OR SELLING

Whether you are a real estate agent for others, selling your property on your own, or selling your property using a real estate agent, this category includes all time spent preparing to sell a property (such as cleaning it or hiring a cleaning service), showing the property to prospective purchasers, conducting open houses for agents and the general public, advertising the property, responding to offers on the property, ordering title insurance, dealing with any defects that inspections or other reports have uncovered, and eventually closing on the property.

And again, remember, you don't physically have to do the various tasks connected with each activity. In other words, you don't have to show a house to a potential buyer or actually do the manual labor of renovating a property. Your work as a real estate professional could be, in respect to the two aforementioned activities, hiring an agent and supervising a contractor.

Rich Dad Tip

- Be sure to note your real estate professional status by properly filing out Schedule E on your tax return.
- Failure to make the proper election to treat all interest in real estate as an activity can result in a denial of your real estate losses and the payment of additional taxes.
- Make certain your tax preparer is aware of this requirement, and seek his or her advice.
- Maintain and retain a log or record to support your activities in real estate.

There are two pieces of good news about qualifying as a real estate professional:

- If you're married and file a joint return, only one of you (either you or your spouse) needs to meet the two conditions. Remember, in Case No. 7, John was the real estate professional and Marsha continued as a dermatologist.
- To document your hours working as a real estate professional is straightforward and quite simple. Keep a regular log showing the dates you worked, how much time you spent, and what you did (e.g., "looked at apartment complexes with Eric Spitzer, my Realtor").

One other way to qualify as a real estate professional is to actually have a job in the trade, such as being an agent, broker, appraiser, or contractor. However, to claim that your rental real estate activities are nonpassive, you must own at least a 5 percent interest in the business that employs you. Please not that if you are an employee of the real estate company and do not own 5 percent or more of the company, you will *not* qualify as a real estate professional.

Important tax tip: However, if you are a real estate agent acting as an independent contractor, you may have an option. Consider forming an S corporation and have the brokerage firm contract with this S corporation for services. Your corporation may then pay you a salary. In this scenario, you will own 5 percent or more (most likely you'll own 100%) of the business that is paying you and will thus qualify as a real estate professional. Again, it is best to check with your tax advisor about the details of this possiblity.

"Flipping" Can Jeopardize Passive Loss

To be taxed on a piece of property at the capital gains rate of 15 percent, you must hold that property for at least twelve months. But you can get taxed at a much higher rate—that of ordinary ("earned") income—if the IRS decides you're not an investor but have the occupation of a broker/dealer of real estate. To put it another way, as a dealer you generate ordinary income, or a salary, because dealing is your trade or business, your occupation.

Some investors use a fix-and-flip strategy. They'll buy a property, spruce it up, and sell it as soon as the market lets them make a gain. This strategy seems to work for some people, especially those who are handy and can contribute their "sweat equity" to the deal. But it is important to know that if you consistently buy and sell multiple properties, the IRS may deem you a broker/dealer in the business of real estate, even if you've owned each property for longer than a year. This means you'll pay ordinary income tax rates (as well as employment taxes) on all of your gains. And thus you won't be able to use the real estate professional strategy to your benefit. Be sure to discuss your specific situation with your professional advisors so you know ahead of time your upcoming tax obligations.

Other Real Estate/Business Strategies

Whether you qualify or not as a real estate professional, whether you pay capital gains or ordinary income taxes, if you are a real estate investor, it may be a business for you. And as a business you are allowed to claim tax write-offs for business expenses. You can set up an office in your home and deduct a portion of the utilities and mortgage (based on floor space) from your tax return. You can write off costs for a cell phone, e-mail service, gas mileage, newspaper subscription, and other reasonable business expenses.

The IRS's Section 162(a) says: "There shall be allowed as a deduction, all the ordinary and necessary expenses paid or incurred during the taxable year in carrying on any trade or business." What is "ordinary" and "necessary" is left open to interpretation. But below is a list of some typical personal expenses that may be substantiated as business expenses if you legitimately use them for your business. Although some of the following expenses may be claimed after you set up the proper business entity. It is important that you consult with your tax advisor as to the deductibility and substantiation requirements for your specific situation:

Personal Expense	Possible Business Expense
Computer, software	Business equipment
Internet service	Utility
Cell phone	Business equipment/service
Automobile	Auto allowance (Alternative: Business vehicle, if entity that holds property owns the vehicle; auto maintenance can be claimed.)
Meals out	Business meals (keep receipts and note purpose of meeting and who attended) 50% deductible
Child/day care	Provided child care (the business adopts a plan to furnish child care)
Child's allowance	Employment for your child (you must write a job description, keep a time sheet, and pay a reasonable wage)

Medical, vision	Medical reimbursement (adopt a medical reimbursement plan to pay all medical, vision, dental, orthodontia costs)
Magazines	Subscriptions (for your use or waiting clients)
Artwork	Office art (enjoy in your office)
Dry cleaning	Out-of-town expenses
Vacation	Business trips (only if they have a business purpose for the trip, and there are specific limitations)
Tuition	Education (authorize employee/owner education)
Seminars	Education (authorize employee/owner and document applicability for your business)
Furniture	Business furniture (where appropriate, such as a desk)
Home costs	Home office or business rental (measure square footage, follow home office guidelines, track all home expenses for reimbursement)

Again, it is important that you discuss your particular facts and circumstances with your tax advisor.

Section 179 Depreciation

Under Section 179 of the U.S. Tax Code, up to a certain amount per year of expenses for depreciable business assets is allowed to be deducted as business expenses. For 2006, the limit is $108,000. This means you can write off 100% of the purchase price of your qualified business assets up to $108,000 instead of depreciating them over several years. See your tax accountant for further information and specific details.

Use all of the deductions and benefits the tax code allows when it comes to investing in real estate. And never forget one of the biggest real estate advantages allowed: the 1031 exchange . . .

Chapter 10

Tax-Free Exchanges

Case No. 8
Blake

Blake was an auto mechanic who knew that the way to wealth was through real estate investing. As an auto mechanic he could only get paid when he repaired a Rabbit or tuned a T-bird. If he wasn't working, he wasn't getting paid.

But by owning real estate, by collecting rents from tenants, he got paid whether he showed up to work or not. And knowing this, Blake set out to acquire real estate according to the most tax-efficient means possible.

Blake had acquired two properties in the last four years. One was a two-story tan-colored fourplex in a strong rental neighborhood. Blake had used deferred maintenance issues (the need for a new roof and air-conditioning units) to obtain a below-market price for the property. The fourplex, even after the improvements were made, provided Blake with positive cash flow each month.

His second property was a duplex in a transitional neighborhood. Blake had hoped that the area would improve at a faster rate and that the tenant mix would improve as well. But this was not happening quickly enough for Blake.

So Blake decided to sell the duplex and acquire another property in an area with greater appreciation potential. He was concerned about having to pay taxes on the tidy gain from the sale of the duplex, so he met with his CPA to better understand his tax situation.

The CPA was glad Blake had come to see him. By doing so, he was able to let Blake in on an incredible tax strategy that would save him $7,500. Blake was intrigued and asked for more information.

The CPA explained that by selling his old property using a "1031 exchange," Blake could defer taxes if he reinvested all the proceeds from the old property into a new property. Blake liked the sound of this strategy and following his CPA's advice engaged in the following:

First, Blake sold the duplex for $100,000. With just $7,500 down, he had only paid $50,000 for it four years ago. So with the sale, he had a nice profit of $50,000 on it. Because he had held it for over one year, the capital gains tax (at this writing) was 15 percent (or $7,500 on a $50,000 gain). Blake's property and residence were in a state that didn't have a state capital gains tax, so all he had to deal with was the federal capital gains tax. The CPA noted that if Blake moved to or held property in a state with a capital gains tax, he would have to factor that state tax in as well.

But the point of the transaction was to defer capital gains taxes until a later day.

The CPA instructed Blake to line up a "qualified intermediary" to handle the monies received from the escrow closing. Blake couldn't touch the money, or the 1031 transaction would fail. The money had to go straight to a qualified intermediary.

The CPA then indicated that Blake had 45 days to identify a new property and 180 days to close on it. So Blake set about to promptly locate a new property.

After two weeks of searching, he found a fiveplex in an appreciating area for $300,000. With the $50,000 held by the qualified intermediary and new financing of $250,000, Blake purchased the fiveplex. The $7,500 in capital gains he would have had to pay the IRS in a traditional sale situation was deferred and could be used tax-free to buy a bigger property.

Blake liked this real estate strategy. He learned that he could continue to trade up to bigger properties as long as each one was held for a year and a day.

Over the next five years, Blake traded up three more times. At the end of this run, he owned an immaculate twenty-four-unit apartment building as well as the original two-story, tan-colored fourplex. Both properties were cash flowing, giving Blake hope that someday soon he could retire from the auto mechanic business with a nice continuing income stream.

And Blake had to pinch himself when he thought about the benefits of 1031 transactions. For he had started out buying a duplex for just $7,500 down, and without putting in any more money along the way, or paying taxes on any gains, he now owned a cash-flowing twenty-four-unit apartment building for essentially $7,500. What a great country.

To understand the 1031 process is to understand six key rules. To explain these rules, we are pleased to include a section written by 1031 exchange expert Gary Gorman. Gary is the author of *Exchanging Up! How to Build a Real Estate Empire Without Paying Taxes . . . Using 1031 Exchanges* (SuccessDNA, 2005).

What is a "1031 exchange"? A 1031 exchange rolls the gain from your Old investment property over to your New. It's called a "1031" exchange because 1031 is the IRS Code Section that governs this rollover. The fact that it is an IRS Code Section means that it is law and if you follow the rules the IRS has to allow your exchange.

So, what do you have to do to have a valid exchange? There are six basic rules that you have to follow, which is another way of saying that there are six things the IRS will look at if they audit your exchange. And before we review the six rules, there is one very important point to know: Section 1031 is a form-driven code section. You must follow all of the rules exactly. Failure to follow one small rule can result in your exchange being disallowed if you get audited. Every form and document that is part of your exchange must be exactly correct.

RULE #1—IT MUST BE INVESTMENT PROPERTY

A 1031 exchange is available only for property held for investment or used in a trade or business. Used in a trade or business means that if you own a bicycle shop, and you own the building that your bicycle shop is in, that building is used in your (bicycle) trade or business. A 1031 exchange does not apply to your personal residence, meaning the house you live in.

While people do exchanges on property used by their business, the vast majority of real estate exchanges are done by people that own other investment property. Under the law that has been in effect since 1991, you can exchange any type of investment property for any other type of investment property. For example, if you sell a purple duplex, you could buy an office building, an apartment building, a warehouse, or even bare land. Or you could sell bare land and buy income-producing property in order to increase cash flow, which is a popular investment strategy.

After Section 1031 was first written in 1921 (it had a different code number back then), people commonly thought that if you had a purple duplex you had to find someone else who also owned a purple duplex and swap deeds with them. You might find Adam, who had a purple duplex and was willing to sell it, but he didn't want yours—he wanted Barb's. Barb wanted Chris's and he wanted Debby's. Debby, luckily, was willing to take yours. This is what we used to call a five-legged exchange, and the problem with them was that if any one of the parties to this transaction backed out, or wasn't able to complete their leg of the transaction, the entire exchange fell apart for everyone.

In the 1970s this concept was challenged by a man named T. J. Starker and his family, who sold some expensive timberland, got the money, and then bought their replacement properties over the next year or two. The IRS challenged their exchanges and the matter ultimately ended up in U.S. Tax Court, which is the Supreme Court of tax law. Starker and his family won, and people immediately began doing "Starker exchanges," which were essentially very unstructured transactions. In order to bring some order to the exchange process, Congress rewrote Section 1031 in 1991, and these transactions are now called 1031 exchanges rather than the archaic "Starker exchange" label, although you will still occasionally hear someone call it that.

Section 1031 does not allow you to do an exchange on property you hold for "resale," although the IRS does not define that term. Essentially, it means property that you buy with the intent of immediately selling it rather than holding it for investment. A classic example of property held for resale is "fix-and-flips." A fix-and-flip is where you buy a distressed property with the intent to quickly fix it up and then sell it. As you can imagine, there are people who are adamant that their fix-and-flip property, which they owned for mere weeks, was investment property. And, not surprisingly, some of these cases end up in U.S. Tax Court. Most of these people lose, although occasionally someone will win one of these cases.

The tax court opinions typically require a "two *tax* year" holding period. This creates a problem because January 1 of year *one* to January 1 of year *two* is two tax years. So is July 1 of year *one* to January 1 of year *two*, as is December 1 of year *one* to January 1 of year *two*. The last two examples are not fair if you are the one that bought your property on January 1, so to level the playing field the IRS seems to favor a "year-and-a-day" test, meaning that a year and a day from any point in time, even leap year, will get you to a new tax year.

The more probable reason for the year-and-a-day rule is that it forces all exchange transactions to be long-term capital gain transactions. Long-term gains apply to property that has been owned for at least 365 days, and are typically taxed more lightly than short-term gains, which apply to property owned less than a year. The IRS doesn't want you turning short-term capital gains into long-term capital gains by doing an exchange. They don't want you, for example, buying a distressed property, fixing it up, and then selling it two months later and doing an exchange. The reason, of course, is that the IRS in that case is losing out on higher tax revenues.

Let's say that you do a 1031 exchange and buy another distressed property and do it again. You do this on ten properties and now it is three years after you bought your first property. You're tired of the fix-and-flip business and so you decide to sell your last property and cash out. Because of all the exchanges you've done, you've built up a large accumulated gain and it's time to pay tax on it. Would this gain be taxed as a short-term gain (at a high tax rate) or as a long-term capital gain (at a much smaller tax rate)? The correct answer is that it should be taxed as a short-term gain, although it would be easy for you to convince yourself that it ought to be long-term because of the three-year time frame between the purchase of your first property and the sale of your last. This is why the IRS doesn't want you doing exchanges on short-term transactions.

The taxpayers who have won court cases where they held the property for less than a year were able to convince the court that their "intent" was to hold the property for more than a year, and that due to circumstances beyond their control they had no choice but to sell the property sooner. In other words, they were able to convince the court that their heart was pure.

Our firm gets calls daily from people wanting to do an exchange on property that they have only owned for months, or even days, before they sold it. We got a call once from an attorney that wanted to do an exchange on a property he was going to sell five minutes after he bought it because he believed that he could prove his heart was pure. (Of course, this involves a higher standard for attorneys.) The facts of the case are that he got a good deal on the purchase, and had listed it for sale at a higher price before he closed the purchase. His buyer was buying the property from him five minutes after the closing of his purchase (on a sales contract that was entered into well before he even owned the property). The so-called proof of his investment intent was the fact that he was a successful stock market day trader, which he considered a form of investing, and he didn't see any difference between day trading and what he was doing with this property. The IRS would have disallowed this exchange.

There are many so-called exchange professionals who preach that you can do fix-and-flip-type exchanges if you can make some type of intent argument. They will tell you that taxpayers have won these types of cases in tax court. The problem with their argument is that the IRS has an unwritten policy of disallowing exchanges of less than a year. Yes, there are people who've won short-term exchange cases in tax court. But the problem is that getting to tax court could easily cost you in excess of $50,000, and once you get there your chances of winning are not good. Play it safe and stick to a holding period of at least a year and a day.

One last thing before we move on to the next requirement, and that is "vacation homes." Do they qualify for 1031 exchanges or not? You could make an argument, as many do, that they are not held for investment or used in a trade or business (unless they are rented) and therefore do not qualify for a 1031 exchange. In fact the IRS says that they do qualify. In a 1981 private ruling a taxpayer wrote in and asked if they could do an exchange on a vacation home that they bought primarily for personal enjoyment, but also partially as an investment. They wanted to buy a larger vacation home that they would also hold primarily for personal enjoyment but also partially as an investment. The IRS ruled that they could do an exchange from one to the other provided they could prove their investment intent.

For years the exchange industry professionals have debated what is investment intent and how do you prove it. Then, in 2004, in a U.S. Tax Court case involving a vacation home in Truckee, California, the court dealt with the issue of investment intent. This vacation home near Lake Tahoe had had very little rental in the two years that were the subject of the court case—essentially all of the usage had been personal use of the property by the taxpayers and their family members.

While Section 1031 issues were not part of this tax court case, the issue of whether or not the property was "investment property" came up. In this case the IRS ruled that the property was investment property based entirely on the testimony of the taxpayer's wife that one of the reasons they had purchased the property was their expectation that it would appreciate in value.

Having said that, we still advise our clients to do something that they can use to prove their investment intent should they get audited. This can be as simple as sending a letter to your attorney and CPA that says that you intend to own the property as an investment with the expectation of appreciation. It is best to do this when you buy the property, but if you already own vacation property and haven't done this, consider doing it as soon as possible. It would be best if you did this more than a year and a day before you plan to sell the property.

RULE #2—45-DAY IDENTIFICATION PERIOD

From the day you close the sale of your Old Property you have exactly 45 days to make a list of properties you might want to buy. You typically want three properties, or less, on this list. The reason for this is that there are no limits on your list if it has three properties or less.

If you put more than three properties on your list, you become subject to the "200 percent rule" of Section 1031 which says that, since your list is more than three (whether it has four, or ten, or forty properties), the total combined purchase price of everything on the list cannot be more than twice the selling price of your Old Property.

Let's say that you sell your purple duplex for $100,000 and you list three properties worth $10 million each, for a total list of $30 million. Is this okay? Yes—because your list only had three properties on it. But what if your list shows four properties for only $75,000 each—is this okay? No. Because your list has more than three properties on it, you can only list $200,000 worth of properties (twice the $100,000 selling price of the Old Property). Since four times $75,000 is $300,000, which exceeds your 200 percent limit, your exchange is "toast." And your whole exchange is toast even if you bought one of the properties. So, be smart—keep it simple and keep your list to three properties or less.

How do you complete your list? You have to list each property in terms that are clear enough that an IRS agent could take your list and go directly to the door of the property. This means, for example, that if one of your properties happens to be in the Phoenix Condominium Towers, you have to list Unit 203—you can't simply say 123 Camelback Road, which is the address of the towers.

You will give your list to your qualified intermediary, a person we will discuss in Rule #4. Just make sure that it is in your intermediary's hands before midnight on the 45th day.

RULE #3—180-DAY REINVESTMENT PERIOD

From the day you close the sale of your Old Property, you have exactly 180 days in which to buy your replacement property, and whatever you buy has to be on the 45-day list. This means that you can buy one or all three of the properties on your list. Just make sure that you actually close the purchase, because "closing in escrow" or doing a "dry closing" does not meet the requirements. Title to the New Property has to be in your name before midnight of the 180th day.

And like the 45-day requirement, these are calendar days, and there are no extensions—if the 180th day falls on a Saturday, or Sunday, or a holiday like the 4th of July, then that is the day. One exception to this requirement that you have to be careful of is that if your 180th day falls after the due date of your tax return (such as April 15), and you have not purchased your replacement property, you will need to extend your tax return. The reason for this is that if you file your tax return without reporting your exchange, then your exchange is toast. And obviously you cannot properly report your exchange if you haven't purchased your New Property.

RULE #4—QUALIFIED INTERMEDIARY REQUIREMENT

You cannot touch the money in between the sale of your Old Property and the purchase of your New Property. By law the money has to be held by an independent third party called a qualified intermediary. Intermediaries have two primary roles: They prepare the exchange documents that are required by Section 1031, and they hold the money during the exchange.

The problem is that almost anyone can be an intermediary. To be sure, the law excludes certain people from being an intermediary (people like your own personal or business attorney, your CPA, or anyone that is related to you), but essentially, virtually anyone can be an intermediary. And this creates potential problems for you and your exchange. There are three potential problems you need to be aware of.

The first is that very few intermediaries have a background in taxation or real estate law. Section 1031 is a very complicated code section with lots of potential traps, yet most intermediaries lack the knowledge or sophistication to really help their clients stay out of trouble. They cover this by inserting "hold harmless" wording in their documents, or making you sign a separate hold harmless agreement. A hold harmless agreement says that you can't sue them no matter how badly they screw up your exchange. You should never sign such an agreement and you should make sure that you delete similar provisions that might be buried in the exchange documents. If the intermediary won't let you remove the hold harmless wording, what they are telling you is that they don't have confidence in their knowledge and abilities, which means that you need to find another intermediary.

The second problem is that Section 1031 is a form-driven code section—meaning that all of the forms and documents have to be perfectly prepared and completed for you to have a valid exchange. There is no room for error in this code section—you either get it exactly right (dot the "i's" and cross the "t's") or your exchange can be disallowed. There are a lot of bad exchange documents out there and you can't assume that because you are paying your intermediary a large fee, their documents are correct, which is another reason why you don't want to sign a hold harmless agreement.

The last problem is the biggest, and that is that they must hold your money in between the sale of your Old Property and the purchase of your New. Since virtually anyone could be an intermediary, there is really no reason why a convicted felon couldn't be your intermediary and hold your money. Make sure you know who you are dealing with.

Related to this is the fact that most intermediaries hold their client's money in a commingled, or pooled, account. This means that they hold everyone's money in the same account. This is tremendously risky for you. A recent court case has ruled that such an account is available to any creditor of the intermediary. If one of the intermediary's employees is on their way to the bank on intermediary business and they happen to hit a school bus and some kids are killed, their parents could sue the intermediary and get your money.

Commingled accounts are also very tempting to less scrupulous intermediaries. In recent years there have been three big intermediary losses—two of them by intermediaries who were day trading with the money in a commingled account.

In the recent court case mentioned above, the court stated a number of times that money held in a separate account for the intermediary was protected from the intermediary's creditors. So, if you get nothing else out of this discussion on 1031 exchanges, please know that you must insist that your intermediary hold your money in a separate account just for you. This is critical—do not let your intermediary commingle your money with anyone else's money. Insist upon a separate account.

RULE #5—TITLE REQUIREMENTS

In simple terms, how you held title to the Old Property is how you have to take title to your New Property. This means that you have to stay within the same tax return—the same tax identification number or Social Security number.

In other words, if Fred and Sue hold title to their purple duplex in their own name (Fred and Sue Jones, for example), they cannot take title to the New Property in the name of their corporation (Jones Investment Corporation), because the corporation files a different tax return.

There are several exceptions to this rule dealing with what the IRS calls "disregarded entities," which are things like revocable living trusts and single member limited liability companies. While a complete discussion of disregarded entities and 1031 exchanges is beyond the scope of this book, you can obtain more information at www.expert1031.com, or ask your qualified intermediary to explain it to you. If they are a good intermediary they should be able to do so easily.

RULE #6—REINVESTMENT RULES

In order to pay no tax, you must do two things: First, you must buy equal or up. If Fred and Sue sell their purple duplex for $100,000, they must buy their New Property for at least $100,000 in order to owe no tax. If they buy down and only pay $90,000 for their New Property, it does not mean that their exchange is toast—they simply pay tax on the $10,000 buy-down. And in a 1031 exchange the entire $10,000 buy-down would be taxable.

The second thing you have to do is reinvest all of the cash from the sale of the Old Property into the New Property. If there was $40,000 of debt and closing costs when Fred and Sue sold their purple duplex and their intermediary received the balance of $60,000, they must reinvest all of the $60,000 in the New Property in order to avoid paying tax. This is true even if they put $5,000 of their own cash into the original purchase of the duplex.

If Fred and Sue are buying their New Property for $150,000, they do not have an equal or up problem since they sold for $100,000 and are buying for $150,000. However, if they get a new loan for $100,000 (which means that they only need $50,000 of the $60,000 that the intermediary is holding) they will pay tax on the leftover $10,000 because they did not reinvest all of the cash. And, as stated above, the entire $10,000 would be taxable. One thing that Fred and Sue could do to avoid this problem would be to reduce their loan to $90,000 so that they use the entire balance of $60,000 held by the intermediary.

Another way that Fred and Sue could have avoided paying tax in both of the examples above would be to buy a second property which would get them to their required equal or up computation and use up any unspent cash. The second property would have to be on their 45-day list, of course.

Finally, contrary to the belief of most tax advisors, there is no requirement that the debt on the New Property be equal to or greater than the amount of debt on the Old Property. You only need to buy equal or up and reinvest all of the cash to avoid having to pay any tax. Many tax professionals, as well as most exchange advisors, are confused about this, but it's true—there is no debt replacement requirement.

What happens to the gain that gets rolled over? This is a common question, and the answer most people want to hear is that it disappears, but it doesn't. Your rollover gains are aggregated until you finally sell your last property and don't do a 1031 exchange. For example, if Fred and Sue roll over a $30,000 profit on the sale of the purple duplex, and buy their replacement property for $150,000, they have a $30,000 built-in gain on that property. If they then sell that property for $200,000 and decide not to do an exchange, their taxable gain will be $80,000 ($30,000 from the first property and $50,000 from the second). In the real world their gain will actually be greater than this because of something called depreciation recapture, but you get the idea. If Fred and Sue decided to do an exchange on the second property, their built-in gain on the third property would be $80,000 and they would continue from there.

Thanks to Gary Gorman for that clear discussion. Now let's put it to use . . .

Transferring Property to Your Heirs Tax-Free

Case No. 9
Ron and Betty

Ron and Betty have been successful real estate investors throughout their lives. In fact, they had been so successful it was now time to plan distributions in such a way so that their children, and not the IRS, were the proper beneficiaries.

Ron and Betty purchased a strip center many years ago for $100,000. The center was now worth $500,000, and the mortgage had been paid off. Knowing that they wanted to transfer assets to their two children, Kenji and Cindie, they met with a 1031 exchange expert to devise a plan.

The first step was to sell the strip center for $500,000 and enter into a 1031 exchange whereby Ron and Betty acquired a 50 percent interest in New Property A. The new property was worth $1 million and was 50 percent owned by the children, Kenji and Cindie. Ron and Betty's contribution was the $500,000 in cash from the sale of the strip center, while Kenji and Cindie's contribution was a promissory note secured by a first deed of trust on the property for the remaining $500,000.

The 1031 exchange expert explained that even if Ron and Betty owned 100 percent of the strip center, it was acceptable for them to only own 50 percent of New Property A. There were two key points to consider in the transaction.

The first was that for Ron and Betty to defer capital gains taxes, they had to buy a property equal to or greater in value, which they did. The strip center was worth $500,000 and New Property A was worth $1 million. The second point was they had to take title in the same name as they held the strip center. Ron and Betty always used limited liability companies (LLCs) for asset protection purposes. For New Property A, they used a tenants-in-common structure whereby Ron and Betty's LLC and Kenji and Cindie's newly formed LLC were listed in title as tenants-in-common owners. As long as these points were satisfied, Ron and Betty were okay and ready for the next step.

After a year and a day of holding on to New Property A, the family began looking to trade up to New Property B. In another six months, they located the right property in a desirable area. New Property A had appreciated, and it sold for $1.2 million. New Property B was purchased for $2 million. Ron and Betty's contribution was their $600,000 share from New Property A. Kenji and Cindie, meanwhile, bought from their $600,000 share of New Property A a $1.4 million interest in New Property B. As such, in the new property, Kenji and Cindie own a 70 percent interest ($1.4 million of $2 million) while Ron and Betty's interest is reduced to 30 percent ($600,000 of $2 million).

Obviously, one can appreciate where this is headed. After two more exchanges, Ron and Betty could, for example, own 12 percent of a $5-million New Property D. Kenji and Cindie, on the other hand, would own 88 percent of such a valuable property. And remember, neither the parents nor the children have paid capital gains taxes as this transfer of wealth has occurred.

And because Ron and Betty own such a small percentage of New Property D, their ownership interest may be subject to IRS-sanctioned discounts. This is because the IRS prudently recognizes that even though 12 percent of a $5-million property may be worth $600,000 on paper, no investor is going to pay that kind of money for a property where they have no say in management or control over major decisions, such as selling the property. So the IRS generally agrees that such a lack of control may account for a 10 to 40 percent discount, let's say a 30 percent discount, meaning that Ron and Betty's 12 percent is really only worth $420,000.

This discount gives Ron and Betty the option of gifting their interests tax-free (at $12,000 per year at this writing) to Kenji and Cindie over a period of years. With Ron able to gift $12,000 each to Kenji and Cindie, and Betty able to do the same, a total of $48,000 per year ($12,000 per gift times two parents, times two children) could be gifted away. Assuming New Property D didn't wildly appreciate, thus driving up the value of Ron and Betty's 12 percent interest, the gifting could be accomplished over a ten-year-plus period. (That is $48,000 per year in gifts to gift out a mildly appreciating $420,000 discounted interest in New Property D.) For a more detailed discussion on gifting and discounts see Garrett Sutton's book *How To Use Limited Liability Companies and Limited Partnerships* (Success DNA, 2005).

Or Ron and Betty could decide to wait until their passing to bequeath the remaining 12 percent to Kenji and Cindie according to their wills, living trusts, or other estate planning vehicles. With the tax-free exemption for federal estate taxes at $2 million for each of their estates (as of this writing), Ron and Betty, assuming they had no other significant assets, could pass the remaining 12 percent in New Property D to Kenji and Cindie tax-free.

Of course, you will work with your own tax and legal advisors on your own situation. But the point to take away here is that Ron and Betty, starting with just a $100,000 investment in their original strip center, were able to pass along a $5-million asset tax-free to their children through the effective use of 1031 exchanges and estate planning strategies.

You can, too.

Now let's focus on a tax savings strategy that hits close to home . . .

Chapter 11

Your Principal Residence

Case No. 10

Emily and Jack

Emily and Jack are a happy couple. Married for several years, they had bought their small, quaint first house in an older part of town at a time when prices were somewhat depressed. The homes were distinctive and had character, and soon other young couples discovered the area. Inevitably, the boutiques and small restaurants followed, and just as inevitably, home prices increased in value.

Emily and Jack's daughter, Sarah, was one year old, and a second child was on the way. After learning the space demands of one child, they realized that with two they would need bigger quarters. But Jack worried they could not afford a larger house.

Then Emily learned of a friend in the neighborhood who was selling her house tax-free. The friend had moved into the area at the same time Emily and Jack had, and the appreciation on her house had been significant. Emily called to wish her friend well in their new house and in the process learned about how to sell your house tax-free.

When Jack heard about the strategy, he immediately called his CPA to confirm whether it was accurate.

To his surprise, it was.

Jack learned from his CPA that the IRS allowed married couples a significant tax benefit if they lived in their primary residence for two of the last five years. The benefit was an exclusion of capital gains of up to $500,000 for married taxpayers upon the sale of the house.

Jack immediately calculated the numbers. He and Emily had purchased the house three years ago for $150,000. They had put 10 percent down, or $15,000, and after three years of mostly interest payments, they still owed $135,000 on the first mortgage. With the improvements and desirability of the neighborhood, their house was now worth $350,000. Their capital gain upon a sale would be the $350,000 sale minus the $150,000 purchase price, or $200,000. But with the exclusion of gains up to $500,000, there were no taxes to pay on the $200,000 profit.

With that, Jack quickly calculated that they could move into a larger house. After paying off their $135,000 mortgage, they would have $215,000 tax-free to put down on a new house. Jack felt comfortable in his financial life to now be able to afford a $385,000 mortgage. Together, Emily and Jack found a beautiful $600,000 new home with four bedrooms and a large backyard for their growing brood to play in. It was hard to believe that, when all was said and done, they had obtained this new house with just their original down payment of $15,000. The tax-free capital gains rule made all the difference for their family.

The Primary Residence Exclusion

One of the greatest tax gifts relates to the taxability of capital gains you earn on the sale of your home, your primary residence. So great is the principal residence tax exclusion that even married couples filing jointly are benefited to the same, if not greater, extent as single taxpayers. Now, some people may argue that there have been, are, and will be greater gifts, but not much beats the simplicity of the rule. The basics of it are immediately easy to grasp: You own a house, you live in it for at least two years, you sell it, and you don't have to pay any taxes on the gain. Gone are the days when the young homeowner (not wishing to sell and upgrade) had to save every receipt for every upgrade, every repair, and every minor item bought at the hardware store. If you have lived in your own home for two years, you probably don't have to worry.

Of course, there are some technical points associated with the general rule. They are pretty simple, so first let's bullet-point the main ones:

- If you are single, your capital gains exclusion is limited to $250,000.
- If you are married, your capital gains exclusion is limited to $500,000.
- You have to own the home and it has to be your "primary residence" for two of the previous five years.

What is your "primary residence"? Basically, it is a home that you personally live in the majority of the year. If you have a house in Palm Beach and one in Lake Tahoe and you spend eight months of the year at the Tahoe home, then that is your primary residence. But keep in mind the "two years out of five years" part of the rule. Let's say that the next year you spend seven months at the Palm Beach house. Then the Palm Beach home is your primary residence that year. Do you see where this is headed? You can "primary" more than one home at once over a five-year period so long as each is your main home for at least two years during that five-year period. Temporary absences are also counted as periods of use—even if you rent the property during those absences (but talk to your accountant about whether you will have to recapture any rental depreciation that you have previously benefited from as a deduction on your tax returns).

Now, don't let the five-year requirement confuse you—it only takes two years to achieve the tax exclusion. The five-year part is a bonus, allowing you some freedom. You don't have to personally use the home as your primary residence for two consecutive years or for the two years immediately before you sell; you just have to use it as your primary residence for two of the previous five years. But it is also a limitation. You cannot live in a house for two years and then rent it for four years and then get the exclusion. You could live in it for two years and then rent it for three years and then sell it (so long as it is sold within the five-year mark from when you first lived in it as your primary residence).

Also bear in mind that married couples do not have to live together. So long as one spouse lives in the primary residence for the two years, then the couple can take advantage of the $500,000 exclusion. But they cannot create a primary residence for two homes at once and get the $500,000 exclusion for both. If they live apart during the two-year period and both sell their primary, then each of them is limited to the single taxpayer exclusion of $250,000 for each house.

If you have a home office or rental as part of your primary residence or run a business out of a portion of your property, your ability to maximize your capital gains exclusion largely depends upon whether the home office, business, or rental was part of your home (in the same dwelling unit) or a separate part of your property (a separate building or apartment). If the business use of your home was contained within your dwelling unit, then upon sale you may need to recapture any depreciation taken for that part of the home. But you will not lose any of the allowable capital gains exclusion ($250,000 for single taxpayers and $500,000 for married filing jointly). If the business use of your home was not a part of your dwelling unit, then you need to bifurcate, or divide, the sale by allocating the basis of the property and the amount realized upon its sale between the business or rental part and the part used as a home.

Remember, only one home can be sold in any two-year period unless you and your spouse live apart, and even then you can each only take the single payer exclusion of up to $250,000. But what if you need to sell a home that you have not lived in for the full two years? The IRS tells us that in special circumstances you can sell a home before you reach the two-year mark and get a prorated exclusion. An example of a prorated exclusion is if you are a single taxpayer and have to sell your primary residence for a qualified reason after living in it for only one year, then you could exclude up to $125,000. In other words, you lived in a home 50 percent of the requisite time, so you can take 50 percent of the allowable exclusion. The special circumstances that qualify you for this safe harbor and allow you to take the prorated exclusion have to do with health (yours and certain qualified individuals such as close relatives), change of employment, or what the IRS calls "unforeseen circumstances" (examples include death, natural or man-made disasters, multiple births from the same pregnancy, divorce). These circumstances also have to cause you to sell your home. Factors used by the IRS to determine causation include:

- Your sale and the circumstances causing it were close in time.
- The circumstances causing your sale occurred during the time you owned and used the property as your main home.
- The circumstances causing your sale were not reasonably foreseeable when you began using the property as your main home.
- Your financial ability to maintain your home materially changed.
- The suitability of your property as a home materially changed.

1031 Exchanges and the Primary Residence Rule

What happens if you do a 1031 tax-deferred exchange of rental property or other property held for investment and then later decide to live in the property that was purchased? As discussed in Chapter 10, it is crucial to your 1031 exchange that both the property sold and the property purchased are held for investment. The property purchased must undergo a sufficient holding period before it is resold or converted into a noninvestment property. Many advisors have suggested that it must be at least a year. So your holding period should be at least a year and a day. After you have complied with the "held for investment" requirement by, for example, renting the property if it is rental property, then what? Well, you could sell the property and pay your taxes on that sale and all previous sales that were perhaps in a series of exchanges or exchange and defer the tax once again, *or* you could live in the house as your primary residence. If you have had a series of gains that you have deferred, this is a way to extinguish your tax debt forever—all you have to do is move into your investment property once the holding period for it to qualify as an investment is over.

Gaining the primary residence exclusion for property that was 1031 property isn't as easy as the simpler primary residence rules talked about above, but it does allow you to take advantage of two loopholes at once! The main difference when primary-residencing a 1031-exchanged property is that you actually have to hold the property for five years. The five-year part here is a substantive rule; you cannot sell after only two years of ownership as you can if you were simply primary-residencing a home that was not exchanged into. But that first year that you had to hold on to the home for investment goes toward the five-year calculation. So you rent it for two years and live in it for three, or vice versa, so long as you kick the whole thing off with a one-year rental period and live in it two of the remaining four years.

A few years after buying a commercial building at $150,000, you realize that it is worth $300,000 and you do a 1031 exchange, into a nice single-family home worth $350,000 (you have to put in an additional $50,000 to complete the purchase). You have now deferred $150,000 worth of gain. Let's say you then choose to rent the home for the first two years that you own it and then you later decide to move into the home. You then live in the house for three years, at which point it is now worth $700,000, and you sell it for this amount. You and your spouse have now effectively wiped out not only the $350,000 gain from the sale of your primary residence but the previous $150,000 gain as well, utilizing the $500,000 exclusion on gains from the primary residence.

Appreciating the interplay between the primary residence rules and the 1031 tax exchange rules can lead to very significant and very legal tax savings.

Now let's consider tax savings on equally important real estate . . .

Chapter 12

Vacation Homes

For many people, their second purchase of real estate will be a vacation home. And while vacation homes can offer a much-needed retreat from city life as well as appreciation in well-located areas, they can also offer an under-appreciated benefit: tax savings.

There are four basic scenarios to understand regarding how vacation home tax rules can be utilized. The best way to review these rules is through a case study, as detailed below. Please note that the rules apply whether your vacation home is a condominium, home, or other type of residence.

Case No. 11
The Edgar Family

The Edgar family was a well-liked group of competitive brothers and sports-men from Buffalo, New York. The four brothers had hunted, fished, brawled, boated, and camped together since their youth. And now, even with families of their own, they vowed to continue their family heritage. Although each brother had a different profession and they all made different amounts of in-come on an annual basis, the brothers were able to scrape together enough money for a down payment on a vacation property. Of course, due to their competitive natures, the brothers, and even more so their wives, realized that they could not own a vacation home together.

The beauty for the Edgar brothers was that their proposed purchase was for four cabins right next to each other on Seneca Lake, one of the prime lakes in the Finger Lakes region east of Buffalo. They could hunt, fish, and boat together during the day without combusting under the same roof after cocktails in the evening. The wives were in agreement, and the four-cabin Edgar compound was purchased.

The cabins were right on the lake, and each was well appointed with four bedrooms, two baths, and a large living and dining area. They were in a desirable area and could be used for both vacations and rentals. Because the cabins were on four separate parcels and each brother was in a different financial situation, all four vacation home tax scenarios were utilized.

Scenario One: Brother Al
Rent to Others for the Entire Year

Al was a machinist. Although he was a talented individual with a mix of skills combining artistry with science, the American economy no longer rewarded machinists.

After he had purchased his cabin, Al's job was outsourced to China. Al knew it would be some time before he found another job. But he vowed to keep the cabin in order to be with his brothers. Still, at the urging of his wife, Amy, he decided to rent the cabin during his period of un-employment.

Renting the vacation home for the entire year provided Al with some excellent tax benefits. He could receive tax-sheltered personal cash flow and a tax loss for sheltering other income. Renting out the cabin for the full year put Al in the real estate business, which thus provided the tax benefits.

Let's look at how Al's rental of the cabin provided him with a tax shelter. Of course, your own situation will depend upon the rents and expenses you generate, but Al was able to rent the cabin for $20,000 a year to a wealthy family from Manhattan.

Profit

Income from Rent		$20,000
Expenses		
Advertising	$200	
Property tax	$5,500	
Mortgage interest	$9,500	
Insurance	$400	
Maintenance & repairs	$1,500	
Total Expenses		$17,100
Cash Profit		$2,900

Tax Loss

Income from Rent	$20,000
Total Expenses	$17,100
Depreciation	$6,200
Expenses plus Depreciation	$23,300
Tax Loss	($3,300)

In Al's case, the vacation cabin provides a cash profit of $2,900 that can be further tax-sheltered by the depreciation deduction of $6,200, generating a tax loss of $3,300 from depreciation. Thus Al pays no tax on the $2,900 in cash flow, and he can use the $3,300 tax loss to shelter other income.

As we've discussed, if you have less than $100,000 in adjusted gross income, you can deduct up to $25,000 in rental activity losses against your nonpassive income including salaries. (The exemption phases out and is inapplicable after your adjusted gross income reaches $150,000 unless, as we discussed, you are a real estate professional.)

In Al's case, the loss could be utilized. Al was out of work, and Amy's teacher salary was less than $100,000. So the $3,300 in tax loss on the cabin sheltered taxes Amy would have otherwise paid on her income.

When Al did get another job and their combined income on a joint return was over $150,000, any tax losses would be "suspended" and carried forward into future tax years. These losses could be used to offset future passive income or be deducted against gain when the property was sold.

This scenario worked for Al and Amy on a tax basis, but still left them missing all the fun with the other brothers. However, in speaking with their CPA, they learned of a little exception in the law they could use to their benefit. As long as they personally used the cabin for no more than the greater of 14 days or 10 percent of the days the cabin was rented during the year, their tax shelter would not be blown.

As it turned out, the family from Manhattan who had rented Al's cabin was going to be out of the country for the 4th of July holiday. They agreed that Al and his family could use their cabin during that week. All four brothers were together, and Al still received the much-needed tax relief the cabin generated for him.

Scenario Two: Brother Bob
Vacation Use and More Than 14 Days Rental

Bob was a mountaineer and a CPA. This was a good thing because when it came to renting out the cabin for 15 or more days and also using it personally for the greater of 14 days per year or 10 percent of the number of days the cabin was rented, one needed a Sherpa guide through the tax regulations.

The four steps to be discussed can get complicated, but there is a silver lining at the end of the process. And while Bob would certainly suggest you see your own tax professional to discuss your specific situation, as a general rule Scenario Two prevents obtaining a tax loss if personal use limits are exceeded. As such, home ownership expenses can't exceed rental income, meaning there is no great tax loss shelter as in Scenario One.

In Bob's case, he liked renting the cabin for 90 days during the year. With kids in youth baseball and bowling programs, the family couldn't get to the lake every weekend. Still, during the summer, he wanted to spend as much time as possible on the lake, and the family logged at least 60 days a year at the cabin.

Accordingly, the applicable percentage for use here is determined by dividing rental days (or 90 days) into 150 days (the total days used—rental plus personal). The resulting rental percentage is 60 percent.

----------------------------- **Rich Dad Tip** -----------------------------

If you discount your daily or weekly rental rate to friends and family, certain fair share rules can come into play which may limit the effectiveness of such rental days. Be sure to work with your CPA in attempting to utilize the complicated laws in this area.

In Bob's case, he rented his cabin out 90 days for $140 per day. The first step, then, is to calculate direct expenses incurred for the rental:

Gross receipts:	
90 days at $140 per day	
Total Rent	$12,600
Less Advertising Fee	$900
Limit on Deductions	$11,700

Bob can write off the $900 fee to find renters, since that expense is directly related to the rental. The remaining $11,700 is the amount Bob can use for vacation ownership expenses. If his expenses exceed this amount, he is unable to deduct them, thus preventing a tax loss from being created.

In step two, Bob deducts the interest and taxes allocable to rental uses:

	Allowable	*Rental Allocation (60%)*	
Limitation Deductions (from above)			$11,700
Property Tax	$5,500	$3,000	
Mortgage Interest	$5,000	$3,300	
Allowable Amount			$6,600
Deduction Limit Amount Remaining			$5,100

So the amount of property tax and interest deductible as a cabin rental expense is $6,600. The remaining balance of $3,900 can be treated as a regular itemized deduction on Form 1040. The deduction limit has now been reduced to $5,100.

In step three, Bob figures out the remaining home ownership expenses that may be allowed as rental deductions:

	Allowable	Rental Allocation (60%)	
Limit and Deductions (from above)			$5,100
Utilities	$2,000	$1,200	
Repairs	$1,600	$960	
Insurance	$400	$240	
Total Rental Allocation Expenses			$2,400
Deduction Limit Amount Remaining			$2,700

As such, the home ownership expense that may be deducted is $2,400 (or 60 percent of the $4,000 in actual expenses). The deduction limit is now reduced to $2,700.

In step four, Bob calculates the amount of depreciation that can be used as a rental deduction:

	Allowable	Rental Allocation (60%)	
Limit on Deductions (from above)			$2,700
Depreciation	$6,200	$3,720	
Allowable Amount			$2,700

The amount allowed is the $2,700, not the higher $3,720. If the allowable amount had been above the $2,700, a tax loss would have occurred, and, again, the intent of the tax is to limit deductions to rental income actually received. So the remaining $1,020 of depreciation ($3,720 less $2,700) is disallowed as a deduction and carries forward to future years.

Remember we mentioned there was a silver lining in all of this? While the detailed calculations prevented Bob from taking a tax loss, the deductions did allow for one positive benefit: Bob was able to offset his $12,000 in rental income. And that is why Bob, ever the CPA, liked Scenario Two. It operated as a vacation home tax shelter.

For more information on this topic, consider reviewing IRS Publication 527, "Residential Rental Property."

Scenario Three: Brother Casey
Vacation Use and 14 Days Rental

Casey owned a picture framing and art supply store in Buffalo. His was a decent business that provided income for the family and enough time off to enjoy the cabin on Seneca Lake. It was not Casey's intent to ever rent the cabin, but a situation came up where he felt compelled to assist.

The family from Manhattan who had rented Brother Al's cabin for the year needed a favor. They were planning a two-week family reunion at the end of August and needed an extra cabin to accommodate all the cousins coming to visit. Brother Bob's cabin had already been rented out, and so Al talked to Casey on behalf of the Manhattan family.

Given that the family had let Al use his own cabin for the 4th of July weekend so that all the brothers and their families could celebrate together, Casey felt obligated to return the favor. It was agreed that the family would rent Casey's cabin for the two weeks at $145 per day.

Casey was worried about the tax situation he had gotten himself into. He spoke to his CPA brother, Bob, about how to account for the $2,030 in income he would be receiving.

Bob told Casey not to worry. While Bob's situation was complicated by the amount of personal and rental use of the cabin, Casey's case was easy. The government provided a tax exemption for short-term rentals.

The rule was that if you rented your vacation home for fewer than 15 days in a year, your rental income was *tax-free*. Thus Casey could keep the $2,030 without paying any taxes on it. As well, he could still deduct all of his mortgage interest and taxes on the property.

Casey liked this scenario and was open to renting the cabin out for two weeks a year into the future. An extra $2,000 tax-free income never hurt.

Scenario Four: Brother Don
Exclusive Vacation Use

Don owned a concrete contracting company. He did work throughout up-state New York and was quite successful. Don and his wife, Jeanne, did not need to rent out the Seneca Lake cabin, nor did they want to do so. Don's work took him throughout the area, and sometimes he would spend the night at the cabin while on the road. Don and Jeanne liked the flexibility of using the cabin whenever they wanted and on a whim, and were not keen on being constrained by obligations to renters.

But while there was no rental income to worry about, Don could still utilize certain tax deductions his other brothers all received. Mortgage interest and real estate taxes were fully deductible for Don. As such, with $9,500 a year in mortgage interest and the $5,500 in real estate taxes, Don could write off $15,000 a year for the major costs associated with the cabin, even though he never rented it out.

This was such an incentive to vacation home ownership that Don and Jeanne looked into acquiring another property. The couple and their two children enjoyed a ski vacation in Colorado every year. Don found a condo at Breckenridge for a reasonable price and put in an offer.

It wasn't until Don was talking to Bob about the tax aspects of the transaction that he learned the bad news. The mortgage interest deduction is only available on your personal residence and one designated second home. The mortgage interest on a third (or fourth and on up) personal residence was nondeductible personal interest, and thus of no tax benefit.

Bob offered Don two solutions. One was to analyze whether the interest expense on the Breckenridge condo would be greater than the Seneca Lake cabin. If so, the condo could become the designated second home. The second option was to have one of the properties be used year-round as a rental property, in the same way Al was treating his cabin. In that case, Don could take the mortgage interest deduction on all three properties.

But Don was more interested in vacations than taxes. He decided to leave things the way they were and bought the Breckenridge condo for his own exclusive use. While he couldn't write off the mortgage interest, he more importantly could enjoy excellent vacations with his family.

As a summary of the four scenarios involving vacation home ownership and their tax treatment, the following table may be useful:

	Scenario One Rent to Others All Year	Scenario Two Vacation Use/More Than 14 Days Rental	Scenario Three Vacation Use/14 Days or Less Rental	Scenario Four Exclusive Vacation Use
Tax and mortgage interest deductions	Yes	Yes	Yes	Yes
Rental cost deductions	Yes	Yes—but not over rental income amount	No—but rent is not taxed	N/A
Rental loss deductions	Yes (subject to passive loss rules)	No	No	N/A

Be sure to work with your tax advisor to properly take these deductions. And remember that vacation properties may be (or may become) some of the most valuable real estate you will ever own. And not just in terms of dollars, but also in terms of family memories and shared experiences. You will want to do what is necessary to protect this important asset, so be sure to consider holding this property in a protected entity, as discussed in Chapter 21.

And so you can enjoy your vacation home into your golden years, let's review real estate and retirement planning . . .

Chapter 13

Real Estate and Retirement Plans

Most Americans are now concerned that company pension plans and Social Security will not adequately provide for them in their retirement years. This fact is keenly underscored by Congress—not in their flowery words and grand pontifications on the stability of Social Security, but in their contradictory legislative actions.

Over the last ten years, Congress has approved increasingly beneficial retirement options designed to encourage Americans to save on their own for their golden years. While no congressman will dare utter the fact that with mind-numbing trillions and trillions of unfunded obligations, Social Security and Medicare are now regarded by many as Ponzi schemes that can never be fixed, Congress has covered itself with retirement legislation. So that twenty years or so from now when the government system inevitably breaks, Congress, the institution, will be able to shake its finger at the American people and point to the IRAs, 401(k)s, Roth IRAs, and the like they have created. And the message will be that the benevolent Congress gave the masses a way to save for their own retirement years ago. What will not be addressed is why the government continued to take 15.3 percent in payroll taxes from workers and businesses for a failed system. But that's an issue between you and the ballot box.

The point is that to provide for your own retirement, it is prudent, as it is in all facets of life, to rely on yourself and not on the government.

When it comes to planning for the future, some real estate investors use their real estate portfolio to provide for retirement.

We have many clients using this strategy. As an example, Denny is a dentist who owns a forty-unit apartment building financed on a fifteen-year note. While his mortgage payments are higher for now, he will own the building free and clear upon his retirement. Denny will receive $12,000 a month or more once the mortgage is paid off. Better yet, because of depreciation and the suspension of losses until real estate gains are offset and realized, Denny's $12,000-a-month profit will be tax-free for a good many years. That monthly income will cover his needs throughout his retirement.

But even more Americans will use the new and improved retirement plans to accomplish the same result.

Case No. 12
Jeremy

As an enrolled agent and tax preparer Jeremy knew the rules about retirement plans. And he knew that since Congress kept raising the amounts one could set aside each year, he should take care of himself. The message was clear that no one else would.

So, over the years, Jeremy had amassed an IRA valued at $125,000. The account was invested in mutual funds and bond funds, which, in the past few years, were only generating a 4 percent return. After factoring in the effects of inflation, it was not a stellar return. Granted, the returns were accumulating tax-free into his IRA. But Jeremy knew he needed a great deal more money to retire on, at least $1 million. And he knew that because this was a traditional IRA (and not a Roth IRA), he would be taxed on the monies when he started withdrawing them from his IRA for his retirement needs at the higher ordinary income tax rates, thus further increasing the money needed.

So Jeremy started looking for a better investment return. Many of his friends had done well by investing in real estate. And his good friend Terry had even successfully invested in real estate using his IRA. This was intriguing, and it led Jeremy to his first real estate investment.

Jeremy knew his market and decided to stay local with his investing. He also knew that when the new freeway to the northern suburbs was eventually built, land values would skyrocket. But because people had talked about the project for years and nothing had been done, land values were still surprisingly affordable. And yet it didn't take 20/20 crystal ball vision to see that the road would someday be built. The traffic on surface streets during commute hours was getting worse. Quiet neighborhoods were not so quiet anymore. Political pressure for a freeway into downtown would certainly increase.

So Jeremy found two acres of land near a proposed off-ramp for the freeway. It was selling for $100,000. He arranged for a trust company to set up a self-directed IRA, which is an IRA that can invest in a wide variety of assets. The trustee then set up a limited liability company (LLC) to hold title to the property for asset protection purposes. This will be discussed in greater detail in Chapter 25. For now, please note that if the IRA took title to the real estate in the name of the IRA and a claim arose involving the property, a judgment creditor could reach not only the real estate but the remaining $25,000 in Jeremy's IRA. By using an LLC, the remaining IRA assets are protected from attack.

Jeremy's IRA purchased the two acres and waited.

In year one, he heard some people claim that because everything was tax-free in an IRA, it meant he did not have to pay property taxes on the two acres. But in checking with his advisors, Jeremy learned that was not the case. If the LLC owned by his IRA didn't pay the taxes, he could lose the property in foreclosure. So with the $4,000 in annual contributions he used to fund his IRA each year, he had the trustee pay the $1,500 a year in property taxes. The remaining $2,500 went into his IRA and was held in an interest-bearing cash account as a reserve for any expenses that came up on the two-acre property.

It was Jeremy's strategy to contribute the maximum amount possible to his IRA. The current maximum for any IRA, be it Roth or a traditional, was $4,000. When Jeremy reached age fifty, he could put in an additional $1,000 a year. These amounts, Jeremy believed, would increase over time.

Jeremy knew he needed a lot of money for retirement and funded the maximum amount each year. Jeremy's patience was well rewarded. Six years later the freeway was built through the northern suburbs. Jeremy's acreage was very well located and eventually sold for $1 million. That money went tax-free into his IRA.

At age fifty-nine and a half, Jeremy began to pull money out of his now $1-million-plus IRA. Because he had used a traditional IRA, and the initial contributions were made with pretax dollars, he had to pay tax at ordinary income rates when he took the money out. (The Roth IRA, as we'll discuss later, is the opposite: Contributions are made with after-tax dollars, but the withdrawals are tax-free.) So if Jeremy's tax rate at age sixty was 20 percent, he would pay the IRS $2,000 on every $10,000 withdrawal from his IRA.

Jeremy's case illustrates the advantages of using IRAs to invest in real estate. But it also highlights a tax disadvantage.

What if Jeremy had used his own money instead of his IRA money to invest in the land? Or what if he used money from a Roth IRA? Would there be any tax difference?

The answer is yes.

If Jeremy had purchased the property using his nonretirement after-tax dollars, he would be subject to capital gains taxes of just 15 percent. Remember, he held the property for over one year so that the lower capital gains rate (versus the ordinary income rate for a less-than-one-year hold) would apply. As we've seen, this 15 percent capital gains rate is less than the ordinary income rate that an IRA is taxed at upon withdrawal. So in many cases, you'll want to consider using your own money to buy highly appreciating real estate. (Note: You must also consider the question, How long will we have the 15 percent capital gain tax rate available?)

Which raises this question: Given the tax difference, why would anyone use an IRA?

The answer, of course, is that IRAs are where the money is held. Millions of Americans have been besieged by stockbrokers, mutual fund companies, financial planners, and all types of investment advisors to set up individual retirement accounts. And almost as many millions have done so.

So when it comes to investing in real estate, many Americans, despite the later tax consequences, are going to use their IRA because that is where their money is held.

So how can you use an IRA in a more tax-advantaged way to acquire real estate?

The answer, which we've alluded to, is to use a Roth IRA. A self-directed Roth IRA, with a trustee investing in real estate through an LLC, can be an excellent tax vehicle. Remember we said that a Roth IRA is made up of after-tax contributions. And because you paid tax on the money going in, you don't have to pay tax on the money coming out.

So if Jeremy had used Roth IRA money to buy the two acres, the million dollars upon sale would not be taxed. And when Jeremy began to pull the money at retirement, there would be no tax. It was almost too good to be true.

Of course, when we hear those words, we are all trained to ask, what's the catch? And there is a catch. But there is also a positive exception after the catch. The catch is that (as of this writing) only people earning $150,000 a year or less can contribute to a Roth IRA. So at the start, high income earners were excluded from the generous tax benefits of a Roth IRA.

But remember how we said that Congress is getting more and more generous with retirement legislation as it becomes clearer and clearer that Social Security is probably beyond repair. As of 2006, anyone at any income level can contribute their after-tax dollars to a Roth 401(k).

This is big. Now anyone can contribute after-tax dollars and pull money out at retirement tax-free. Plus, 401(k) plans, whether Roth or regular, allow contributions at this writing of $15,000 per year, with workers fifty or older able to contribute an additional $5,000 per year. And while a Roth 401(k), as an ERISA plan, does not allow for investments into real estate, you can in many cases roll your Roth money from a Roth 401(k) plan into a Roth IRA plan. Once there, you can use your Roth IRA to invest in real estate.

And from there you are given some excellent planning opportunities, such as allowing your beneficiaries, like your children, to draw money out tax-free from your Roth IRA after you have passed on. With all the benefits available, it is important to know the landscape of plans. Here are some key questions and answers:

WHICH RETIREMENT PLANS CAN INVEST IN REAL ESTATE?
Retirement plans such as IRAs, Keoghs, SEPs, and Roth IRAs are not subject to the same limitations as ERISA (Employment Retirement Income Security

Act of 1974) plans. These more restrictive plans include 401(k)s and many corporate defined-benefit pension plans.

IRAs, Keoghs, SEP IRAs, and Roth IRAs (hereinafter collectively referred to as "IRAs") are not subject to ERISA limitations (which prohibit certain types of investments). So while ERISA plans, such as the popular 401(k)s, cannot invest in real estate, IRAs can. IRAs may also be self-directed, meaning that you can retain an independent trust company to serve as IRA trustee and direct them where to invest your retirement monies.

WHAT CAN'T IRAS INVEST IN?

IRAs cannot invest in S corporations, life insurance, or collectibles (such as paintings, antiques, gems, coins, and Oriental rugs). Almost all other investments are fair game, so, for example, you can invest in real estate, bonds, trust deeds, notes, annuities, and limited partnerships.

WHAT TYPE OF REAL ESTATE IS AN ACCEPTABLE IRA INVESTMENT?

Your plan can invest in raw land, subdivided or improved land, single-family homes, apartment buildings, multi-unit homes, co-ops, and commercial property. If your plan purchased real estate for cash (no loan) from an unrelated party and you never use the property for personal reasons (nor do certain family members), then the investment is rather simple.

CAN AN IRA USE DEBT TO ACQUIRE REAL ESTATE?

Yes, but there are several restrictions.

First, the loan must be "nonrecourse," meaning that the lender may look only to the IRA-owned property as security for the loan. If the loan isn't paid back, the lender can proceed only against the property. They have no recourse, or right, to proceed against any other assets, meaning your other retirement monies.

Which is good for you, the borrower, but is also a reason why not many lenders make nonrecourse loans. They want as much security as possible. (You would, too.) So then how do you obtain financing?

There are several ways. You can have the seller carry back a note. Seller financing is a good way to proceed. You can also have a friend make the loan using his or her own funds or IRA funds. Remember that if you fail to make the payments, your "friend" can end up with the property. Finally, if you put enough money down (say, 50 percent or more), some banks may make a nonrecourse loan. With a large down payment, some lenders will feel comfortable in having only the property as security.

Another restriction is that you, as the plan beneficiary, cannot personally guarantee or even sign for the loan. As such, the plan and your plan trustee must sign the loan papers. Not all trustees are going to do this, so check ahead of time what your trustee is willing to do to assist in the securing of financing.

Another issue is that any income or profits related to the loan are subject to UBIT taxes.

WHAT ARE UBIT TAXES?
UBIT stands for "unrelated business income tax." It is the tax on income and profits related to your leveraged, or financed, part of the transaction. So for example, if you purchase a property for all cash (meaning there is no financing involved), you will not have a UBIT issue.

If financing is involved, the tax is based on net income after all expenses and deductions are taken into account. As well, your first $1,000 of net income is not subject to the tax.

Assume your IRA buys a fourplex for $400,000. You put $200,000 of your IRA money in as the down payment, and the seller finances the $200,000 balance. Your net annual income is $10,000. The UBIT is calculated according to the relationship between the property's tax basis (purchase price plus improvements less depreciation) and the average amount of debt and the property during the preceding twelve months. (As the debt decreases each year, so will the UBIT rate.)

Thus, in our example, with a 50 percent debt to tax basis ratio, the UBIT is calculated as follows:

Net Income	$10,000
Less Exclusion	$1,000
Taxable Amount	$9,000
50% UBIT Ratio	$4,500
Trust Tax 37.5%	$1,687.50

Remember that once this tax is paid, the balance (or in this case $8,312.50) remains in your IRA tax-free and can accumulate tax-free.

WHAT ARE THE DISQUALIFIED PERSON AND PROHIBITED TRANSACTION RESTRICTIONS?

Your plan cannot buy real estate from a disqualified person or enable an investment for yourself or another disqualified person.

Your plan may also not purchase real estate and then have a disqualified person use it while the plan owns it. A disqualified person includes:

- The owner of the plan
- The owner's spouse
- The owner's descendants (children) or ascendants (parents)
- The spouse of a descendant (daughter-in-law or son-in-law)
- A fiduciary of the plan or person providing services to the plan
- An entity where at least 50 percent of the beneficial interest is owned by a disqualified person or an aggregate of disqualified persons (i.e., 50 percent or more of the entity is owned by one or more disqualified persons)
- A 10 percent owner, officer, director, or highly compensated employee of such an entity

Remember, because the property must be purchased for investment purposes only, your business, your family members (except siblings), or you may not live in or rent the property while it is on the plan.

Beware of promoters who state that family vacation homes and other family use properties can be purchased with your IRA. Buying property with IRA funds for personal use is a prohibited transaction. As such, the IRS will treat the account as if all assets were distributed to the owner at their fair market value on the first day of the applicable tax year. If the value is greater than the owner's basis in the IRA, a tax on the gain will be due.

Steer clear of promoters who would put you in a prohibited transaction. Such transactions include:

- Using your IRA as security for a loan
- Borrowing money from it

- Selling property to it
- Buying property for personal use
- Receiving unreasonable compensation for management of it

WHAT ARE RMDS?

RMD stands for "required minimum distribution." While you *may* start to withdraw money from your IRA upon reaching age fifty-nine and a half, you *must* start receiving RMDs by April 1 of the year following the year you reach age seventy and a half.

The RMD changes each year and is determined by dividing the account balance as of December 31 of the previous year by the applicable IRS life expectancy tables. As a general rule, the older you get, the more you must withdraw. Your IRA trustee or administrator can assist with calculating your RMD.

It is important to note that Roth IRAs are not subject to RMDs during the participant's lifetime. They are, however, subject to RMDs after the owner's death.

Rich Dad Tip

If your IRAs are invested in real estate properties, consider your situation as you approach age seventy and a half. If your real estate is illiquid and you are facing the requirement of minimum distributions, it may be time to sell one or more of the properties.

Now let's consider another excellent tax strategy for purchasing real estate . . .

Chapter 14

Using Pretax Dollars to Buy Real Estate

Case No. 13

Carlos

Carlos owned Something Fishy, Inc., an aquarium sales and service business. He sold the expensive angelfish and koi and the less expensive goldfish and guppies to fish lovers throughout the city. And then, for the large percentage of his customers that didn't want to actually deal with cloudy water and its causes, he provided a mobile tank cleaning service. Business was good and he used after-tax profits from his S corporation to buy duplexes and four-plexes around town. He knew he didn't want to be in the aquarium business forever, and his goal was to build passive income from real estate for his retirement years.

While Carlos had been good at acquiring real estate for his own account, he, like many others, had never known about a tax-advantaged strategy for buying business real estate. This secret was revealed to him when he met with an attorney about asset-protecting his duplexes and fourplexes.

The attorney asked about protecting his business real estate, assuming that Carlos owned the stand-alone aquarium retail building he used. When Carlos said he leased the building from crusty old Hector, who would never fix anything on time, the attorney smiled and said he had the last tax-advantaged real estate acquisition loophole for him to consider.

Carlos was interested.

The attorney explained that Carlos, like virtually all business owners, needed a location for business operations. A location—be it a retail store, an office building, a warehouse or even an equipment storage yard—was a business necessity. As such, rent was a necessary business expense that had to be paid first before profits were calculated.

With rent as a write-off, why not rent to yourself? Or, as the attorney further explained, why not let your business, which used pretax dollars for rent, buy you, the new landlord, a piece of real estate?

The light was coming on for Carlos. He had never considered such an option. As a visual person he asked the attorney to chart it all out. The attorney complied with the following:

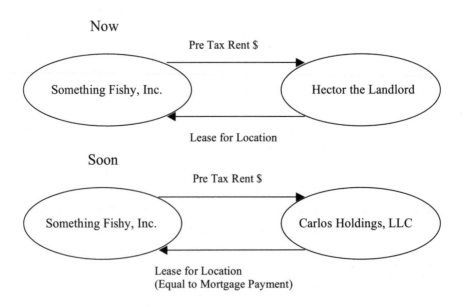

Now

Pre Tax Rent $

Something Fishy, Inc.   Hector the Landlord

Lease for Location

Soon

Pre Tax Rent $

Something Fishy, Inc.   Carlos Holdings, LLC

Lease for Location
(Equal to Mortgage Payment)

The attorney explained that Carlos would find a new location to purchase for the aquarium business. (He could also try to negotiate with old Hector to buy the existing location.) Once the new spot was located, Carlos would form an LLC or LP (limited partnership) to acquire the property. He would use after-tax dollars for the down payment on the building. Using pretax dollars from the business for the down payment would be inappropriate and could lead to a finding that the business owned the building. The attorney explained that for asset protection purposes you wanted the real estate to be separately owned. In this way, if the business were sued, the real estate would be better protected, since it would be an asset owned in a single-purpose LLC separate and apart from the business.

It was further explained that after Carlos paid the down payment with his own funds, the rest of the payments—the mortgage, utilities, property taxes, and the like—would be paid by the business. That is, after Carlos' initial down payment, all other expenses would be paid by the business. The beneficial use of pretax dollars was underscored by the attorney. These were monies that the business could write off before calculating profits and before the payment on any profits of federal, state, local, and payroll taxes. These were full one-hundred-cent dollars (and not after-tax fifty-cent dollars) put to good use, increasing Carlos's real estate portfolio.

The attorney further noted that there was no limit to the number of locations the business could buy for Carlos. If he wanted to expand into a second location in the fast-growing west side of town, after paying the down payment the business could pay the mortgage and buy him another commercial property.

Using your business to acquire real estate for your own personal portfolio is a strategy any business owner can pursue. And not only do smaller entrepreneurs like Carlos pursue it. Some of the world's largest corporations do the same thing. There was no better example of this strategy than McDonald's. In fact, it could be said the company wasn't in the hamburger business but rather the real estate acquisition business. As they expanded through selling franchises, most often they would own the real estate "under" the franchise location. For while being known for flipping burgers, the company didn't flip its properties, and, as a result, McDonald's now owns billions and billions of dollars in real estate around the world. And what works for Mc-Donald's can work for you.

Carlos liked the whole strategy. He asked what other work had to be done to cement the deal. The attorney suggested that a lease between the business and the LLC owning the property would be appropriate. He also suggested that the business make one payment to the LLC each month. The LLC from its own separate bank account would then pay the mortgage, insurance, and the property taxes. The business would still pay the utilities and other operating expenses. The attorney noted it was important for the LLC to be seen as a distinct and separate entity.

Carlos found a new location for his business and started having his business buy him real estate.

Now let's review some miscellaneous tax strategies . . .

Chapter 15

Three Extra Tax Strategies

Three extra tax strategies for real estate are often overlooked. In the right situations, they can work quite well for investors.

Installment Sale

There are several methods through which one can sell property now and be taxed on it later. We have already discussed one of the main tax deferral strategies, the 1031 exchange. Another method is the installment sale.

An installment sale is a sale of property where the sale price is paid in installments and at least one payment is received after the tax year of the sale. So, for example, an installment sale could involve receiving a 10 percent down payment on a red brick duplex in December and a 90 percent full payment of the balance in January.

Through this method, a taxpayer can avoid paying some of the tax on the gain in the year of sale. So that in our red brick duplex example, not all of the taxes on any gain would be due in December when only the 10 percent down payment was made. Instead, any taxes on gain would be spread out over the two tax years in which the payments were received. This can be a valuable technique, especially when, as in our example with only 10 percent down received in year one, not all the money is received the first taxable year. It is not pleasing or painless to pay taxes on profits you haven't yet received.

The installment method not only allows you to defer taxes. It can help with the marketability of your property as well. Because sellers have the flexibility to defer a substantial part of their gains, they may in turn be more flexible with the structure of an offer to their ultimate benefit. For example, accepting only a small cash down payment at the start may allow more buyers to get into the property. Thus sellers have increased the market of potential buyers of their property. And since price and terms are interrelated, a low down payment allowing the buyer to buy into the property may provide the seller with the negotiating leverage to obtain an overall higher sales price.

Under current tax law, the capital gains rate is 15 percent on properties held over one year. So by deferring from one year to the next may not save you a great deal of money when the tax rate is constant. But what if the tax rate were to go down in future years? (Not likely but always possible.) Under that scenario, deferring taxes into future, lower-rate years would be beneficial. Similarly, what if you have short-term capital gains on the sales of properties held less than a year? These gains are taxed at your ordinary income (i.e., salary) rate. Consider the consequences if you retired in two years so that, with no salary income, your tax rate dropped from 35 percent to 15 percent. You certainly could save money by deferring gains into future, lower-tax-rate years.

On the other hand, if you elected not to be taxed under the installment method, then you would pay tax on the entire gain in the year that any money is first received. Again, if your current tax bracket is lower than it will be in future years, then paying the taxes now at a lower rate may be an option. For most people, however, deferring any tax may be the better choice, especially since paying taxes ahead of gains can be a difficult out-of-pocket experience. Be sure to work with your tax professional to analyze which scenario is best for you.

Under the installment method, the seller typically accepts a promissory note from the buyer to pay off the balance of the purchase price in future years. (Hopefully, this promissory note is secured by a deed of trust against the property.) Any gain from the sale of property is prorated and based upon the ratio that the gross profit from the sale bears to the total contract price, and taxes are then due on the prorated gains in each year in which the payments are received.

Case No. 14
Joe and Jane

Joe purchased a duplex for $148,500 and two years later sold it to Jane for $180,000. Jane paid Joe a down payment of $50,000, and Joe carried back a purchase-money mortgage in the amount of $130,000 to be paid over thirty years beginning the following year. Joe's gain from the sale (assuming he had no other expenses) would be $31,500 ($180,000 less $148,500). By using the installment sale method, Joe only has to claim 17.5 percent of the down payment as capital gain. This percentage reflects the ratio between the $31,500 total gain Joe will realize from the sale and the $180,000 contract price. Thus Joe only has to claim $8,750 (or 17.5 percent times the $50,000 down payment) as capital gain the first year. Assuming a capital gains rate of 15 percent and no other offsets, Joe will owe $1,312.50 in taxes in the first year.

Each year thereafter whenever Joe receives payment, he will only have to report 17.5 percent of the sales price payment as capital gain. As a separate matter, if you receive interest from the loan or the property, such monies will be taxed at your ordinary income rate. Of course, if you do not charge a reasonable interest rate (generally over 5 percent as of this writing), the IRS will impute (or assert) a rate for you.

Those classified as "dealers" by the IRS may not use the installment method of reporting sales. If you are a dealer and you sold your property through an installment sale, you would have to pay tax on the gain up front, regardless of when or whether you actually received the money. As a general rule, dealers are those who are in the trade or business of selling property, meaning they are active and consistent sellers of property (flippers beware!). Be sure to work with your tax advisor to analyze if dealer status applies to your specific situation.

Incomplete Contract of Sale

A dealer is permitted to defer his tax obligation if the contract for sale is incomplete. It is important to note that because a contract for the sale of real property has been entered into does not mean that a "sale" for tax purposes has occurred. In order to be a taxable event, the property transfer must be a completed sale. Whether a contract is a completed sale depends upon the obligations of the parties to the sale and the contract language. If the sale is considered to be incomplete, then the seller does not have to pay any tax on his gain until the entire contract is paid off and the title is transferred. This tax strategy can be useful for dealers of real estate.

So what determines if the sales contract is completed or not completed? In a private letter ruling, the IRS summarized when the sale is complete:

1. Whether the amount of and right to the purchase price is fixed and unqualified.
2. Whether the obligation to convey title on final payment of the purchase price is absolute.
3. Whether the buyer has taken possession or has the legal right to possession.
4. Whether the buyer has otherwise assumed the benefits and burdens of ownership.

It is clear that the presence of all these factors would compel the conclusion that a sale has occurred; moreover, since a single factor is not controlling, the absence of any one of them would not compel the conclusion that a sale had not occurred.

Let's review each of the factors individually, as none but number 3 is particularly self-explanatory.

Whether the amount of and right to the purchase price is fixed and unqualified. If you are selling a piece of property, you are going to have a fixed price; otherwise, there would be nothing to enforce should there be a default in payment. So this is one factor you will certainly want to meet. But fear not, there are three others to beat.

Whether the obligation to convey title on final payment of the purchase price is absolute. This requirement essentially refers to whether or not the contract has nonrecourse language. With no-recourse language, the seller may never receive the payment of consideration and therefore is under no absolute obligation to deliver the title. In a relevant case where the contract at issue specifically said that there was no recourse, the tax court stated that the sellers did not have an "unqualified right to recover the consideration for their old residence . . . until they were paid in full." The tax court then upheld the sale as incomplete based upon this one factor. Unfortunately, the appeals court disagreed and overturned the decision, saying, "the 'no recourse' paragraph of the contract should be looked on as only one of the conditions of the total transaction." So having the no-recourse language will help you on your way to an incomplete contract, but you will need at least one additional factor to get you there.

Whether the buyer has taken possession or has the legal right to possession. Does the buyer have possession of the property? Most likely, yes. It would be very difficult indeed to get a buyer to agree to pay you for possession when they have to live elsewhere. One more factor is met.

Whether the buyer has otherwise assumed the benefits and burdens of ownership. You need to have this question answered in the negative in order to have the incomplete contract. Make sure when you draft your contract that all or most of the following are true:

- The buyer is not responsible for insuring the property.
- The buyer does not have the right to rent the property and keep the profit.
- The buyer does not have the duty to maintain the property.
- The buyer is not obligated to pay taxes, assessments, and charges against the property.
- The buyer does not have the right to improve the property without the seller's consent.
- The buyer does not have the right to obtain legal title to the property by paying off the contract at any time.

If the majority of the above are true and there is no-recourse language in your sales contract, then for federal purposes you most likely have an incomplete contract.

It is important to bear in mind that the incomplete contract for sale strategy also relies on state law. How each state defines title transfer is important. Do not try to put this strategy into effect without a complete understanding of its rules and the laws of the state in which the property is located. Be sure to work with your legal and tax advisors to make certain the incomplete control of sale will work for you. If it works, dealers may be able to defer taxes into future years.

Charitable Remainder Trust

Another tax strategy involves charity.

A charitable remainder trust (CRT) is a way for a philanthropic-minded owner of a property that has greatly appreciated in value to earn an income tax deduction, contribute to a worthy charity, and provide an income stream for beneficiaries—all at the same time, and while the property owner/donor is alive.

There are two notes of caution surrounding CRTs. First, it is imperative to know that once a CRT is formed, it is irrevocable. The property will remain in the trust and out of your reach. You can't change your mind once the trust is formed and funded. However, the charitable beneficiary can be changed, if desired.

Second, you must have a charitable intent. Beware of promoters selling CRTs as a way to avoid taxes. If you think you might want the assets to work for you in the future, do NOT set up a CRT. If charity is your intent, here is how a CRT can work:

- You donate your property to the CRT, receiving a tax deduction calculated on the current value of the interest the charity will receive. (And because the property is no longer considered part of your estate, it will not be subjected to estate taxation after your death.)
- The CRT can sell the property without incurring tax on the sale.
- The CRT will invest this principal, and while you're alive, the profits will go to specified beneficiaries (such as your children), based on the amount of income the assets generate and the payout percentage the donor has specified. (As of this printing, the IRS requires a minimum distribution of 5 percent of fair market value of the assets.)

- After your death, the charity will receive the principal. Again, the principal will not be there for your children or other beneficiaries upon your passing. Still, for some a CRT is a good tax strategy.

Case No. 15
Tyson

Tyson thought that he had it all in 1999: a great job, a big and ever-growing stock brokerage account, a fat 401(k) plan, and the vision and means for a luxurious retirement in paradise. By 2002, everything had changed. The great job was grating on his nerves with worthless stock options offering no incentive, the brokerage account was broke, the 401(k) plan was thin, and retirement was a distant vision. Tyson would be working for a lot longer than he ever anticipated.

But Tyson had made one smart and totally unintended investment decision along the way. He never thought about it during the dot-com boom. It was almost more of a nuisance then. But now, with real estate values rising, it was becoming his biggest asset.

Tyson lived in Albany, California, a quaint, small, and desirable city north of Berkeley along the east side of San Francisco Bay. He had purchased his two-bedroom bungalow-style house in 1982 for $95,000. He was single, the house was comfortable, and he liked the neighborhood and his neighbors. Until the rowdies moved in next door.

They were students at the nearby University of California. Six of them lived, laughed, and yelled in the adjoining two-bedroom bungalow. The wild neighbors consistently proved that the music of Aerosmith and the Grateful Dead did not get any better the louder it got. The neighborhood was kept awake every Thursday, Friday, and Saturday night as well as Monday nights during football season. All of the neighbors, led by Tyson, complained to the absentee landlord, the police, the community board, and the city council and to whoever else would listen.

Finally, a city councilman dropped by Tyson's house as an all-night party was being held at the Animal House bungalow. With this shocking revelation of rowdy neighbors, the government wheels began to move.

The owner of the bungalow had moved to Southern California. He was getting sick and tired of the nasty neighborhood letters and police complaints.

When the city councilman called demanding a solution to the problem, the landlord offered to sell the house for $125,000, a price that was $15,000 above market in 1985. When this high-handed solution was offered to the neighbors, no one bit. Except Tyson.

He realized that by controlling the house next door he would better be able to enjoy his own property. He was not a real estate investor. Instead, he considered the purchase a necessary quality-of-life expense.

Over the years, Tyson rented the bungalow to quiet professors and solitary writers. The neighborhood revered him as the neighbor who stepped up for everyone's peace and tranquillity. But then a funny thing happened. As Tyson's high-tech options, stocks, and retirement began to fade, the bungalow began to appreciate. More and more families and professionals wanted to live in Albany at the same time prices throughout the San Francisco Bay Area shot up. The bungalow was now worth $675,000, and with the mortgage long since paid off, Tyson owned it free and clear.

With no stock portfolio to speak of, the bungalow was now his most valuable asset. And as Tyson neared retirement, he considered ways in which to tap into the totally unintended pool of equity that sat next door. Tyson looked into a 1031 exchange, but that did not appeal to him. He was an accidental real estate investor, and he did not really want to own more real estate. He looked into selling the house but didn't quite like the idea of paying a capital gains tax.

Then Tyson learned from a lawyer friend about charitable remainder trusts, or CRTs. By placing the house in a CRT, the house could be sold tax-free. While the sales proceeds pass into a charity upon the donor's death, the trust pays the individual an income in the form of an annual fixed dollar amount or a fixed percentage of the asset's or proceeds' value.

Tyson liked the sound of this strategy. Because he had never married, he had no children to consider for estate planning, so he liked the idea of being able to benefit his favorite charity. And because charity begins at home, he also liked the idea of a fixed annual income through his retirement years.

The lawyer made certain Tyson understood the key downsides to using a CRT. Once established, the trust was irrevocable, meaning that the principal was beyond his control. If Tyson had a medical emergency or wanted to send his nephew to college, the trust monies (absent his annual payments) could not be accessed.

Tyson acknowledged his understanding that the trust principal would be placed irrevocably beyond his control. And with that, Tyson's lawyer friend set up the CRT and the house next door was contributed into the trust. The house was sold by the CRT without having to recognize any capital gains. The proceeds were then invested into low-risk bonds and index funds. The CRT provided that Tyson would receive a 6 percent annual payment based on the total value of the trust's assets.

The result was that Tyson received $40,000 a year from the trust. This money was subjected to income tax, but when Tyson was fully retired, he was in a lower tax bracket.

Tyson appreciated the annual income he received and the irony of how his retirement plan came about. Once a year, at the annual 4th of July picnic, he and the old neighbors turned up the Grateful Dead real loud and remembered the rowdies and the rich rewards for getting rid of them.

------------------------------ **Rich Dad Tip** ------------------------------

- Beware of promoters who sell CRTs as a way to avoid taxes. You must have a charitable intent and be willing to give up access to a large pot of money for CRTs to be appropriate.
- Be sure to work with your tax and legal advisor when setting up a CRT. The rules can be complicated and onerous.

Now that we have maximized our tax advantages, let's learn the legal side of things . . .

Part Four

Legal Strategies

You have just learned many of the key tax advantages to owning real estate. Now it is time for an equally important task in today's litigious society: learning the legal advantages necessary to protect the property, as well as you and your family, from the risks of ownership.

It is important to note that the legal strategies to be used, just like the tax strategies previously discussed, do not happen automatically. There is not some benevolent protector out there who instinctively structures everything for you to maximum advantage. Instead, if you want maximum advantage, you need to take two affirmative steps. First, you and your advisors must understand and appreciate the strategies. Second, and more important, you and your team must move to implement these strategies on your behalf.

So as soon as you are in contract to buy that first piece of property, you need to start thinking about how to protect it. And if you already own real estate in your individual name, you must immediately consider the many risks of such ownership and the legal advantages our legal system offers to better protect you. Please note that when we speak of protection, we are speaking in very broad terms. We want to protect not only the property you will or have acquired but also all of your personal property, your other real estate, and your other assets as well.

The concern for protection is basic. Real estate involves risk. And when risk is not properly managed, demands, litigation, and money judgments can arise. These can lead to the exposure (and loss) of your personal assets.

What are some of the risks associated with owning real estate? First and foremost is the risk of injury. If a tenant or a tenant's guest falls at your property, you can be held liable for allowing a dangerous condition to exist. (Whether or not you knew of the problem may or may not be determinative.) You'll want to have insurance coverage in place to cover such risks. But insurance companies don't cover every claim. Many insurance companies have denied coverage to the Gulf Coast claimants on the basis that Hurricane Katrina did not bring about wind damage. If you can't rely on your insurance company in every case, what can be done? Read on and learn the legal advantages our system offers the rich (and all of us) to better protect valuable assets.

Real estate also involves obligations. You will sign contracts and agreements and mortgage documents. And there is a risk that you may not be able to perform all of the promises you have made. Will you be personally responsible for all of your obligations? It depends on how your affairs are structured, and how well you have utilized the legal advantages and strategies that exist.

Another underappreciated risk comes from environmental liability. If there are toxins on your property, whether you put them there or not, you can be held liable for potentially huge remediation costs. Innocent landowners, whose only misstep was to be involved in a toxic property's chain of title, have been wiped out, both financially and emotionally, from environmental liabilities.

For these and related reasons, it is imperative that you know the legal and financial risks before you buy a property. And once again, equally important is knowing, appreciating, and actually implementing the legal advantages our laws and courts afford you.

These strategies have been used for centuries by the rich to protect themselves. And they are available to all of us, right now, by taking affirmative steps forward.

So in using the legal system to our advantage, let us start by protecting your primary residence . . .

Chapter 16

Homestead Exemptions

Case No. 16
Kenny

Kenny, the entrepreneurial superstar, was under tremendous stress. Even more than in all those board room showdowns that had yielded millions in stock options and pay. Kenny was used to that kind of pressure. He was used to the business media spotlight in and out of the halls of commerce. He was so well known in the business world that he endorsed mutual funds and hair restoration clinics.

But Kenny had just been through a different kind of pressure: a molestation charge. It was all so ludicrous. Like all handsome, famous, ultra-wealthy entrepreneurial superstars, Kenny had never heard "no" from any of his adoring female interns. All the Jens and Kellis, Ambers and Angelinas were eager to hook up with him. Yes, he was married—but could Kenny help it if he was popular?

Once again, a young lady frequented his hotel suite. But in a first for Kenny, she later told police detectives she'd been molested by him. A warrant was issued, Kenny was charged, and the headlines rippled in waves from Fox to CNN. His lawyers heatedly declared their client's innocence. At a news conference, a shaken Kenny—his tearful wife by his side (her net worth being threatened, too)—admitted to partying with the young woman, but insisted it was "consensual."

A media circus began to hound the family and friends of Kenny's accuser, prying into her life. Kenny's aggressive lawyers questioned the accuser's amorous history, alcohol use, and mental state. It became too much. She couldn't continue. The prosecution dropped the case. Kenny—no longer the hot commodity for commercial endorsements—moved on with his career.

But a civil suit loomed. The young woman's lawyers filed a suit in California, where Kenny lived. Under California law, a sizable fortune with seemingly no limit could be awarded for pain and suffering, plus economic and punitive damages. Kenny was appalled, his wife furious. Fortunately, they could afford the best counsel.

Their expensive attorney advised the couple to move to Florida. Sell the oceanfront house in California and go to the East Coast. Florida, he said, has amazing homestead laws to protect your assets from sleazy, selfish, gold-digging claims.

Kenny asked what "homestead" meant. The lawyer explained it's a method of guarding the equity in your house. You file a homestead with your county recorder. Each state has its own laws governing homesteading. In California, a homeowner can protect up to $75,000 in equity. If your house is worth $600,000, and you paid the mortgage down to $525,000, you'd have $75,000 in equity. A creditor couldn't reach it.

But Kenny and his wife lived in a $10.6-million mansion. Because all of their loans had been paid off, they had $10.6 million in equity in the house. A $75,000 homestead exemption is not much of a deterrence, advised the attorney. The plaintiffs could still go after the remaining $10,525,000 in equity.

Then why move to Florida? Kenny asked. The attorney responded that Florida has an unlimited homestead exemption. As long as the house sits on an acre or less, creditors cannot touch your house. Whether it is fully encumbered or completely paid off, creditors cannot force a sale of your house in Florida.

So Kenny and his pragmatic wife sold their mansion on the Pacific and moved into one on the opposite coast. They promptly filed a homestead and enjoyed the maximum protection under Florida law.

As this fictitious example illustrates, homesteads can be very valuable in protecting a very vital real estate asset—your personal residence—from claims.

Homestead exemptions in the United States date back to the early 1840s and the early years of the Republic of Texas, which had just broken away from Mexico (remember the Alamo?) and was self-ruling. Texas wanted to lure settlers to leave the United States and develop the land. They offered complete homestead protection for landowners from the claims of creditors. This economic development inducement worked brilliantly. Ranchers and farmers immigrated to the young republic to homestead and enjoy the security the homesteading offered. Before long, homestead laws were adopted by U.S. states whose legislators recognized them as a beneficial tool for economic development. Indeed, European farmers arrived by the boatload to these homestead states in the 1870s and 1880s.

Today homestead exemptions vary by state, not only in the limit of equity protection but in the size of a property's acreage. New Jersey, Pennsylvania, and Delaware (whose histories differ drastically from states in the South, Midwest, and West) offer no homestead exemptions. Texas, Oklahoma, Kansas, Iowa, South Dakota, and Florida offer homestead protection for an unlimited dollar amount. A chart explaining each state's homestead laws can be found at www.successdna.com.

There are some general rules. One is that a person can possess but one valid homestead at a time. Another is that homesteads usually apply only to real estate owned and occupied as a principal residence. (The good news is that condominiums and co-ops are generally protected; some states even include mobile homes.)

The homestead exemption is not a panacea against all legal claims. It doesn't shield the homeowner from debts on the property secured by a mortgage or a deed of trust. Nor does it defend the property from IRS liens and the payment of taxes, mechanics' liens, child support, or alimony payments. But it does protect the personal residence from seizure or forced sale due to general creditor claims, such as for personal or business loans, credit card balances, or accidents.

Florida's homestead laws give the greatest protection. The Sunshine State's supreme court decided that converting nonexempt property (such as cash and other assets subject to immediate seizure) to a homestead with an unlimited exemption (even a multimillion-dollar house, as long as it sits on no more than an acre) is fair and just—even if the homeowner's purpose is to cheat an existing creditor. This is why Florida, to someone like Kenny, feels like a prudent investment.

With your primary residence guarded to the greatest legal extent, it makes sense to defend yourself from personal liability in each of your other real estate activities. To more completely grasp why this strategy should be a part of your financial future, let's take a peek back into history . . .

Chapter 17

Land Ownership and Notice Requirements

The legal relationship between landlords and tenants can be traced to medieval Europe, where the king reigned over all the land. The king would allow a select group of lords to each take control of a parcel of land in return for their contributions of money, military service, favors, and loyalty. The lord was given absolute control over his parcel of land and answered to no one except the king. This is the origin of the term "landlord"—the idea of one being the lord of his land.

The lord would often give others the right to live on his land as long as they performed all of the necessary maintenance. These people who worked the lord's land were called serfs in feudal times, referring to their service to the lord. They would work the land, care for animals, and construct homes and other buildings to make the land valuable, but they received no rights—or respect. They were never in the position to actually own the land they worked. This is the origin of our modern idea of tenancy. In order to have the right to use a piece of land, there are certain responsibilities expected of the tenant. The word "tenant" comes from the Latin word *tenere*, which means "to hold."

Today "tenant" refers in legal terminology to the person who holds certain legal rights to the land.

During England's feudal times, lords owned their land only until their death, at which time the land would revert back to the king's ownership. If the lord's family wanted to continue holding the land, they were charged a hefty fee. It wasn't until 1290 that owners gained the right to freely sell or transfer their land. This change made families even more protective of their land because they had the opportunity to hold it for generations and even centuries.

Fortunately, for habitability purposes, the relationship between landlords and tenants has evolved over the years. Landlords are expected to keep their rentals at least up to code and habitable. Tenants are no longer expected to rent a place "as is." Mechanical skills have become less valued by society, thus making it harder to demand that tenants make all their own repairs and perform all maintenance. Therefore, landlords are now responsible for many aspects of property maintenance. Tenants have also gained the right to quietly enjoy their property. This means in part, at least in most jurisdictions, that the landlord cannot come onto the property without notifying the tenant in advance.

So while most of the laws concerning the landlord-tenant relationship have evolved with time, they can all be traced back to the feudal model of kings, lords, and serfs practiced in medieval times. So, in order to lord over your real estate, it is important to know the types of ownership.

Four Types of Ownership

Modern times have brought four types of ownership. These four types and their characteristics are as follows:

1. *Fee Estates:* This type of estate, also known as "fee simple absolute," provides absolute ownership for an indefinite period of time. Though use is somewhat limited by governmental land use restrictions, a fee owner has the right to do whatever he or she wants to do with the land. This also allows the owner to sell, lease, or give the land away as he/she sees fit. When buying an estate, this is the most desirable type of ownership, since it allows you to do what you want with your land.

2. *Life Estates:* This interest occurs when the title holder grants the tenant possession of the property, lasting the tenant's lifetime. The lifetime tenant is responsible for taxes and repairs until his or her death, at which time the possession of the house reverts back to the title holder.

3. *Estates at Will:* This occurs when a fee owner allows a tenant to use the property for free. Estates at will terminate at the will of the fee owner once he or she has given the tenant proper notice.

4. *Leasehold Estates:* This occurs when a fee owner grants a tenant the right to possess the property for a predetermined amount of time. This is the typical landlord-tenant agreement in which the fee owner retains the title while the tenant possesses and uses the property for the term of the lease.

There are different types of leasehold estates, characterized by their measure of time and term. These variations are:

• *Fixed-Term Tenancy (or a Lease):* This is tenancy for a fixed term. At the date of termination, the tenant's possession automatically comes to an end. However, entering into a new lease at this time can extend the agreement and continue the tenancy.

• *Periodic Tenancy (or a Rental):* Rental or periodic tenancy agreements can be year-to-year, month-to-month, or week-to-week. The time period is determined based on the time between rental payments. The most common type of periodic tenancy is a month-to-month agreement. These types of agreements can only be terminated with timely notice. In the case of a month-to-month rental, a thirty-day notice of termination from either the landlord or the tenant is considered to be proper notice.

• *Tenancy at Will:* This is similar to an estate at will when a tenant possesses the property for an undetermined amount of time without making payments. Unless otherwise specified, the agreement terminates with the death of either the tenant or the landlord. When terminating the agreement before such an event, the landlord must give the tenant proper notice.

Since the terms of each leasehold agreement are so different, each type also has a different definition of what characterizes proper notice should either the landlord or the tenant wish to terminate the lease. For example, the fixed-term tenancy agreement expires on a certain date. No notice must be given in this situation, since the terms of the agreement specify this date as the date of termination. If a tenant stays past this date without negotiating a new lease, procedures to evict the tenant can proceed.

Notice for periodic tenancy agreements is given in accordance with the period between rental payments. This means that a tenant making weekly payments requires only a week's notice. A tenant on a month-to-month agreement must be given thirty days' notice. If the tenant remains on the property after the period of notice has run out, the landlord may evict the tenant.

While all these periods of notice may vary according to state law, the general rule is that thirty days' notice must be given to a tenant at will.

Once a lease, rental, or at-will tenancy agreement expires, either automatically or by giving notice, the tenant is considered to be holding over. This results in "tenancy at sufferance." Once a tenant is holding over, he or she does do not require any notice, because any agreement you made no longer applies. These tenants can be evicted.

As a landlord you most certainly will have to evict a tenant at some point. While this is not something that anyone likes to do, owning rentals is a business, so any tenant who is not paying what is owed or is otherwise hurting your business must be removed.

It is recommended that you recruit a knowledgeable local attorney who represents landlords in eviction cases *before* you even buy your first property. Ask people you trust, such as your CPA, friends, and others who own rentals, for an attorney they would recommend. While most times you will be able to handle an eviction on your own, it is reassuring to know that someone is behind you if things ever turn ugly.

Now you know that there are many types of lease agreements and that each of these tenancy types requires a different notice requirement. Knowing the notice requirement for your agreement is key in evictions. Some requirements can even differ by state. As a landlord it is important that you are knowledgeable about eviction laws in order to properly serve your tenants and to protect yourself against lawsuits.

Case No. 17
Cari and Jake

Cari owned an old Victorian house located near the university. The house had been renovated so that it now contained two apartments. A professor who just moved to the area with his wife and two young daughters lived on the top floor. He loved the location of the house because of its proximity to his classroom. And he was always timely with his rental payments.

Jake, an absentminded herpetologist, lived on the first floor. He was forgetful with his rent and forgetful about whether his amphibians, snakes, and various other crawling creatures were in their cages or not.

Needless to say, the professor, his wife, and especially their children did not enjoy the creepy crawlers on the stairways and the porch. They had complained more than once to Cari about Jake. She began to realize that Jake was a problematic tenant and she would have to do something about it.

Jake's lease was a periodic month-to-month agreement, yet he usually forgot to pay the rent on time, if at all. Cari knew from her previous experience with rentals that Jake's periodic lease only required her to give him thirty days' notice in order to terminate the lease. If he did not move out by the time the thirty days were up, she would be able to evict him.

However, Cari knew if she didn't do something sooner than that, she might lose the responsible tenants she really wanted to keep: the family living upstairs. Once Jake was late with his next payment, Cari contacted her attorney to see if there was anything she could do.

He advised Cari to serve Jake with a three-day notice to pay rent or to leave the property. The notice stated the exact amount of rent Jake owed, which is a requirement in most states for such a notice. The notice also stated that if the rent was not paid within three days, the landlord would forfeit the lease and take hold of the property.

After four days, Jake called Cari and said he was ready to pay the rent. Cari refused to take the rent, telling Jake that he had missed the deadline and he now must vacate the apartment. Jake hung up the phone while hissing expletives.

Cari went to her attorney and asked him to file an unlawful detainer action to evict Jake, who claimed that he had tried to pay Cari the rent he owed but that she would not accept it. However, the court noted that Jake's lease agreement was terminated only after he had not paid the rent within the three days stated in the notice and that Cari had opted to forfeit Jake's right to possession.

Jake and his creepy creatures were evicted from the building.

This example shows you that sometimes you do not have to wait the required thirty days or more to end a lease agreement. However, a three-day notice like the one given to Jake cannot be used if a tenant fails to pay late charges. This is considered only a minor breach. But if a tenant has not paid rent, conducts criminal activity on the property, or is destructive to the property, the lease agreement can be promptly terminated. The three-day notice is delivered and the lease is terminated, thus restoring possession to the landlord.

If a tenant still refuses to leave the property, eviction proceedings must follow. If the tenant still doesn't leave after you've won your eviction proceeding, the sheriff may have to be called to forcibly remove the tenant.

Some states also differ on these laws. For example, some states serve a five-day notice instead of a three-day notice. In order to learn your state's laws, consult with an attorney in your area. Keep in mind that even if two states have the same laws, one state's court may be more lenient or strict with the tenant than another state's court.

But of even greater consequence than notice is landlord liability . . .

Chapter 18

Landlord Liability

The need for landlords to legally protect their assets stems from the heavy responsibilities the laws impose on landlords in managing their properties. Consider the following case:

Case No. 18
Karen, Guy, Bruce, and Davy

Karen lived in Viewmont, which in the last five years had been "discovered." Now it was a regular occurrence for artists and authors, families and empty-nesters from large cities and suburbs to move into the scenic little mountain town. In response, Karen decided to turn her quaint two-bedroom brick house near the town square into a rental property. Stretching her assets, she then bought a larger house in a new development on the outskirts of town. Karen felt that both properties should continue to appreciate in value as Viewmont's population swelled.

Karen was the only psychologist for a hundred-mile radius and had managed her small practice very well. She had conservatively husbanded her savings with frugal spending and was not burdened by the costs of raising a family. Prudent in her affairs, she quickly grasped the business of a first-time landlord and screened prospective tenants until she settled on a couple of artists: Guy and Bruce, who came with impeccable references.

They proved a good choice. They paid the rent on time, kept the house clean and tastefully decorated, and showed a talent for gardening. The only problem was the walkway to the front porch. It was uneven and cracked due to tree roots underneath. Guy had tripped on one of the large cracks and had asked Karen to fix it. Guy suggested that at the very least, better lighting on the walkway was needed so the cracks would be highlighted on dark evenings. Karen said she would consider the requests, but nothing was ever done.

Three months later Viewmont was hit with a series of fierce winter storms. Even the old-timers couldn't recall such heavy snowfall. The mercury plunged; the drifts piled up and froze over, turning the city's streets into empty corridors of ice for several days. Karen drove her truck over to the rental house as soon as she could. The pipes were in good order, and the furnace was working well. She left her tenants a snow shovel and a bag of deicing pellets she had purchased at a home-supply store.

As the residents of Viewmont dug out of the blizzard, another storm rolled in. Davy, an acquaintance of Guy and Bruce's, visited late one evening. The uneven walkway was frozen and, as usual, not well lit. Davy slipped and fell hard, fracturing his elbow and smacking his head so hard he suffered a bad concussion. He racked up tens of thousands of dollars in medical bills and could not return to his waiter's job for several months.

After visiting a personal-injury attorney, Davy sued not only Guy and Bruce but Karen, too. Through his attorney, Davy claimed that Karen, through the exercise of ordinary care, should have ensured that there was adequate lighting at the house and the walkway was properly maintained.

Karen, through her attorney, said that her tenants were responsible for such maintenance. Neither side would budge, and the case went to trial, at which a jury sided with Davy. The fact that Karen had known the walkway was not well lit and could be dangerous—even bringing a shovel and a deicer to her tenants—was determinative. She had failed to ensure it was safe and clear. The jury applied the law as it exists in most states: If the landlord is aware of a dangerous condition on her or his leased premises and does not take steps to remedy such a condition, the landlord can be liable for injuries resulting to others.

Karen's insurance company asserted that she had wrongfully allowed a dangerous condition to exist on the property. The company, as certain lesser insurance companies will do, declined coverage of the claim. Karen had not taken the steps to protect her assets. She lost a great deal of them at trial.

The Duty of Care

Over time, the legal concept of duty of care has evolved in concert with the objectives of another concept: public policy. Public policy is the overall vision guiding jurists and lawmakers to achieve a social good. In the case of Karen's walkway, that social good is the prevention of unnecessary and avoidable injuries to innocents such as Davy, who was just walking to his friends' front door.

Case law and legislation by lawmakers across the country have established the public policy that landlords exercise reasonable care in managing their properties to prevent foreseeable injuries to others. Consequently, this duty of care is owed by landlords to all people—whether they live on the premises, are visiting as guests, or even trespassing. That last category pushed the concept of duty of care into a gray area in respects to trespassers who are on a property with intent to commit a felony, such as theft. Resulting public outcry after several court decisions held that property owners owed a duty of care to those injured while illegally on a property led to laws in many states negating landlord liability to criminals. Had Davy, for example, been a burglar skulking up the walkway at night unexpected by the tenants, with the intent of breaking into Karen's house, she would be free of liability in most states.

Aside from that exception, a landlord who is cognizant—or should have been cognizant—of a perilous situation on his or her property will be held responsible for injuries incurred on that property. A point the courts will consider in deeming liability is the cost and availability of insurance to cover the risk. If a landlord fails to carry an easily purchased and reasonably priced insurance policy, it can cost the landlord even more. (Whether your insurance company will cover the claim is a separate issue.)

The best overall strategy for a landlord is threefold: to understand and meet the requirements of duty of care; to carry enough insurance to cover unforeseen claims; and to have further protection with the proper legal entity.

The Duty to Inspect

Inherent in the duty of care to prevent injuries is that a landlord has a duty to inspect the property for unsafe conditions. A reasonable inspection is required every time the landlord renews, extends, or first enters into a rental agreement. Negligence in inspecting the premises at such times leaves the landlord vulnerable later on to being charged with foreknowledge of an unsafe condition that the landlord should have found during the inspection.

Case No. 19
Eddie, Judy, and the Bar

Eddie and Judy were very hard workers and had turned a small mom-and-pop convenience store into a little chain of E&J Markets on the central California coast. Having grown confident in business, they sought out new opportunities and decided to buy a failing restaurant atop a ravine overlooking the bay. The lot itself, of which the restaurant occupied a third of the acreage, was valuable. The view of the water, especially at sunset, was spectacular. But their time was quickly stretched too thin, so Eddie and Judy leased the restaurant to Vic, who was hot on the idea of building up the bar end of the business, filling the Bayside Grill by booking entertainment and instituting happy hours and other specials.

Vic renovated the bar, added new outside doors, and extended the dance floor. The crowds did come. They ate, they drank, and they danced to the bands. Then tragedy struck. One late-night reveler left and never made it to the parking lot. Instead, he somehow happened around back behind the building and ended up tumbling down the ravine, incurring a spinal injury.

Eddie and Judy were stunned to be named in the lawsuit. It seemed like a cruel joke. They were just the landlords—not operators of the restaurant-bar. They had received no notice from Vic that patrons were straying behind the property in the area of the ravine drop-off.

The jury, however, took a different view. The plaintiff's attorney successfully argued to the panel of twelve average citizens that the landlords had allowed a dangerous condition to exist.

The duty to inspect premises to ensure they are safe from dangerous conditions applies when (1) the lease is renewed, extended, or initially entered into; or (2) the landlord is granted the periodic right to inspect, or to approve of construction.

The jury decided that if Eddie and Judy, the landlords, had performed a periodic inspection as granted in their lease with Vic, they would have recognized that someone turning the wrong way out of the bar's doors and—instead of proceeding into the lighted parking lot—wandering behind the building (ignoring the Dumpster and the muddy, unpaved ground) could approach the edge of the ravine and topple down the slope.

Never mind the Private Property sign that was posted behind the restaurant. Never mind that the previous owner had never mentioned any instance of a customer going behind the restaurant. The landlord has a duty to the public to execute reasonable care in inspecting the property. This meant that Eddie and Judy should have inspected the restaurant-bar after Vic's renovations.

The Duty to Disclose a Dangerous Condition

The lengthy list of a landlord's duties may include an affirmative requirement to warn tenants of current problems. Laws vary by state, but certain decisions in one state (often, it seems, California) that seem outrageous at the time end up being adopted into the mainstream.

Case No. 20
Roberto and the Teenage Partiers
Roberto owned a four-unit apartment complex across town from his house. Times were tough, and the town's vacancy rate for tenants rose, so Roberto relaxed his policy of a minimum six-month lease and went to month-to-month to fill up his investment property, which now had two empty units. A recently divorced mother and her teenage daughter moved into one of these units. No red flags went up in Roberto's mind, because the mother was

gainfully employed, passed the credit check, and prepaid the first and last months' rent plus the damage deposit.

It wasn't until three months had passed that the other tenants began complaining about music blaring late at night from the mother and daughter's apartment. Roberto left several unanswered telephone calls at the unit and even stopped by and knocked during the day, but no one came to the door. He mailed a notice to the mother warning her about the loud music and pointing out that the landlord-tenant contract forbade such behavior.

A week later Roberto discovered spray-painted graffiti on the retaining wall of the parking lot. He knocked on the door of another tenant's apartment. Velma, a retired nurse and longtime tenant, told Roberto that rowdy adolescents frequented the new tenants' apartment late at night. In fact, since nothing had been done about the pounding music, Velma was ready to file a police report. Why, Roberto asked, wasn't the teenage girl's mother controlling her daughter and her friends? Velma replied that she believed that the mother had gotten a new sales job with a pharmaceutical company and was often out of town.

Roberto filed a police report about the graffiti vandalism. Then he consulted his lawyer and began eviction procedures. He sent a thirty-day notice to terminate the mother's lease. He felt bad, but decided that an empty apartment was better in the long run than a bad tenant.

Roberto's luck seemed to be looking up when, the following week, he succeeded in renting the empty fourth unit to a new tenant: Priscilla. She was a quiet, serious-faced schoolteacher, new in town, and agreed to put down extra money on her damage deposit since she owned a cat.

Priscilla wasn't so lucky. Two weekends later a drunken driver plowed into her car just after midnight as she was pulling into the parking lot after seeing a movie. Priscilla, who was wearing her seat restraint, suffered whiplash and a broken nose. Her Honda Civic was nearly totaled. The other driver, who was pulling out quickly without the headlights on, was a minor who had become intoxicated at the problem apartment.

Roberto was named in Priscilla's lawsuit. The court ruled in her favor, finding that the landlord—who was well aware of criminal behavior at his apartment complex—owed a duty to his tenants to either provide extra security while problems persisted or warn his new tenant of the danger. The judge held that Roberto's failure to perform either of these duties created a risk that Priscilla or other tenants might suffer harm. She was awarded damages.

This is the law in California and several other states. As it may become the law in other states over time, you need to plan and act accordingly.

Because this is such an important area, it is worthwhile to consider a second similar case.

Case No. 21
Bradley, Howard, and James

James owned a small apartment complex downtown. He had recently found a tenant for a studio that had been empty for some time and was feeling relieved to have it rented. Everything seemed to be going smoothly until the new tenant, Bradley, moved in.

Almost as soon as James handed over the keys, Howard, the tenant living next door to Bradley, began filing complaints. From the beginning, the two did not get along at all. At first, Howard only complained about Bradley's loud music and rowdy gatherings of friends. Bradley complained about Howard's small poodle and its constant yapping.

But what began as minor annoyances escalated quickly. Other tenants told James that they frequently heard the men exchanging words with each other on the balcony. Howard's complaints became more serious. He accused Bradley of vandalizing his car and breaking one of his windows with a rock. James had tried talking to them, but at this point told them to contact the police when disputes developed.

One evening their dispute became violent when Bradley assaulted Howard. Howard filed a suit against both Bradley and James. The judge ordered Bradley to pay for assault damages and pain and suffering. James was also held liable in the suit.

While James was not found directly liable for the assault against Howard, the judge ruled that a landlord cannot disregard actions of a tenant that disturb a fellow tenant's quiet enjoyment of the property. Because James repeatedly fielded complaints from Howard without taking action, the judge ruled that he was liable as well.

The judge said that when a tenant signs a rental agreement, there is an implied covenant of quiet enjoyment. Because of this, it is the landlord's responsibility to intervene if the tenant's ability to use the space has been compromised.

Because Howard complained about increasingly bigger issues, James should have evicted Bradley for causing a substantial disturbance to other tenants. Landlords may also get an injunction against disruptive tenants.

The court has ruled that tenants are entitled to quiet enjoyment of the property—this being implied by the signing of a rental agreement. The landlord must ensure that tenants are not being seriously disturbed or harmed by other tenants.

Implied Warranty of Habitability

In addition to the duty to act reasonably in inspecting and maintaining a property, a landlord is legally bound to rent property fit for human occupancy. This seems obvious, but it took a great deal of time before the nation's courts reached such a requirement. Do you recall the discussion of British feudal heritage in Chapter 17? It won't shock you to learn that in the days of yore, some greedy landowners, smug with their great power, were pleased to offer whatever foul, nasty little hovel they liked to the unwashed, unlanded masses. Such peasantry and riffraff should feel fortunate to even have a roof over their wretched heads, was the attitude of these landlords. No matter if the roof leaked with every rain, the walls were drafty, the water wasn't potable, and raw sewage ran outside the door.

This attitude, protected by law, prevailed in Britain, America, and other Commonwealth countries for centuries. Landlords could lease whatever filthy rat's nest they cared to, and if the tenant didn't like it, he could move on to the next dank hole. The courts consistently backed the landlord's position that if the rental contract did not specify livable conditions, the landlord was not obligated to provide them.

Not surprisingly, few landlords cared to provide decently habitable lodging, given the expense of doing so. And tenants, bereft of options, typically had to settle for a pigsty, since there would be nothing but fouler pigsties down the pike. Ultimately, though, society paid a price for the dearth of clean living conditions. As societies shifted from agricultural to industrial and cities grew exponentially, street after street of squalor incubated diseases, such as typhoid, cholera, and the plague, creating a public-health nightmare. Still, landlords sustained a take-it-or-leave-it mentality.

What began to turn the tide was the democratic system itself. Upwardly mobile citizens who'd grown up in sordid rental situations entered the judicial system. The benches were no longer the sole province of the privileged. Judges whose childhood memories were scarred by unheated homes with no running water and inadequate toilet facilities had little compassion for stingy landlords. Still, an obstacle to requiring habitability standards was contract law—which held sway in common-law courts. A landlord-tenant contract could include whatever the parties agreed to. If the provision of sanitary conditions wasn't in writing, too bad.

But a second factor came powerfully into play. Massive outbreaks of cholera, typhoid, hepatitis, and other diseases were ravaging cities. The public good was imperiled, and judges found a way to circumvent the constraints of contract law by deciding that habitability was *implied* in every rental contract.

Public policy had won out over contract law. A warranty of habitability existed from the start. And this implied warranty made perfect sense: Why would a tenant want to live in a place unfit for humans?

The ramification for you, the landlord, is that you must maintain and manage your residential property to ensure its habitability. In the end, it is a sound public responsibility. And by the way, it is a responsibility you cannot delegate to a property manager. Although the property manager is hired to notify you about problems and needs of the property, the buck stops with you in the eyes of the law. In fact, you are ultimately responsible for your property manager's actions as well.

In light of all this, it is clear that landlords bear far-reaching liability for their investment or rental real estate. As a landlord your greatest risk will stem from dangerous conditions you allow on your property. These conditions include, but aren't limited to:

- Poorly maintained locks, doors, gates, lights, walkways, and safety measures
- Broken fixtures
- Unfinished repairs

- Continuous criminal activity
- Dangerous animals

The failure to remedy a dangerous condition will result in potential landlord liability. Your first concern should be to never let such a condition arise. Tend to your property conscientiously, keeping it well maintained and in good repair. Give your tenants a clean, decent, safe place to live.

Of course, life is unpredictable, and problems can come straight out of the blue. No matter how unexpected, fluky, or downright bizarre the happenstance may be, responsibility for any resulting damage will fall squarely on you. You're the landlord. You're responsible. It's that plain. And that important. So you must take the intelligent steps of protecting yourself.

The two primary ways of protecting yourself are insurance and entity usage. These will be discussed in the next chapters.

Chapter 19

Insurance

Case No. 22

Greg and Benjamin

Greg and Benjamin were old friends from college who recently began investing in real estate. They bought two buildings next door to each other on Monroe Street in an old area of the city that had recently been renovated into a bustling neighborhood of boutique shops, galleries, and jazz cafés. The old brick buildings had been turned into apartments that were in high demand because of their newly cool location.

Though they both knew they had made a great investment, their management philosophies could not have differed more. Greg could be described as a bit of a risk-taker. He owned real estate rentals in another section of town and had never had a single problem. Therefore, he did not want to pay the expense of insurance that he didn't need. He decided to pay for only the minimum liability insurance and held the property in his own name because he didn't want to pay the initial and continuing fees of a limited liability entity.

Benjamin, however, was much more cautious than Greg. He always remembered his grandmother's advice about insurance. She used to say that insurance was like an umbrella on a cloudy day: If you carried one, it definitely would not rain that day. But if you didn't have your umbrella with you, it surely would pour. He took this advice to heart and took every step possible to make sure he protected himself and his property.

Benjamin purchased a comprehensive commercial insurance package from his broker, which included liability insurance covering any injuries to third parties on the property. Since he would be hiring people to do repairs and maintenance, he made sure he covered any injuries to them by purchasing a workers' compensation policy. His insurance also covered any additional construction costs required to bring the building up to code. He was also covered for loss of rent should more construction or another interruption take place. Additionally, he bought an umbrella override policy that offered another $2 million in extra protection. After consulting with his attorney, he decided to hold the property in a limited liability entity instead of in his own name so he could never be held personally liable in the event of a lawsuit. While Greg poked fun at his cautious ways, Benjamin believed his peace of mind was worth the extra expense.

It took an unexpected accident for the two friends to realize the true value of proper coverage. One winter afternoon, after an unusually bad snowstorm followed by a week of rain, floods plagued the city. With the location of the two apartment buildings at the bottom of a hill, the damage to the Monroe Street buildings was particularly severe.

To Greg's and Benjamin's relief, no one had been injured in the flood. However, the flood had damaged the personal property of almost every tenant in both buildings. One of Greg's tenants, Sandra, who lived on the ground floor and worked from home, had all of her files and business equipment destroyed. She would not be able to work for months.

After all the tenants had been relocated and things had started to settle down, Greg and Benjamin had to take a close look at rebuilding costs. It was at this point that the consequences of their different management priorities became very clear. The city notified Greg and Benjamin that if they chose to rebuild, the new buildings would have to be built to code, including handicap access, and flood abatement regulations. Because the buildings were positioned at the bottom of a hill, these additions were not going to be cheap.

However, because of Benjamin's comprehensive coverage that included increased construction costs, the additions were covered by his insurance.

Benjamin also received a monthly payment from the insurance company to pay his mortgage and other expenses while he was not receiving rent. His insurance was able to handle all of the claims filed by his tenants for their property damage.

Greg's situation, on the other hand, was causing him quite the headache. His insurance would only cover exactly what was lost—the older building. Any costs to construct the required improvements would have to be paid with Greg's own money. The insurance company did not cover lost rent, like Benjamin's did, and the mortgage payments were still due. In addition, Greg's tenant Sandra would not be able to work for quite some time because of her business losses, and Greg's low liability level was not enough to cover her claim. Because he held the apartment building in his own name, he could expect that Sandra's attorneys would seek recovery from Greg's personal assets. All of these extra expenses had to be paid out of Greg's own money. Greg was forced into bankruptcy and had to sell the land on Monroe Street.

Benjamin was able to purchase Greg's land from him—a move that aided them both. The plans for a new apartment building with eight units were approved. Benjamin made sure the new building was properly insured and was held in a limited liability entity. Even though Benjamin knew that the probability of another freak accident occurring was slim, he also knew how reassuring it was to be fully covered.

Insurance Broker

The insurance broker is an essential part of the team you assemble when you purchase your real estate property. You must look for an experienced professional who strives to find personalized options for your business or investment. What you don't want is someone who is just interested in selling you the most expensive policy and collecting premiums.

A broker with years of experience can offer coverage pertaining to certain laws and requirements that clients are probably unaware of. For example, in Napa, California, all new single-family homes are required to have interior fire-retarding sprinkler systems. With this requirement in place, a policy providing only replacement coverage would be inadequate. A broker in that area would be familiar with such a requirement and would advise his clients to consider coverage for an increased cost of construction in the event of damage. This way, if the home is ever damaged and needs to be rebuilt, the required installation of the sprinkler system will be covered by the insurance.

Brokers can also advise clients on other types of coverage that are commonly overlooked. One example is the non-owned and hired auto coverage. If you have an employee who is making a delivery or deposit for your business in his or her own car and gets into an accident, you could be held liable if attorneys find out that the employee was on an errand for your business. The non-owned and hired auto policy would cover your defense costs and claims in this type of suit.

If you own a business and have just one employee, your broker may also suggest that you consider employment practices liability, which would cover any claims of wrongful termination, discriminatory actions, or sexual harassment filed against you. Whether these claims are legitimate or not, having the proper liability insurance offers peace of mind should a lawsuit be filed. If you have an employee who handles large amounts of money for you, consider insurance that covers employee dishonesty, including embezzlement and theft.

Finding an insurance broker you trust can help ensure you will be fully covered. The benefit of having a broker's advice is that your insurance coverage can be custom-tailored to your needs.

Rich Dad Tip

The insurance industry, in the face of record claims, is now in the process of reconsidering coverage on certain properties. If a number of water damage, storm damage, burglary, or other claims have been filed against one property, insurance companies are now refusing to insure the property. Coverage is not based on the owner, who may have a spotless record, but on the property's history. As a potential buyer of the property, you need to know if it can be insured. Your bank will most likely not give you a loan if it can't.

The property's profile is found on an insurance industry database known as the Comprehensive Loss Underwriting Exchange, or CLUE. Since only the current property owner can order a CLUE report (online at www.choicetrust.com), buyers may want to require sellers to provide them with a clean and insurable CLUE report. A negative report may force owners to pay much higher premiums with a nonstandard carrier, such as Lloyd's of London.

And remember, with insurance companies finding reasons not to insure you and even more reasons not to make good on claims, you need to protect yourself as best as you can.

While insurance is the first line of defense, the correct use of entities is the second line of defense. And given the track record of the insurance industry in providing consistent, reliable, and exception-free coverage, the use of entities as a second line of defense is a necessity.

Before we discuss how to use entities to hold real estate, it is important and instructive to know how *not* to hold real estate . . .

Chapter 20

How Not to
Hold Real Estate

There is a great deal of misinformation out there about how to hold your real estate. Many think that simply taking title as joint tenants or tenants in common provides asset protection. The truth is otherwise . . .

Case No. 23
Johnnie and Jillian
Johnnie Jason was a welder with his own truck, his own clients, and his own set of problems. First and foremost was Jillian, who never seemed happy about the way things were.

Johnnie and Jillian had married six months earlier. Out of the blue, two weeks after the wedding, she demanded that she be put on the title of the ranchette Johnnie had been living in and using as his office/warehouse for the welding business.

Johnnie was a bit surprised by this sudden demand. Jillian had never made mention of an interest in property ownership. But as Johnnie had learned from his fishing buddies, things seemed to change once you got married.

Jillian was very specific about how she wanted the title to be held: joint tenancy with right of survivorship. She said she had learned from her girl-friends that was how to do it. When Johnnie asked what the words meant, Jillian shook her head. She didn't know what it meant besides knowing that it was how it had to be done.

Johnnie managed to get out to go fishing the next Saturday morning. He asked the guys why Jillian's girlfriends told her specifically to change the ti-tle to the ranchette from his name to joint tenants with right of survivorship. His friends started smiling, then chuckling, and were soon convulsing with laughter. "She's getting ready to poison you," said one.

Johnnie was not laughing. He demanded to know what they meant.

Buzz was a real estate guy. He explained to Johnnie that the joint tenancy part meant the two of them had an equal undivided interest in the entire property. The wife didn't own the kitchen and the husband the den. Instead, they owned everything equally. He laughed and said the right of survivorship part meant that upon Johnnie's death Jillian automatically owned the entire property. It was unlike other forms of holding title that could be separately willed or given to others at death. With a joint tenancy, the surviving joint tenant ended up with the joint.

Which is why, Buzz added, if you were going to slowly poison your spouse and get away with it, you'd want all your properties titled as joint ten-ancies with right of survivorship. No muss, no fuss, no need to go to court. It was automatic. The survivor got the property.

Johnnie demanded to know how they all held their title. The guys started looking at each other back and forth, and finally all admitted to holding their title as joint tenants with right of survivorship. Their wives had insisted.

So Johnnie gave in to Jillian's demand and filed a grant deed with the county recorder, retitling the ranchette to: "Johnnie and Jillian Jason, as joint tenants with right of survivorship."

Several months later Johnnie had a problem in his welding business. A big commercial job had gone horribly wrong. Worse yet, Johnnie had forgotten to renew his insurance the month before the accident. Because he operated as a sole proprietorship and didn't use a protected entity like a corporation, he was being sued personally for everything he owned. Jillian was not pleased.

When the judgment was entered, the creditors immediately went after all of the Jasons' assets, which were the truck, some tools, and the ranchette. With no asset protection entities or titlings in place, they lost everything. Johnnie had owned the ranchette free and clear. Now the lawyers and creditors with the judgment got it. It was promptly sold, and the Jasons were on the street.

Jillian threatened to divorce Johnnie. Her standard of living had plummeted. He begged for a second chance. He found work as a journeyman welder. They would come back. But they were living paycheck-to-paycheck in a small one-bedroom apartment. Jillian didn't feel like seeing her friends anymore. She found a job at a dollar store on the other side of town and kept a low profile.

Then Johnnie met Hal on a job. Hal liked Johnnie's work and invited him to become a partner in his welding business. Soon Johnnie's financial situation improved. Jillian was happy when they were able to afford the down payment on a new house.

A question arose on how to take title to the new house. Jillian was displeased that the joint tenancy had not protected her interest in the last house. One of her girlfriends told her the other way to hold title was as tenants in common. As a tenant in common Jillian would own a separate fractional share of the property, which she could freely sell or gift to whomever she wanted. Her friend said it would be her property, protected and free from the claims brought against Johnnie. After the last go-round, Jillian liked this approach.

And so at the closing, the escrow officer was instructed to prepare deeds to the new house that read: "Johnnie and Jillian Jason, as tenants in common."

Because Johnnie now realized that Jillian liked to have a stake in things, he decided to title his interest in the welding business with Hal the same way. Since the business was a general partnership, their interest was issued to Johnnie and Jillian Jason as tenants in common.

Eventually, Johnnie learned why Hal wanted him in the business. Hal had a drinking problem he managed to cover up quite well. But in time, Johnnie began to notice the missed deadlines and the periods of shoddy workmanship.

Then Hal went on a runner. He disappeared for three days. When Johnnie got the call, Hal was in jail for vehicular manslaughter. He'd crashed the company van through a crowded city park. There were several fatalities.

Soon thereafter, Johnnie learned the consequences of doing business through a general partnership. It was worse than a sole proprietorship. As a sole proprietor he was personally responsible for his own mistakes. As a general partner he was responsible not only for his own mistakes but for Hal's as well. It was liability times two.

Then Johnnie learned the consequence of also listing Jillian as a partner. She, too, was legally responsible for Hal's actions.

As expected, lawsuits were filed. Because it was Hal's third alcohol-related accident, the insurance company used a little-known exception buried in the boilerplate contract to deny coverage. Hal, Johnnie, and Jillian were held personally liable for the damage. Hal had no assets.

The Jasons' major asset was once again their house. The tenancy in common titling did not protect them. Because they were both responsible general partners, the judgment was against both of them. The attorneys went straight for their individual tenancy in common interests in the house. Their interests were attached and the house was sold, subject to the existing bank mortgage, to help satisfy the judgment.

Jillian could take no more. The Jasons were divorced. Starting over, Jillian moved to Florida, where an unlimited homestead exemption existed. A creditor couldn't reach your house in Florida. Johnnie moved to Texas, where the same was true. With his run of luck, he needed to live in a state with unlimited protection for homeowners.

As the case illustrates, asset protection is not gained by holding title as joint tenants or tenants in common. But since over three-quarters of all real estate owned by U.S. married couples is held jointly, understanding the consequences is important.

Joint Tenancies

Joint tenancies are a form of shared property ownership, used most commonly by married couples. Joint tenancies allow for undivided ownership, meaning each tenant owns the entire property and is granted all rights to use and occupy the property. Because each partner fully owns the property, one partner cannot decide to sell his or her share without first breaking the joint tenancy and creating a tenancy in common, which we will discuss shortly.

One of the main reasons married couples choose to own property in a joint tenancy is that it offers survivorship, which tenancies in common do not offer. Survivorship means that upon the death of one of the partners, the surviving tenant automatically owns the entire property. Therefore, one partner cannot bequeath his/her interest in the property to someone else upon a death. Instead, the deceased joint tenant's ownership simply ceases to exist.

Survivorship is important to many married couples because it ensures that each spouse knows how the property interest will be treated upon the other's death. If there is an unexpected death, this quick and automatic transfer of ownership allows the surviving spouse to use or sell the property without having to wait for the property interest to go through probate. At the same time, couples must be aware that, as our last case illustrated, joint tenancies do not offer asset protection.

As well, joint tenancies can lead to unexpected consequences. Suppose that John and Daisy are an older couple, each with a child (John Jr. and Daisy Mae) from a previous marriage. John and Daisy have talked about putting in place a will and trust so that there is an equal distribution to the children, but for now they own their main asset, a valuable gated-community home, as joint tenants with rights of survivorship.

Unfortunately, John and Daisy were in a horrible head-on collision. John died immediately. Daisy died in the emergency room. Upon John's death, all his ownership in the home, pursuant to the operation of the joint tenancy, immediately passed to Daisy. Then, three hours later, when Daisy died, everything passed to her next of kin, Daisy Mae. John Jr. received nothing, even though the house represented his father's total assets.

This result was not what was intended. While John and Daisy had talked about leaving assets to both children, their titling of the property and their lack of a will or trust led to a different result. And once Daisy Mae owned the house, she stopped taking John Jr.'s calls. A lack of planning led to a permanent split between the survivors.

Be sure to understand the consequences of joint tenancy before taking title by that means.

Tenancies in Common

Tenancies in common are the most common form of shared property ownership. In this type of tenancy, each partner owns a separate fractional interest in the property. Both partners have the right to do as they wish with their share, meaning they can sell, transfer, or bequeath their share to someone else. In turn, whoever takes over the share that is sold or transferred also has the same rights and privileges as the former tenant had.

Tenants in common have the right to use and/or receive income from their part of the property as they see fit. Tenants in common can enforce their fractional rights to the property in several ways: They can physically divide it, divide it by sale, or request separate accounting and payments that correspond to their share only.

Tenancy in common does not provide survivorship. Therefore, there is no automatic transfer of ownership to the surviving spouse. This means if a married couple owns their property as tenants in common and each spouse does not specifically dictate to whom their share transfers, default rules of inheritance will apply through what is known as intestate succession. This unfortunately does not always divide the property the way the owners would have liked. For example, in most states, intestate succession directs that children get any property ahead of parents or siblings. If your kids are rich and rotten and you want to benefit your poor sick mother, you'd better have a written will, or otherwise the children will take your property under intestate succession and probate.

Tenancy in common results in the partners owning specific and divided portions of the property. It is similar to a corporation. If each partner owns 50 percent interest, like a corporation, they can sell their half-interest to whomever they want without affecting the other's interest. However, this means that unless you have a prearranged buy/sell agreement, you are stuck with whomever your partner decides to sell or transfer his/her interest in the property to, whether you get along or not. It also means that if your partner in the property gets sued and loses, you may have a new partner. This could be someone who wants to partition (divide up) the property and sell it. Tenancies in common can lead to unpredictable results. They are not an asset-protected titling strategy.

Tenancies by the Entirety

Tenancy by the entirety is another, less common form of joint tenancy that originated in old English law and custom. Tenancy by the entirety can only exist between married partners. This agreement is unlike that of joint tenancy in that both partners don't individually own the entire property. Instead, the property is owned by the unity—the "entirety"—of the two.

In joint tenancies, the husband can sever the tenancy and therefore can remove his wife's right of survivorship by selling his interest in the property. Because of its paternalistic origins, a tenancy by entirety was designed to protect the wife's financial interest should she be widowed. Therefore, the husband cannot sever the tenancy. He can only sell his right to use the property during his lifetime and his right to survivorship. If he dies, the wife maintains her right to survivorship.

While the old-fashioned ideals behind this type of tenancy have made it less desirable in modern times, many states have found value in using them. Because in this type of agreement one spouse is prevented from dissolving the other's right to survivorship, states have interpreted this idea to fit other situations. Tenancy by the entirety is now used to prevent creditors from seizing the couple's property based on the financial obligations of one spouse. However, while some states have used this form of tenancy to protect assets, the U.S. Supreme Court ruled that tenancies by the entirety do not protect against federal taxes (see *U.S. v. Craft*, 122 S. Ct. 1414 [2002]). Because each state treats tenancies by the entirety differently and they don't offer full asset protection, it is best to consult with your local advisor before you decide on using this type of tenancy.

Protection and Title

Even though you hold your property jointly with a partner, this does not limit your liability as a real estate owner. Keep in mind that with tenancies in common, a creditor can seek a court order to sell the property to satisfy a judgment. This means that if one co-owner has a judgment entered against him or her, even if it is unrelated to the property itself, that tenant may be forced to sell his/her share. This would leave the remaining owner in tenancy with a new partner he/she doesn't know and may not see eye to eye with. Therefore, if you decide to own property with a partner in a tenancy in common (which we do not suggest), try to ensure that your partner is free from financial problems.

Joint tenancies do not offer any asset protection even though they make it harder to seize property. However, a determined creditor can get at the property. If there is an existing claim that a creditor wants to settle, they can convert the joint tenancy to a tenancy in common and then sell the property to satisfy the claim. So much for any preexisting notions of protection.

It is also important to note that contrary to popular belief, living trusts do not offer asset protection. While living trusts, also known as revocable trusts, provide probate avoidance and estate planning opportunities, they will not protect your real estate from the claims of creditors.

So if it is not as joint tenants, tenants in common, or in a living trust, how do you hold real estate? The full answer is next . . .

Chapter 21

How to Hold Real Estate

As we have seen, there is risk in owning real estate. In doing so, you are dealing with tenants, vendors, and even strangers who interact daily with your ownership of the property. And one of them can become injured (or can at least appear injured) and sue. While insurance is the first line of defense, not every claim will be covered. Insurance companies find reasons not to cover you. As well, you are operating in the most litigious society on earth. There is a litigation lottery mentality at work in our country. If you own assets, there are predators out there willing to play the angles within the legal and medical system to take them from you.

Protection is paramount.

Case No. 24
Albert

Albert had been an electrician for over thirty years. He ran his business as a sole proprietor from a building he had always rented. He ran his business his way, and never gave in to the pressures of others. He was a creature of habit who avoided change at all costs.

His son, a successful businessman, constantly advised Albert that he should be holding his electrical contracting company as a corporation, not as a sole proprietorship in his own name. He was worried that his father was vulnerable. However, Albert didn't believe in paying the extra costs involved in owning a corporation when he didn't see the need for it. He had owned his business for thirty years in his name without a single problem. So he shrugged off his son's suggestions.

Then Albert's landlord, Carlo, informed him that he was moving to Italy to live closer to his family. He didn't want to have to deal with the maintenance of the building from overseas, so he had decided to sell it. He wanted to give Albert the first opportunity to buy the property.

Buying the building was the last thing Albert wanted to deal with. He was quite content renting from Carlo. Carlo sensed Albert's hesitation and explained to him that if he didn't buy it, Carlo would be forced to sell it to someone else who could possibly raise Albert's rent or even evict him if there was a new vision for the property.

So Albert finally decided that buying the building would be in his best interests. Before closing, Albert met with Carlo and the loan officer. The loan officer asked him how he'd like to hold the title to the property. Albert was confused by this question—if the property was his, why wouldn't he hold it in his name?

Carlo tried to explain that there are several options available for holding title to property. He suggested that it would be smart for a small business owner to own his property as a limited liability company or even in a limited partnership. Carlo said these entities could offer Albert protection in the future.

Not surprisingly, Albert would have nothing to do with forming an entity to hold his real estate. He believed that these were useless services designed by greedy professionals to steal money from hardworking business owners. Against the advice of both Carlo and the loan officer, Albert insisted that the loan be made directly to him, in his name only, and that his name appear solely on the title.

Then the inevitable nightmare occurred. A fire broke out in a million-dollar home after Albert did some electric work there, causing a great deal of damage. The family sued him for negligence. Albert's insurance policy could never cover the full amount of the settlement. A lawsuit was filed, and Albert's assets were left completely exposed.

Because he owned everything in his name and did business as a sole proprietor, attorneys were able to reach his business and the building he owned. If he had listened to the advice of those around him and owned his business as a corporation and the real estate as an LLC, he would have had much greater protection.

By refusing to even listen to the advice of the knowledgeable people around him, Albert lost everything. This is the first lesson from Albert's story. Listen to the advice others offer to you. This doesn't mean you have to follow it—just be open to it. Robert Kiyosaki learned from his rich dad that investing and business are team sports. This is why it is so crucial to surround yourself with experts that you trust.

The other lesson to be learned from Albert's experience is that you should consider holding your real estate in an entity for protection purposes. A properly formed and maintained entity can discourage an attack. Holding real estate in your own name invites attacks.

So how are you best protected when owning real estate? The answer comes down to six words:

Limited liability companies and limited partnerships. These are the entities of choice for protecting your real estate holdings.

Why?

Because limited liability companies (LLCs) and limited partnerships (LPs) provide the greatest asset protection possible. Unlike a corporation, where a creditor can attack your shares and control the company, in most states a creditor cannot assert voting control over your LLC or LP interests. They can't force you to sell the property. They can't vote in new management. Instead, they only obtain what is known as a charging order, a right to receive distributions from the entity. And because you remain in control, what if you decide not to make any distributions? The creditor gets nothing. But then who pays the taxes on any undistributed gains? It is the person holding the charging order. Until the IRS rules otherwise, the creditor pays the taxes.

It is not attractive for creditors to obtain a charging order where the result is that no distributions are received and yet taxes must be paid on any undistributed profits. In fact, knowing that your assets are held in LLCs and LPs may be enough to prevent a lawsuit from being brought in the first place. Lawyers know that lawsuits involve two battles: winning in court and collecting. If they sense it will be difficult to collect (and that as part of a contingency fee arrangement they may personally have to come out of pocket to pay taxes on any undistributed profits), the case may not be brought in the first place.

That said, there are several key points to discuss in regards to asset-protecting your real estate.

First, beware of corporate and legal form promoters who guarantee 100 percent bulletproof asset protection. Yes, you will be better protected by using these entities. But no one in good conscience can offer a 100 percent guarantee. We do not live in a static society. Laws change, and future court decisions may minimize current protections. You will do the best you can in our current framework, but there are no absolute guarantees. Please be very clear that someone who offers a 100 percent asset protection guarantee is 100 percent of the time trying to separate you from your money.

Second, in California there are court cases that have minimized the protection of LLCs and LPs. There certainly is no 100 percent guarantee in California. There is a bankruptcy case in Colorado that has minimized protections. Other states may follow.

So how do you deal with the less-than-favorable decisions in California, Colorado, and other states with plaintiff-friendly court systems?

The best defense is to organize your LLCs and LPs in the two states that have excellent asset protection laws in place. Nevada and Wyoming both have statutorily enshrined the charging order as the exclusive remedy for creditors. Meaning that someone with a judgment against you can't force a sale of your own property to collect. Instead, they must by law wait for distributions to be made. And as we've discussed, that is not a satisfactory means for collecting money, and thus is both an aid toward settlement (at, for example, ten cents on the dollar) and a deterrent to litigation in the first place.

Suppose you acquire a large apartment building in California. You know you need to use a protective entity but are aware that California law (or your own home state's law) does not offer the best protection. How do you deal with the situation?

Before we discuss asset protection, we need to consider a state taxation issue. California and Texas have an extra tax on LLCs. If you have gross receipts (not profits but just revenues) of $250,000 a year or more in your LLC, you pay an extra tax to the state of California. At a minimum, the tax is $800, but with millions in gross receipts you will find yourself paying thousands of extra dollars for the privilege of using an LLC in California. So on larger properties, you will use a limited partnership, which is not assessed the extra gross receipts tax. Please note that Texas also has an extra franchise tax on LLCs (4 percent on profits over $125,000 a year), which leads many to use LPs in that state as well.

Of course, the issue with the LPs is that they require a general partner to manage them. And a general partner is personally responsible for everything that happens in a limited partnership. So if you list yourself as an individual, you haven't really protected yourself. You're still personally responsible.

Thus the key to using an LP is to make sure that the general partner is another corporation or LLC. In this way, you encapsulate the unlimited liability of the general partner into a limited liability entity. So for California, Texas, and all other states, your LP structure will look like this:

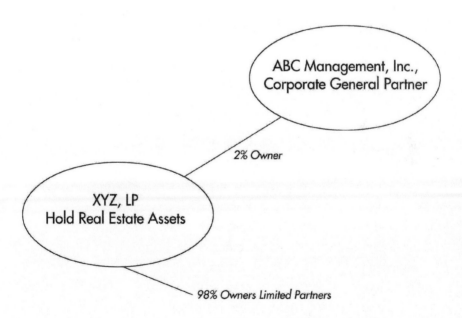

ABC Management, Inc.,
Corporate General Partner

2% Owner

XYZ, LP
Hold Real Estate Assets

98% Owners Limited Partners

The beauty of the limited partnership structure is that with as little as 2 percent ownership, the general partner can exert complete control over the affairs of the limited partnership. This is an excellent way to handle properties with family members or investors involved. As limited partners they can be restricted from asserting demands or control over the investment. Absent fraud, the general partner reigns supreme.

The problem with properly structuring a limited partnership is that it requires the formation and maintenance of not one entity, but two. To do it right, you need not only a limited partnership but a corporation or LLC to serve as the general partner.

In an expensive state like California, where the annual entity fee is $800 per year, the costs can add up. But there are two points to remember.

First, the extra $800 may pale in comparison to the many thousands of dollars in extra California or Texas state taxes to be paid on an active LLC.

Second, you can use your corporation (or LLC) to be the general partner of more than one LP. In other words, you only need to pay the formation fee and annual $800 fee (in California) once, not every time you form a new LP.

An example is as follows:

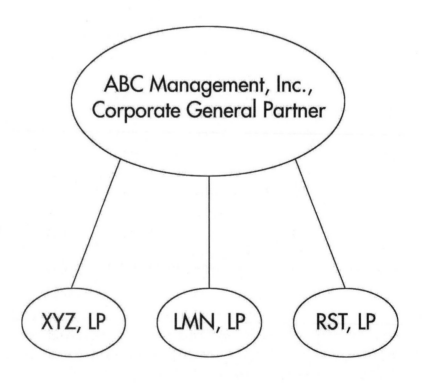

In this illustration, ABC Management, Inc., is the corporate general partner for three separate limited partnerships.

Assume the three LPs own real estate in California, but you want the better asset protection features of Nevada and Wyoming law. How can entities be accomplished? Very easily.

First, you form the LPs in Nevada or Wyoming. It is suggested with multiple entities that some be formed in Nevada and some in Wyoming. In this way, if a plaintiff is coming after you, he will have to fight in not one state, but two. That use of multiple favorable jurisdictions can be a deterrent to litigation.

Once the corporate general partner and the LP(s) are formed in Nevada and/or Wyoming, then you must qualify them to do business in the home state where the real estate is located. This is a fairly simple process and brings you into the home state's tax system.

Beware of promoters who state that by incorporating in Nevada, for example, you don't have to pay taxes on money generated in California or any other state. That is bad advice that will land you in trouble.

Let's assume you own three apartment buildings in California. You form ABC Management, Inc., and LMN, LP, in Nevada. RST, LP, and XYZ, LP, are formed in Wyoming. All four entities are then properly qualified to do business in California, a process that involves presenting the out-of-state formation documents to the California secretary of state's office and paying the annual fee.

How will asset protection work in this case? First, we must distinguish the types of attacks that may be brought. The first attack is brought by a tenant who falls at the apartment owned by LMN, LP.

Can this tenant get a judgment and reach the assets of RST and XYZ? No, his claim is against LMN. The other real estate, and your personal assets, are protected by using LLCs and LPs.

But under California law, because the claim involves the real estate and the real estate is located in California, California law applies. And California law, under current precedent, could allow the tenant to reach the assets within LMN, being just the apartment building. But, again, remember even in this liberal California scenario, the tenant does not reach your other assets.

The second attack can come as a claim not involving the real estate. Suppose you get into a car wreck and your insurance has lapsed. The claim has nothing to do with the apartment buildings you own. The attack then comes not at the operational level, but at the ownership level:

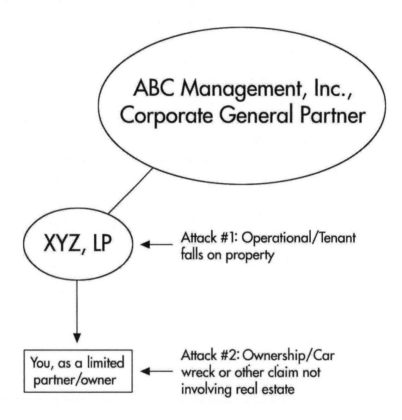

Because Attack #2 does not involve the real estate but is, rather, an outside claim, the law of the state in which you are organized will in a vast majority of the cases be the law that is applied. And by organizing in Nevada and/or Wyoming, a creditor is going to have to live with the charging order procedure as the exclusive remedy. As we've seen, the charging order is not a sure path toward collection and is thus a deterrent to litigation.

Additional information on the proper use of LLCs and LPs can be found in Garrett Sutton's book *How to Use Limited Liability Companies and Limited Partnerships* (SuccessDNA, 2005).

Land Trusts

There is a great deal of buzz about using land trusts to hold real estate. Amid all the chatter, it is imperative to note that:

Land trusts offer zero asset protection.

While certain other advantages, including privacy, are available with land trusts, be very cautious of the promoters who would talk you into a land trust as an asset protection device. We shall discuss the concept of a beneficiary ahead, but for now, know that if you as an individual are the beneficiary of a land trust, you are personally responsible for whatever occurs on the property. That is not asset protection, and you have just paid for a trust document that doesn't do what you needed. For true asset protection, the beneficiary of a land trust should be an LLC or LP. In that case, why not set up an LLC or LP to begin with? You'll save the money on a land trust that way. Consider the following:

Title held by: **Land Trust** Beneficiary: you, an individual Consequence: no asset protection	Title held by: **Land Trust** Beneficiary: an LLC Consequence: asset protection via the LLC	Title held by: **LLC** Owner: you, an individual Consequence: asset protection without expense of a land trust

As you can gather, it is our position that in many cases a land trust is superfluous, since an LLC or LP is required for the necessary asset protection anyway. However, because so many people are curious about land trusts, we shall discuss them here.

It is first important to note that, unlike LLCs and LPs, each state is different when it comes to recognizing land trusts. Some states have yet to officially accept them, so make sure you are aware of your state's position regarding land trusts before you set one up.

A trust is an arrangement in which one person (the trustee) agrees to hold the title to the property of another person (the beneficiary) for that other person's benefit. This type of trust is distinctive in that the trustee holds both legal title, meaning the trustee is listed as the owner in official records, and equitable title, meaning the trustee is entitled to the property. In most trusts, the trustee holds legal title only, with the beneficiary holding equitable title. In fact, in these other trusts, if one person holds both legal and equitable title, it is considered a merger and the trust dissolves.

Although land trust trustees hold both types of title to the property, they aren't required to do much more than sign the mortgage and other official documents when needed. The beneficiary has no legal interest because the trustee holds the title. However, the beneficiary's interest in the property is considered personal property. (And remember, personal property held by you as an individual can be reached by creditors.) The trustee is entitled to the possession and use of the property. He or she is also in charge of all the duties related to the property, including rent collection and the payment of taxes. However, some states require that the trustee have more duties in order for the trust to be recognized.

So why hold property in a land trust? The main advantage associated with land trusts is privacy. Your personal name does not appear on the trust or on any documents. Of course, you still would have to reveal your beneficial interest if asked in court or under oath. Otherwise, only your trustee would have to know you are involved. What, then, is the benefit of all this secrecy?

The main reason is that creditors (or anyone else who might want to know what assets you have) can easily do a search of the assets held under your name. If you hold your property in a land trust, it will not appear as one of your assets because the beneficiaries are not listed in public records. Only the trustee's name appears as the owner. When a search of your assets doesn't turn anything up, it may be enough to deter litigation. It should be noted that this same level of privacy can be gained using a title-holding LLC with a nominee manager.

Using land trusts can have certain tax benefits. When transferring your beneficial interest to someone else, transfer taxes do not apply, the reason being that the owner (the trustee) actually stays the same when interest transfers between beneficiaries. This can save you money, especially with deals involving large commercial buildings. Transfers involving land trusts are relatively simple. Since the beneficial interest is considered personal property, only a signature is required to transfer it. (Of course, transfers of interests in LLCs and

LPs are just as easy.) Land trusts do not file their own federal tax returns. The taxable activities of the land trust are reported on the individual returns of the beneficiaries.

A land trust can be a good option when owning property with several partners. When documents need to be signed, only the trustee's signature is required. There is less hassle because not everyone has to sign and notarize documents. This type of ownership can also be beneficial in the event of the incompetency, divorce, or death of one of your partners. Only that person's interest will be affected, and everyone else's interest will not be involved. However, you do need to have a plan outlined should one of these events occur.

As with LLCs and LPs, land trusts can be used to avoid probate. In most states, property held in a land trust can pass to whomever one chooses without delay.

The whole idea behind a land trust is that you are giving your property to someone you can trust. This means you must be sure your trustee is someone you know will not sell or mortgage your property without your permission. Banks can serve as trustees and are usually a trustworthy option. However, they can charge steep fees for this service. Asking your attorney to be the trustee can also be worth considering. In some states, you can create an LLC or a corporation to act as the trustee. However, when you choose this option, the names of the officers, directors, members, and resident agent will all be on the public record. To preserve your privacy while using this option, recruit someone to be listed as the sole officer and director, while you act as the sole shareholder (since this doesn't go on the record). For additional privacy and protection against creditors, a limited liability company can be used to own the beneficial interest in a land trust as well. If you decide to use an entity to be either the trustee or the beneficiary, be sure to have your attorney advise you about the correct way to do so.

Now let's review how one entrepreneur came to his own asset protection strategies the hard way . . .

Chapter 22

Asset Protection Lessons

Case No. 25

Sammy

Sammy was an astute real estate investor. He had started out as a carpenter working for a company that both built homes and did remodeling jobs. Sammy learned his craft and more. He was a people person and got to know some of the clients. He soon realized that the clients who spent $10,000 with the company to remodel a property were turning around and making $50,000 when they later sold the property.

Sammy liked being a carpenter/jack-of-all-trades, but he liked to make money even more. So he started by buying at a discount a run-down property that he could fix up in his spare time. While he experienced a few setbacks and had some learning pains, when the remodeling and painting were completed, Sammy earned a $20,000 profit after the sale.

That was enough to launch Sammy into his new career. Since then, Sammy has been buying distressed properties, fixing them up, and selling them. In the last six years, Sammy has also been fixing up duplexes and fourplexes and keeping them for his own portfolio. To further his real estate options, in the past year Sammy started building spec houses for sale and for profit.

Sammy had assembled a good team of professionals. He had learned from his CPA and attorney that each of his three real estate activities—remodeling for quick sales, holding and keeping, and building homes for speculation, or spec home sales—required a different legal strategy and a different means of taking title. His strategy was as follows:

1. *Remodel for quick sales.* This is the strategy Sammy first started with, and it continued to constitute a significant portion of his profits. Still, as more new investors were getting into "buying and flipping," the sale prices for distressed real estate were increasing. Sammy knew what his margins were and wouldn't bid on dilapidated yet overpriced properties as others were doing. Nevertheless, there were plenty of good fixer-uppers in his area to acquire. Sammy maintained good relations with the local brokers, always paid full commission, and never tried to wrangle a broker out of a commission. As a result, Sammy always heard of the best deals first and could take his pick of acceptable properties.

Because Sammy was flipping several properties a year, he was subject to ordinary income taxation. This meant he had to pay a 35 percent tax (the highest federal income tax rate as of this writing) on all his flips instead of only a 15 percent capital gains tax rate (at this writing).

It is important to understand why Sammy had to pay the higher tax rate. There are two reasons.

First, when Sammy flipped, he rarely held on to a property for over one year. Instead, he would acquire, remodel, fix up, and sell all within a period of months. The faster, the better. But by selling his fixer properties within less than one year, he did not qualify for the capital gains rate. To get the lower 15 percent rate, you must have held on to the asset for over one year.

On these properties, Sammy didn't want to wait a year. He wanted to turn them and cash out as quickly as possible. If there was a higher tax rate, so be it.

Of course, as mentioned, there was a second reason Sammy had to pay the higher tax rate. And that was because flipping properties was his business. It was how he earned his salary.

When you earn money through a trade or business, whatever this activity may be, that income is subject to ordinary income rates. When you are flipping two or more properties a year, or if all you do is fix up properties (even at the rate of just one per year), your income may be subject to income tax withholding at rates from between 10 and 35 percent. This income may also be subject to payroll taxes of 15.3 percent on the first $94,200 of income and 2.9 percent Medicare withholding above $94,200 (as of this writing in 2006).

This brings us to the best way to take title for Sammy's (and for your) flipping activities.

While in a large majority of cases, you will want to take title to your real estate in an LLC, for flipping you will want to consider using a subchapter S corporation. The reason for this, as with so many other things in life, has to do with taxes.

In a business-operating LLC, all monies flowing through the entity to the owner can be subject to payroll and Medicare taxes. The same is not true for a passive holding LLC. So we must distinguish between an LLC that passively holds real estate and one that conducts a trade or business, including a business operating as a real-estate-flipping LLC.

An LLC that passively holds real estate for investment purposes offers excellent asset protection. As well, all monies flow through the entity (i.e., there is no tax at the entry level as in a C corporation) to the individual. Because the individual (Sammy, you, whoever) usually has another job, payroll taxes do not attach to this stream of income. Likewise, receiving rents from investment real estate is not classified as trade or business income to which payroll taxes apply.

The result is different with a business-operating LLC. Sammy's business of turning fixer-uppers (or any other service business where the LLC members are active in the business) conducted through an LLC results in all monies flowing through being subject to payroll taxes.

As we all know, Social Security withholding does not lead to glory, or glorious returns. The system is broken and may never be repaired. So if we can pay our fair share without going overboard, instead of paying every last dollar into the system, we will be better off in the long run. The principle here is that you can spend your own money more wisely than the government can. It is a timeless and enduring principle to be followed.

Instead of having all monies flowing through a business-operating LLC be subject to payroll tax, consider using an S corporation. In the S corporation, you will pay yourself a reasonable salary and pay payroll taxes on that salary. But any profits over and above your salary can be flowed through the S corporation as dividends. You will pay ordinary income taxes on this income, but unlike the business-operating LLC, you won't pay payroll taxes on it. Again, payroll taxes—even the 2.9 percent Medicare tax on salaries above $90,000—can really add up, especially when you consider it may go toward a benefit you'll never see.

The question, of course, becomes: What is a reasonable salary? Can you have a lucrative S corporation with $1 million in profits and pay only a $10,000 salary and flow through $990,000 in payroll-tax-free profits?

The IRS is all over this one. You've got to remember that the IRS is made up of some pretty smart tax collectors who aren't that easily fooled. Their position on this issue comes down to the question of marketplace salaries. Could you hire someone skilled enough to manage a company that makes $1 million in profits per year and pay them a salary of $10,000? The answer, of course, is no. Neither you nor I would work to benefit someone else so greatly for such a pittance in return. The question then becomes: What is an appropriate salary in such a case? Given the profits, a justifiable salary would be more in the range of $100,000 a year.

Work with your CPA to come up with an acceptable salary level. Comparison information for your industry and region can be found at www.salary.com. By paying yourself a reasonable salary and payroll taxes on that amount, you are then free to flow profits through your S corporation as dividends and avoid payroll taxes on those monies. By using the lower end of the acceptable salary range, you will avoid an IRS audit and not pay more than your fair share of expensive and nonproductive payroll taxes.

As a result of the foregoing, Sammy conducted his remodel and fixer-upper business through an S corporation. Working with his CPA, he paid himself a reasonable salary and flowed his profits through the entity for payment on his individual tax return at ordinary income rates.

2. *Hold and keep.* As Sammy analyzed each new property, he would always ask himself whether it was one to flip or keep.

While he knew how to accelerate the return on his money by quickly flipping properties, he also knew that his long-term retirement needs would be in part satisfied by rental real estate income. Sammy's goal was to acquire one new apartment building per year. Typically, his ideal candidate was a duplex or fourplex that needed some repair. In such cases, he could buy below market and perform improvements over time at his convenience. When he didn't have a quick flip to work on, he could keep his crew busy on his hold-and-keep properties.

Sammy always held his hold-and-keep properties in an LLC, or, in California and Texas, where extra taxes are placed on LLCs, he held them in LPs. He valued the asset protection benefits of keeping his properties in separate entities, especially after suffering two lawsuits early in his career. The first lawsuit arose when he operated his construction business as a sole proprietor and held his first investment property, a duplex, in his individual name. A client had sued Sammy over some very careless work a subcontractor had performed. The plumber had gone out of business and left the state, leaving Sammy holding the bag. A judgment was rendered whereby Sammy's sole proprietorship was held liable for the significant damages. Since the sole proprietorship offered no asset protection whatsoever, all of Sammy's personal assets were fair game for collection. And because Sammy hadn't used a protective entity to hold title to his duplex, the property was completely exposed to the claims of the judgment creditor.

As a result, Sammy lost all of his sole proprietorship assets, his trucks and equipment, as well as the duplex. All lost to satisfy the claims for damages he did not cause. It was a bitter experience Sammy vowed would never happen again.

Sammy immediately started operating his construction business for flipping properties through an S corporation. He began acquiring hold properties with a vengeance, putting them all into an LLC. Before long, he had seven fourplexes and one triplex in his one LLC.

Then the second lawsuit was filed.

A tenant had fallen at the triplex. Normally, an A-rated insurance company would have covered the claim. But Sammy's insurance company was C-rated, and after paying huge brokerage commissions to attract the business, it had very little money left to actually cover any claims. The insurance company argued that Sammy had intentionally maintained a dangerous condition on the property. They argued that such intentional conduct was exclusion to the policy, meaning they didn't have to cover the claim.

Sammy was furious with the company and the insurance agent who sold him the commission-rich and coverage-poor policy. The "dangerous" condition was a stairstep that had just broken. It wasn't intentionally maintained that way. Sammy and his attorney considered bringing a bad-faith lawsuit against the insurance company for failing to cover the tenant's claim. But that involved a great deal of time and money, and all of Sammy's extra time and money were now being spent defending the tenant's claim.

As it turned out, the tenant prevailed against the LLC that owned the triplex. The good news was that Sammy's construction business and personal assets were not exposed to the claim. The bad news was that the judgment allowed the tenant to proceed against all of the LLC's assets. Two of the fourplexes were owned free and clear. The tenant's attorney was able to attach the fourplexes and sell them to satisfy the claim.

It was after this experience that Sammy came to appreciate that one did not want to own too many properties in one LLC or LP. By holding eight properties in one LLC, a tenant with a claim involving one of the properties can reach the equity in all eight properties.

Sammy decided that in the future, only one property would be held in each LLC. Putting too many properties in one LLC created an attractive target for the professional litigants of the world. It was well worth the increased annual LLC filing fees for Sammy to segregate his real estate into individual LLCs. It was a form of insurance, in case his insurance company failed to protect him as promised.

Sammy knew that some states make it expensive to use individual entities for each parcel of real estate. For example, California charges a minimum of $800 per year per entity for a weak asset protection law. Sammy knew that to better his legal position, he needed to pay the extra, yet reasonable fees for entities formed in Nevada and Wyoming. For Sammy, after losing two fourplexes to a tenant's claim, the increased protection was another form of insurance and well worth the extra cost.

And so Sammy used an LLC or LP to hold each of his hold-and-keep investment properties.

3. *Spec home sales.* Whether building one home for speculative sale purposes or building a subdivision full of identical tract homes, Sammy knew that a unique protection strategy was needed. This was because more and more lawyers across the country were bringing lawsuits alleging damage from mistakes during construction, known as construction defect litigation. Plaintiffs' lawyers were filing lawsuits on behalf of homeowners alleging monetary damages due to settling, cracks, improper construction practices, and the like. These suits were especially prevalent in California and Nevada, where a ten-year statute of limitations allowed suits to be brought a decade after a house was built. Lawyers were targeting subdivisions built nine and a half years earlier, and as Sammy perceived it, were stirring the pot with homeowners to identify both real and imagined problems for which a contingency lawsuit could be brought.

Sammy and his lawyer realized that a new strategy had to be used to confront the construction defect litigation explosion.

Each time Sammy built a spec home (a home built on the speculation that someone who had nothing to do with the designing and planning will buy it "as is") he used a new structure. Again, because of its asset protection benefits and efficient flow-through taxation of income, Sammy used a separate LLC for each custom home he built. In California and Texas, because of the extra state taxes on LLCs, he would use an LP with a corporate general partner as his developer entity.

The key to Sammy's strategy was to keep each entity active after the house had been sold. This was to thwart the aggrieved homeowners and their lawyers who had ten years to bring a construction defect claim. By keeping the entity alive during the ten-year statute of limitations period, any claim would be brought against the LLC or LP, not personally against the people who dissolved the entity. And nine-plus years later, after selling the spec house, what was in that surviving LLC or LP? That's right: nothing. The entity that built and sold the house was not a very attractive target.

But isn't it expensive to keep an entity alive for ten years? What about all the filing fees and tax returns? As Sammy knew, it isn't a burden if done the right way.

As far as tax returns are concerned, once each house was sold, a final tax return for the entity was prepared. The LLC or LP could stay alive but have no activity and thus not have to file an ongoing return. In terms of annual filing fees, some states are more expensive than others. In California, it is $800 per year per entity. Including a $125 annual resident agent fee, the ten-year cost per entity is $9,250.

But what if your California entity was originally formed in a low-cost state such as Wyoming? That was Sammy's money-saving strategy. The developer entity was formed in Wyoming and qualified to do business in California. Qualifying in California was required, since the house was being constructed in California. But once the house was sold, the entity no longer conducted any California business. It was free to stop paying California fees and only had to pay the minimal Wyoming fees of $50 per year. Assuming the same $125 annual resident agent fee, the cost of maintaining a Wyoming entity for ten years was only $1,750, versus $9,250 for California. By forming the entity in Wyoming, qualifying in California for only as long as necessary, and then keeping the entity alive in Wyoming until the ten-year statute of limitations ran out, Sammy was able to affordably protect himself and his other assets.

By using only one developer entity per one or two houses, a litigant nine or more years later was left to sue an empty shell, not an attractive or lucrative target. Of course, a litigant could always sue the builders and subcontractors involved on the job for all the alleged construction defects. But again, the incentive for the plaintiffs' lawyers is to bring as many homeowners into one contingency lawsuit as possible.

They prefer to represent a homeowners' association of thirty to three hundred or more homeowners. The more aggregated claims, the more money to be made. That incentive is greatly diminished when the claim is to be brought against a developer entity that developed not an entire tract of homes, but just one or two spec homes.

And so Sammy kept each developer entity alive in Wyoming for ten years. Sammy's CPA prepaid the $1,750 ten-year holding cost to the law firm in Wyoming. For Sammy, the money was a cost of doing business passed on to the buyer and an affordable form of additional insurance. Once the statute of limitations had run and any defect claims were time-barred from being filed, Sammy had the choice of dissolving the entity or keeping it alive and using it only for the next spec home. After all, it had a ten-year history at that point, and the formation fees had already been paid.

Sammy's three strategies for remodels, holdings, and spec home developments served him well, and he prospered without any further devastating litigation.

Now let's consider protecting your prized real estate . . .

Chapter 23

How to Protect Your Primary Residence and Other Asset Protection Strategies

There are four ways to protect one of the most valuable assets you will ever own: your primary residence. You know one of these ways, another one we have discussed, and the other two may surprise you.

The way you know is through insurance. But let's consider this method. It is ironic that you can never ensure that insurance will insure you. As with Sammy's case, there are exceptions buried deep in the four-point, magnifying-glass type that let insurance companies off the hook. Which leads us to ask: How did paying all those premiums benefit us?

As well, insurance companies are notoriously petulant. If they don't like your state and its rates, they'll pick up their marbles and go home, as they do every decade or so in California. A great insurance rate today that contributes to an acceptable investment analysis and eventual property purchase may later turn into an inability to even acquire any insurance at all. They set the rates and then, because you accepted them, punish you by withdrawing from the state. Can we insure some order around here?

So while insurance is the first line of defense for any real estate holding, because it is never bulletproof we need to develop other, secondary lines of defense.

For your primary residence, another line of defense is one we discussed: the homestead exemption. Again, each state has different rules and dollar limits. A summary is found at www.successdna.com.

The remaining two defense lines may surprise you. The first is debt.

Many people assume that debt does not provide asset protection because debt is money owed to someone else. This is true. But while you owe the money, remember that protected assets are in the eye of the attacker.

As an example, suppose you live in Nevada and own a $500,000 house with a $200,000 mortgage on it secured by a first deed of trust. You have $300,000 in equity and have just put a homestead on your house, which in Nevada offers $350,000 in homeowner protection.

How does an attacker see your situation? They don't care that you owe the bank $200,000 on your mortgage. All they care is that the bank has a secure and superior claim to the first $200,000, which means they can't get at it. But the remaining $300,000 is now protected by a homestead exemption, so they can't get at that either.

In this case, and in many like it, mortgage debt is to your advantage because it discourages and prevents an attacker from coming after you. (You may also be better off taking the equity out of your house using debt so you can invest in more real estate or other income-producing assets. However, that discussion is for another time.)

But what about the situation where your primary residence has appreciated so much there is a great deal of unprotected equity above the mortgage and the homestead exemption? This is happening in communities across the country. How do you protect so much equity?

The last line of defense is the single-member limited liability company. As you already know, a limited liability company (LLC) is an excellent way to hold real estate. You can elect favorable flow-through taxation and, especially with LLCs formed in Nevada and Wyoming, achieve outstanding asset protection.

Until recently, however, personal residences were not held by LLCs. This was because the mortgage interest deduction could not be claimed through an LLC. Additionally, the $500,000 tax-free gain for married couples on the sale of a principal residence was not allowed through an LLC.

All this changed when the IRS issued regulations extending such tax benefits to personal-residence-holding LLCs as long as certain requirements were met. (Please note that while the tax-free gains and mortgage interest deductions can now be achieved, homestead exemptions are still only for individuals, not for their primary-residence-holding LLCs.) The two key requirements are that the LLC must be a single-member LLC and a disregarded entity for income tax purposes.

A single-member LLC is, as it sounds, an LLC with a catch. The single-member part refers to one member or one membership interest holder. The catch is that the holder can be a husband and wife, together, for example, as joint tenants. Or the single member can be their living trust, in which both have an interest and which makes sense for estate planning purposes.

The upshot is that because most primary residences are owned by husbands and wives together, the flexibility of a single-member LLC allows for that holding to continue with added asset protection.

Qualifying as a disregarded entity for income tax purposes is easy to do once you have a single-member LLC in place. You simply do not apply for an employer identification number (EIN) and instruct your CPA to flow all the LLC tax items onto your personal tax return. The single-member LLC is considered disregarded for tax purposes because there is only one member (or—remember—two people according to the catch). And with only one member, the tax flows from the LLC directly to the member.

Three questions frequently arise at this point:

First, what if a single-member LLC (for example, ABC, LLC) is owned by another LLC (XYZ, LLC), which is owned by two members? How do tax returns get filed? In that case, ABC, LLC, is a disregarded entity and the tax obligations flow to XYZ, LLC, which, with two members, is not disregarded and must file a return. This strategy is used when a series of single-member

LLCs are owned by one multiple-member-holding LLC. The use of disregarded entities can really cut down on the need to prepare a myriad of tax returns.

The second question relates to asset protection. If the LLC is a disregarded entity, don't you then lose all the limited liability protection?

The answer is no. The fact that for tax purposes the IRS considers it a disregarded entity doesn't mean that for legal purposes the asset protection is compromised. The LLC, if properly formed and maintained, provides limited liability protection to its members, whether disregarded by the IRS for tax filings or not.

However, we have mentioned that single-member LLCs may not be afforded complete asset protection in California and Colorado. And on this issue, you may have to consult with your advisor to weigh the alternatives. If protection is more important than taxation, you may want to use a multiple-member LLC in those states.

The third question involves lenders and the transferring of title. Some lenders don't appreciate why you would title your home (or any other real estate, for that matter) in a protected entity. They think you are trying to hide assets or avoid your obligations when you do so. In short, they don't get it.

And with this scared-of-their-shadow mentality, many lenders will threaten to assert a due-on-sale clause if such a transfer is made. Meaning they'll call the loan and you'll have to refinance your loan. And the new lender still may not let you take title in your LLC. If you have a good loan with low interest rates in place, it may be an expensive hassle to refinance.

But let's look at the transfer to be made. Has there been a sale? You've only transferred title from yourself (as individuals) to yourself as members of an LLC you completely control. There has been a transfer but no sale.

Some intransigent lenders will not accept this argument. They will claim that their due-on-sale clause is really a due-on-transfer clause. You'll have to read the loan document to see if this is accurate or not.

If you are dealing with such a lender, you have two options. The first is to transfer title to a land trust.

Land trusts look a lot like living trusts, which, as mentioned, are used for estate planning and probate avoidance purposes. Many people hold title to real estate in the name of their revocable living trust. While excellent vehicles for estate planning, living trusts, contrary to a widespread misunderstanding, offer no asset protection. For this reason, banks and other lending institutions are okay with borrowers taking title in the living trust name. (You can just hear their rationale: "They can't hide their assets or avoid their obligations with a living trust.") Of course, there is also a federal law dictating that due-on-sale clauses cannot be exercised on transfers to living trusts.

With a problem lender, you inform them that you are transferring title to your trust. The trust is a land trust, which, like the living trust, offers no asset protection. In order to achieve this important objective, the beneficiary of the land trust is not you, but rather your LLC. By virtue of owning the LLC, you own the property in the land trust. Ultimate ownership is still the same. We have just added an LLC to accomplish our estate planning objectives. In this way, title is out of your name personally and your beneficial interest is held by an LLC. A table helps illustrate:

Before	**After**
123 Elm Street	123 Elm Street
Title held by "John and Mary Smith as joint tenants"	Title held by "Elm Street Land Trust" Land Trust
	☐ Beneficial Owners
	Elm Street LLC

The second option is to switch from a problem lender to an accommodating lender. Some lenders are waking up to the fact that in this day and age, asset protection is a legitimate concern. One group actually assists people to take title in the name of the LLC or LP. You may want to check out the LLC Loan Network at www.llcloan.com.

Two final and related points should be made here. Just because you take title in the name of the LLC or LP doesn't mean that you won't have to sign a personal guarantee. Even accommodating lenders need the security of a personal guarantee. (If you were in the lender's shoes, you would, too.)

But signing a personal guarantee with a lender doesn't mean you are personally responsible to the rest of the world. That guarantee is between you and the bank. It doesn't extend to vendors, tenants, potential litigants, and others. Your real-estate-owning LLC (or land trust beneficially owned by an LLC) will provide you with asset protection and, unless you sign other personal guarantees, protect you from personal liability.

The next logical argument then becomes: How can I avoid even a personal guarantee to the bank? What if I own twenty valuable properties in one LLC? Won't the financial strength of that one super-LLC negate the need for any sort of personal guarantee?

Resolving this issue comes down to a weighing of asset protection values. Yes, with twenty valuable properties in one super-LLC, a lender may look to the assets of the super-LLC for security and repayment and thus not require a personal guarantee.

However, what if a tenant falls at one of the properties and sues the super-LLC? They could reach all of the assets, all twenty properties, in the one LLC. Better asset protection could be achieved by spreading those twenty properties out into ten separate LLCs, each holding two properties. In this way, the litigious tenant may reach only two, instead of twenty, properties. Segregating assets into separate LLCs is good asset protection.

Of course, the question then becomes: How many properties do you put in each LLC? In my practice, I have many clients (and myself included) who for maximum protection will only place one property into one LLC. In states like California that charge a minimum of $800 per year per LLC, a number of LLCs can get expensive. Still, I don't recommend putting more than three properties into one LLC. The decision, of course, is up to you, but putting scores of properties into one super-LLC in order to avoid a personal guarantee is not a great asset protection strategy in my mind. I would prefer to segregate assets for greater limited liability and deal with personal guarantees to the bank. If you've analyzed the property and know your business, the personal guarantee should not be a huge issue. On the other hand, the unknown of doing business in America, the out-of-the-blue litigation and the ever-changing legislation, argues for the segregation of assets and maximization of asset protection.

Chapter 24

Structures for Your Real Estate/ Tax Considerations

Now that you realize how important it is to hold real estate in an entity, what kind do you choose? You know the legal benefits of using structures to own real estate, so we need to reveal the tax considerations that go along with them. First we will review the different types of business structures and their particular tax considerations. The four ways you can be taxed on your property are:

- Personally held property
- Partnership (including LLCs and LPs)
- S corporation
- C corporation

The following are descriptions of the types of entities available for holding real estate as well as their tax advantages or disadvantages.

Personally Held Property

There are no distinct tax advantages or disadvantages to holding property simply in your own name. However, the danger lies in holding property without the protection offered by a limited liability business structure.

Partnership

The flexibility associated with partnership tax law makes it highly favorable for holding real estate. Because distributions from a partnership come out at basis, not at the fair market value of S corporation distributions, you can easily move assets in and out without tax consequence. A partnership also provides an ideal structure for doing a Section 1031 like-kind tax-deferred exchange. Because income from partnerships flows through to individual owners, taxes are paid on the individual level.

There are two types of partnerships. The general partnership is never recommended because, as previously discussed, they offer absolutely no asset protection.

On the other hand, a properly formed limited partnership is a reliable entity for holding real estate. By properly formed, we mean one that has a corporation or LLC as a general partner, thus encapsulating the unlimited liability of a general partner into a limited liability entity.

Another reliable entity for holding real estate is the LLC that is taxed as a partnership. Like the properly formed LP, the LLC taxed as a partnership offers excellent limited liability along with beneficial flow-through taxation.

The use of one entity over the other may be decided on the basis of state taxation. California and Texas levy extra state taxes on LLCs and not on LPs. Many people will choose to use an LP in those states to save on taxes.

For people in other states, the expense of an extra entity (be it a corporation or LLC) to serve as an LP general partner may tip the scales in favor of an LLC. Be sure to consult with your advisor as to which entity is best for you.

S Corporations

S corporations are flow-through entities, meaning that the taxable income earned will flow through to the individual owners and will be taxed at their individual rates. However, property distributions from an S corporation to the individual shareholder owners are done at fair market value, which can mean extra taxes. This can be a big issue and it will be discussed later.

The benefit of an S corporation is that the earnings are not subject to self-employment tax, as they are in partnership taxation. But for real estate holdings with passive income, which aren't subject to self-employment tax anyway, there would be no extra benefit in holding through an S corporation. This is the reason that an entity with partnership law is recommended for real estate holdings.

However, if you flip properties with your real estate business, this could be considered active trade or a business, and your income would be subject to self-employment tax. As discussed in Sammy's case, this would be a good situation in which to use an S corporation.

C Corporations

The capital gains rate for the corporate level is much higher than the individual rate, so it is not usually a good choice for holding real estate. The only time it might make sense for real estate investing is if the company is publicly traded or if there is foreign ownership of the corporation. If this isn't your situation, consider using a flow-through entity such as a partnership that can provide much lower tax rates if your individual owners of the partnership are, in fact, individuals.

Joint Ownership—Possible 1031 Exchange

If you plan on holding your real estate with multiple partners and the property may be used for a future like-kind exchange, the property should be held as tenants in common. If you hold the property as tenants in common, you still are able to use a single-member LLC to protect your interest. For example, you and your partner hold title in the property as tenants in common. Your individual LLC and your partner's individual LLC will be named as the individual owners on the title. By using this format, you will be in compliance with the new rules regarding multiple owners and future Section 1031 exchanges—and you will get the asset protection you need. That said, you can also do a 1031 Exchange using an LLC or LP as long as the new property is held by the existing LLC or LP.

Limited Liability Company (LLC)

The tax considerations of an LLC are quite unique because an LLC can choose how it wants to be taxed. For example, when using an LLC to hold real estate, it is best to have the LLC taxed as a partnership if there is more than one member. With partnership taxation of an LLC, a Form 1065 (U.S. partnership return) must be filed. If there is only a single member of the LLC, report taxes on the Schedule E of the Form 1040. This is the same form you would use if there were no LLC involved, but you will still have asset protection.

The LLC (or LP) is the ideal structure for holding real estate because of the tax considerations involved. These considerations include the capital gains treatment, the tax benefit for flow-through passive losses, and the potential distribution of assets.

1. CAPITAL GAINS

The LLC and LP are both flow-through entities, meaning the gains and losses flow through to the individual taxpayer. If the property is sold in the future, the profit from the sale is subject to capital gains. The reason you will want to have individual tax rates apply to this sale is that the capital gains treatment for individuals is much less than that for corporations.

2. TAX BENEFIT

Flow-through entities, such as the LLC and LP, may also allow passive losses to flow through. This usually will happen if you have used the previously discussed tax benefits, such as Benefit #2, "Accelerating Depreciation" and Benefit #3, "Real Estate Professional." You will want these tax benefits for yourself.

3. DISTRIBUTIONS

While S corporations can provide the same flow-through of capital gains and tax benefits as LLCs and LPs, they do not provide the same flexibility regarding distributions. For example, you own a large piece of property that later gets divided into two parcels of land. You now own two pieces of property, and most likely will not want to hold them in the same entity. If you were holding the property in an S corporation and wanted to transfer one piece of property out, the property would have to distribute at fair market value. This would be a taxable event because the value of the property has most likely appreciated since you bought it.

However, if the property were held in an LLC or LP, one parcel of property could move out at whatever value it is held on the books as. Therefore, this event would not be taxable. This is the advantage of holding real estate in LLCs or LPs when it comes to distributions.

Now that we have selected the right entity, let's focus on selecting the right property . . .

Part Five

Selection Strategies

With your familiarity of the tax and legal advantages utilized by successful real estate investors, it's time to select the right property for you to invest in.

As soon as you make the decision to start investing, you will be subjected to everyone's opinion about where they think you should invest. You will surely hear about the hippest, hottest real estate markets of the moment. This year it's Phoenix, Charlotte, and Reno. Next year it will be Teton Valley, Idaho, and Oklahoma City. However, you should not be overly concerned with trends. While trends and demographics are important, it is also important to know that there will always be real estate deals available in every market. In other words, if you don't live near one of the anointed hot spots, don't forgo investing altogether—you can find a deal no matter where you are.

Put your energy into thoroughly analyzing the property, conducting the necessary due diligence, and performing the investigative review. By using the following tips and secrets about these processes, you can make any real estate deal a great opportunity.

As we have just learned, there are powerful tax and legal advantages associated with real estate investing. The knowledge and use of these important strategies will benefit you in all of your real estate activities.

Chapter 25

Property Analysis

Although you are understandably enthusiastic about your real estate investment, you cannot jump in without first doing some preparatory work. The most important step to take before you even start running numbers is to come up with a plan.

In this plan, you first must clarify the specific purpose your real estate will serve. Are you buying this property in order to develop and resell it, or are you hoping to capitalize on the cash flow it will generate? Becoming clear on exactly what you want will help you narrow your search.

Investing for Cash Flow

Be aware that investing for cash flow is much different than investing as a real estate speculator. Cash flow investing is a slow process. While you won't get rich quickly, the investment will most certainly pay off eventually. If this is your goal, you must focus specifically on creating cash flow by following these steps:

1. Specify the type of property you'd like. Are you picturing a single-family home or multifamily units? How much money do you have to invest? How much of a loan can you qualify for?

2. Stake out locations. It is recommended that your first investment be located near you. You will hear plenty of promoters say that with the Internet and communication access, investing locally really is an outmoded concept. But it is clearly the case that (a) the promoters want your money and (b) you will most likely be familiar with trends in your own area and it will be easier to work with a local real estate agent. You may want to consider looking for properties in working-class neighborhoods—they usually require less money down than high-end properties, meaning more return for your money.

3. Once you've picked out a few specific neighborhoods, assess the area. Walk around and ask around to determine the state of the neighborhood. Neighborhoods are always changing—it is your job to figure out if the area is improving or declining. If someone tells you the neighborhood is "stable," you just might reasonably interpret that to mean it is declining. What do you see when you look around? Are the houses well maintained, and is there obvious pride in ownership? Or do you see numerous For Sale signs? Use your real estate agent as a resource here. He or she can provide you with the comparative values of the properties over the years. Have the prices gone up or down?

4. Identify properties you may be interested in. Ask everyone you know whether they are aware of a property for sale. Don't think that your real estate agent is your only resource. The team you have assembled, including your broker, appraiser, accountant, and attorney, can be great sources of information. Keep in mind, however, that just because someone you trust recommends a property doesn't mean you don't have to do your investigative work.

5. Assess the state of the property. Once you have found a property in which you are interested, you must gather information on the surrounding properties to get an idea of the value. To do this, investigate comparable values, comparable rents, and the relative values of the properties in the neighborhood. Keep in mind that an ideal investment property is generally at the middle or lower end of value for the neighborhood. Evaluate the cosmetic state of your property. What does it look like? Are there things that could be easily fixed (i.e., not structural) with little effort or money that would make a big difference in the aesthetic appeal? Get feedback from your home inspector on this.

Also consider the numerous ways to increase your cash flow. Some ideas:

- Update the look of the property. Sometimes inexpensive remodels such as new paint, flooring, or wallpaper can make all the difference in the world. These simple and inexpensive changes are more likely to get noticed by the typical renter than more expensive and involved structural changes.
- Add a garage or carport. Most people would rather park their cars inside. If the cost of this improvement is reasonable, it just may be justified by the increased amount of income.
- Add a fence. If the other properties around yours have fencing, you might want to put one in.
- Consider building a storage unit. Apartment owners always need more space to keep their belongings. If your property has some extra room, you could bring in extra income from renting these units to your tenants.
- Install laundry facilities. If your apartment building doesn't have laundry facilities, think of how quickly those quarters could add up. Consider adding washers and dryers for your tenants' use.

Property Development

Keep in mind that while investing in property for development purposes can make you very rich, it also can just as likely make you bankrupt. Buying a property to develop requires a different type of analysis than buying for cash flow. Property development is considered a trade or business whereby profits are taxed not at the lower capital gains rate, but at higher ordinary income rates. If this is your first attempt at investing for property development, it would be a good idea to surround yourself with an experienced team to advise you. Remember that every property, and thus its legal considerations, will be different.

Property Analysis Calculation

You can make an offer "subject to inspection and financing" on a property so you don't delay the process while you do research. However, at some point before closing, make sure you run the numbers through the following steps:

Step 1: Calculate how much cash down the property will require:

Down payment (required by mortgage broker) _____

Closing costs _____

+ Estimated fix-up costs _____

+ Carrying time for fix-up (number
of months times monthly payment) _____ _____

+ Carrying time for marketing
  (number of months times total payment) _____

  TOTAL _____

Now you must determine if you have, or are able to get, this much money.

Step 2: Calculate cash-on-cash return:

Rent received monthly   A _____

Monthly payment, including taxes
    and insurance and expenses   B _____

Cash flow (A minus B)   C _____

Your investment (from Step 1 above)   D _____

The cash-on-cash % formula is:

$$(12 \times C) \div D$$

Do these calculations before you finalize an offer. If your final calculation does not equal your established minimum return, don't carry through with the deal.

What If Property Values Go Down?

Keep in mind that in cash flow investing, your rent determines your income. If the property value goes down slightly but you are still able to charge the same amount of rent, you will see no change in your cash flow.

However, if your property depreciates so much that you are forced to charge less rent, you would see a decreased income from the property. You would have a negative cash flow—but only for the period of time that the rents are down. This should be a temporary problem because rents will most likely return to their normal level eventually.

Although we have advised you that the geographic location should not be the sole basis for your decision, some geographic areas are predictably influenced by the economic conditions there. These are characteristics that you can capitalize on if you are aware of them.

For example, geography and the economy make a difference in certain areas of the northeastern United States. In some cities, you can purchase a duplex or two-family home for as low as $20,000. Property values are not increasing, and income levels are dropping. Many people are even moving away. However, properties rent for $500 to $800 per unit. By plugging these numbers into the calculation chart, it is easy to see that buying property in this area can bring in huge returns.

Another, entirely different example is shown by the property values throughout California. Some areas are increasing by 20 percent or more per year, showing great appreciation potential. However, rents are not keeping up with this growth, so it is not easy to bring in positive cash flow on such properties. Hoping to recoup negative cash flows with annual appreciation gains has worked in the past. Will it work forever?

Either one of these situations could be profitable, but which one depends on your own finances. If you have some cash reserves, investing in expensive but still appreciating areas in California can be profitable. However, if you have little extra cash, purchasing a cash-flowing property with a little money down may be the way to go. Any number of scenarios like this can be profitable—you just have to find one that works the best for you.

Investing for Appreciation

Investing for appreciation can be a successful strategy, but it can also be a risky one. First-time investors can make big mistakes if they are blinded by dollar signs and don't consider these crucial scenarios:

How long would you be able to keep the property if you lost your current job? Since investing for appreciation usually means you will have little, if any, cash flow, how can you afford this property? How many such deals could you afford?

What will happen if you can't sell the property as quickly as you had planned? For instance, if it takes you many years to sell the property in order to double your money, your actual return may be less than if you owned a property for cash flow.

After considering these warnings, realize that investing for appreciation will only be truly successful if the circumstances are right for both you and the property.

HOW TO ANALYZE PROPERTIES HELD FOR APPRECIATION

First, identify what type of market you are about to enter. A buyer's market has more sellers than buyers. This can be a great situation for buying property—you can get good deals, since there are a lot of properties to consider but not many buyers. The only catch is that if the market continues to decline after you buy, you could have gotten an even better price if you had waited.

In a seller's market, there are more people looking to buy than there are properties for sale. In this situation, it may be hard to find a good deal unless you look for properties that need some work. Real estate agents may not even bother with this type of property in a seller's market. They may be more interested in quick and easy sales. Therefore, you may have to deal with the seller directly.

Once you identify a prospective property, enlist your real estate broker's help to find valuation trends for that area. Since the best indicator of future appreciation will be the past recessionary cycles, look to identify patterns in the appreciation. Does the property appear to be increasing in value with every cycle? If there seems to be an identifiable cycle, are you able to determine where the property is in the current cycle?

If the property and local appreciation fit your profile, then review the cash flow again. Consider how long you could hold the property if your funds dried up, as well as how long it would take to sell it if you needed to do so. In certain cases, the appreciation may be strong enough to overcome these concerns.

Chapter 26

Legal Due Diligence

Buying any property is a big step—one that should not be taken without some in-depth research. This investigative process performed on a property in which you are interested in buying is called legal due diligence. Properties can have any number of problems or claims associated with them, from structural or electrical problems to environmental and hazardous-waste issues. These are things you need to be aware of before you buy. It is always best to find out exactly what you are getting yourself into.

How to Prepare the Offer

If you are wondering how it is possible to perform a lengthy investigation without slowing the buying process, the answer is you must write an offer in which the due diligence is included as a contingency for purchase. This way, if your investigation turns up something you don't like, you will be able to back out of the deal, no questions asked, with all deposits refunded. These clauses in offers usually read like this:

> This offer is contingent upon Buyer's inspection of the property and acceptance of its condition within 30 days from acceptance.

You can choose a shorter time period in which to perform the inspection. Some states have a ten-to-fifteen-day range for inspections. In any case, for a thirty-day period, if the seller accepts your offer on October 1, then you have until October 31 to inspect the property and decide whether you will accept the property as is, back out of the deal completely, or request that certain repairs be made.

Your offer can include flexibility, which means you can have several contingencies that may allow you to back out. These contingencies may include:

• *Financing Contingencies:* A condition of your offer should be that you successfully obtain suitable financing and show proof of loan commitment within a certain time frame.

This Agreement is contingent upon Buyer obtaining the following type of financing: a _____ [e.g., FHA, VA, Conventional, Rural Development, etc.] with an interest rate not to exceed _____ % payable over a period of _____ [e.g., 15, 30] years at a _____ rate [e.g., fixed].

• *Appraisal:* The property should have to appraise for at least what you agreed to pay for it. If it does not, the buyer can void the contract, or the seller may agree to reduce the price.

Within 7 calendar days of acceptance Buyer, at his option and expense, may have the property appraised by an appraiser licensed in the State of _____. If the appraised value is less than the amount of the purchase price contained in this Agreement, then this contract is voidable at Buyer's option and all earnest monies shall be returned; if Buyer chooses to void this Agreement in accordance with this paragraph, then Buyer shall notify Seller in writing of such decision and provide Seller with a copy of said appraisal within 2 business days of receipt of the appraisal.

• *Professional Inspection:* You will want to have the property inspected. A general inspection contingency can cover a variety of concerns.

For example, certain properties should have environmental tests, such as land that once housed a gas station. You may also want a home tested for radon, lead paint, toxic mold, termites, the water tested for purity, structural soundness, electrical, mechanical, and plumbing inspections, etc. However, the contingency language will have a time frame in which these inspections must take place, so you will want to get on locating the proper inspectors immediately. It is important to understand that a general home inspection service will not cover many of the types of inspections you want conducted on the property. Home inspection services are not conducted by structural engineers or persons with any level of expertise in plumbing, electrical, or similar specialties, nor do many check for building code violations such as snow loading, earthquake protection, or hidden defects. Inspection by a qualified, licensed structural engineer is advisable, as is using a plumber or electrician or other specialist for specific areas of concern.

Buyer shall have the right to conduct any inspections, investigations, tests, surveys, and other studies on the subject property at Buyer's expense. Buyer shall, within _____ business days of acceptance, complete these inspections and give Seller written notice of disapproved items.

If Buyer does not give Seller written notice of any items disapproved of within the time period specified, Buyer shall be deemed to be satisfied with the results of any such inspections.

If Buyer does give Seller notice of disapproved items within the time period specified, then Buyer shall also provide Seller with copies of any pertinent inspection reports. Seller then has the option of correcting the deficiencies within _____ days of receipt of notice of disapproval or voiding the contract and returning all earnest money deposits to Buyer.

• *Personal Inspection:* A personal inspection contingency will give you an easy out should you want to back out before its expiration. It should be worded subjectively, allowing you to get out of the contract simply because you decided you did not like the property after all.

Buyer shall have until _____ to personally inspect the subject property and give Seller any written objections regarding any aspect of the property that does not meet Buyer's subjective approval. If Buyer does not provide any written objections by this date, Buyer will be deemed to be satisfied with the personal inspection. If, on the other hand, Buyer gives written notice of disapproval by _____ [date above], this contract shall be voidable in writing at Buyer's option and all earnest monies returned.

• *General Due Diligence:* A general due diligence paragraph is also a very good idea, especially if you plan on adding a guesthouse or developing the property in any way. You will want the offer to contain a due diligence period so that you can obtain approval for your plans from the proper authorities.

Seller shall grant to Buyer a period of thirty (30) calendar days from the date of acceptance in which to conduct any due diligence investigations regarding the subject property, including governmental regulations regarding the division or development potential of the subject property. Buyer shall give Seller written notice within this same time period in the event that the Buyer should determine that any of the items of due diligence should prove to be unacceptable, at which time this contract shall be voidable at the Buyer's option and all earnest monies returned.

• *Survey:* It is a good idea to have the land surveyed or the corners marked. Your approval of the corners can be a condition of the sale.

Seller shall have the property surveyed and the property corners marked by a professional, licensed engineer in the State of _____ by _____. Buyer shall have until _____ to inspect the marked property corners. Buyer shall give any disapproval in writing by _____. If for any reason Buyer disapproves of the property corners, then this contract shall be voidable at the Buyer's option and all earnest monies returned.

• *Review of the Plat, Covenants, Conditions, and Restrictions:* Plats often have notes that contain restrictions not found in the covenants or deed. It is important that the plat and any other restrictions on the property be reviewed by an attorney and that any restriction be approved by the buyer.

Buyer shall have until _____ to review the plat and any covenants, conditions, or restrictions affecting the property and to give Seller any written objections. If Buyer does not provide any written objections by this date, Buyer will be deemed to be satisfied with the plat and all restrictions affecting the property. If, on the other hand, Buyer gives written notice of disapproval by _____ [date above], this contract shall be voidable in writing at Buyer's option and all earnest monies returned.

• *1031 Language:* If you are purchasing the property through a 1031 exchange, it is important that your contract mention this as well as provide that the closing must occur within the bounds dictated by the exchange and that the Seller will cooperate with these needs.

Seller herein acknowledges that it is the intention of the Buyer to complete an IRC Section 1031 tax-deferred exchange. Seller agrees to cooperate with the Buyer in any manner necessary in order to complete said exchange at no additional cost or liability to Seller.

• *Review of Title Commitment:* You will want your title commitment reviewed by an attorney, as the commitment will tell you if the Seller has marketable title as well as list items of record that affect the subject property.

Within _____ business days of acceptance Seller shall provide Buyer with a commitment of title insurance policy showing the condition of the title to said premises. Buyer shall have _____ business days from receipt of the commitment within which to object in writing to the condition of the title and any of the liens, encumbrances, or exceptions set forth in the commitment. If Buyer does not so object, Buyer shall be deemed to have accepted the condition of said title. If Buyer does make written objection within the above time frame, then Seller can either clear any title defects or objections to any exceptions within _____ business days of written notice or this contract shall be voidable in writing at Buyer's option and all earnest monies returned.

• *Approval of Any Leases Associated with the Property:* If you are purchasing rental property where any leases or tenancies are in place, you will want the offer to be contingent upon your review of those agreements.

Within _____ days of acceptance Seller shall provide Buyer with any rent or lease agreements currently in effect along with an affidavit or letter stating whether or not such rent or lease agreements have been strictly adhered to by both the landlord and the tenant. If such agreements have not been strictly adhered to, the letter shall list any defaults or waivers in detail. Buyer has _____ days from Buyer's receipt of any such agreements and said letter to provide written notice to Seller that such agreements or their current status is not acceptable and thus void the contract and have all earnest money deposits returned in full.

• *Water Rights/Mineral Rights:* If water rights or mineral rights are a concern, be sure to make the review of those rights a condition of the offer.

Seller shall deliver to Buyer within _____ days of execution of this Agreement, copies of all documents relating to water or mineral rights. Buyer shall have _____ days from receipt of such documentation to object to the condition of said water or mineral rights and to declare this Agreement void and all earnest monies returned.

• *Contingent on Another Closing:* If you need to sell your present home prior to closing on the home that you are offering on, it is important to make closing your own sale a condition of your offer. Otherwise, you may find yourself making two mortgage payments instead of one.

*This offer is specifically contingent upon the Buyer closing on the
following property: [insert legal description of property] within
_____ months of the acceptance of this offer.*

• *General Contingency:* One attorney I know likes to put a general
contingency in any offer—something to the effect of:

*Within 30 days of acceptance, Buyer may back out of this contract
for any reason with no further obligation and full return of his
earnest money deposit.*

You can make a sales contract conditional on anything you would like. For
example, you could make winning the lottery in July a condition of closing.
But, remember, these contingencies are put into the offer and as such could
be the basis for a rejection or a counteroffer.

Each of the above contingencies gives you one more chance to back out
of the deal if you aren't completely satisfied with what you find. Buyers
should not hesitate to use the acceptable financing clause. If you are not able
to obtain financing that you feel comfortable with, you should be able to get
out of the deal completely.

At the end of your inspection period, many good brokers will prepare a
written statement for you to sign in which you accept the condition of the
property, therefore removing the contingency on the offer. If you do not
want to accept the property after your investigation, you don't sign the
agreement.

Sometimes, if communication isn't as strong, it will be assumed that if
the agreed-upon date comes and goes without you contacting the broker or
seller, you have accepted the property's condition and are willing to proceed
with the sale. If you are not planning on purchasing after your investigation,
it is best to send a written letter before the deadline to the seller or broker,
or both, to notify them that the deal is off. If you do not do so, and they assume you are going to purchase when you are not, you may end up forfeit-
ing the deposit you have already paid. However, this may still be better than
being sued for the entire amount of the transaction.

In all cases, whether you want to buy or call the deal off, it is best to clearly communicate your intentions in writing to both the seller and the broker before the deadline so that no party involved makes an incorrect assumption.

Inspections—the Repair Addendum

Chances are any property you are considering purchasing has minor superficial issues you'd like to correct eventually. Home inspections should not focus on these little imperfections, since every home has its fair share. Your pre-purchase inspection should be aimed at uncovering problems that aren't so minor—meaning issues with the foundation, roof, or heating, plumbing, and electrical systems.

If problems are found in any of these components, you will want them to be addressed and resolved before you take possession of the property. You can request that these repairs be completed before closing by drafting a repair addendum, a summary of required repairs acknowledged by the buyer, Realtor, and seller. Not only will this ensure that you won't have to face these expenses immediately after purchase, it reduces the risk that lawsuits will be filed disputing the condition of the property.

Any major problems found during the inspection will be summarized in the inspector's report. A detailed description of the problems will need to be transcribed into the repair addendum, thus communicating the findings to the seller. Always include a copy of the inspector's report so the seller can reference it. Then list, in the order you would like them completed, the repairs you would like the seller to address before reinspection.

Include as much detail in the description of repairs as possible. First list the specific part of the system that needs to be repaired. Use language that communicates your expectations clearly. If you want a component completely replaced, be sure to use the word "replace" rather than "repair." Make a request that once the work has been completed, you will receive copies of receipts.

After work has been completed, another inspection of each of the items included in the repair addendum is required. This should be done well in advance of the final walk-through and closing just in case additional work is still required. If this is the case, another inspection report and repair addendum signed by the buyer must be presented to the seller.

Title Insurance and the Preliminary Title Report

The title report holds all the specific information about a particular piece of property: the physical details, the type of ownership, and exactly what rights are granted to the owner of that property. Sometimes there are flaws in the title that can bring about challenges for the owner. Title insurance can offer protection against such difficulties.

Many of the flaws found in titles are very subtle. Because of this, many lenders require title insurance and will not loan money until they receive a clear and insured title report. Most title insurance protects against defects in, or liens or encumbrances on, the title to a piece of property. The insurance company will help in defending against challenges to your title to the property. However, insurance companies will only agree to insure against certain things. You must be aware of what coverage your company is providing.

The first step in obtaining title insurance is to receive a preliminary title report. This is the product of the insurance company's review of public records that relate to the property in question. However, in most states, the preliminary title report cannot be relied upon as a representation of the status of title to the property. It will, however, inform you what exactly the insurance company is willing to insure you against.

When you receive the final title report from the insurance company, it will include all the risks the title company has refused to insure against. This is important to note because should there be a problem in the future, your insurance company will not involve itself regarding any of the matters it has chosen to exclude coverage on.

When you receive the title report, time spent carefully inspecting it will be well worth it. You should consider having your lawyer look it over as well. If you close a real estate deal and then realize your insurance does not cover problems that were disclosed in the preliminary report, there is no going back. At that point, you will not be able to rework the terms of the purchase agreement in order to protect yourself. It is important that you know exactly what the title contains and how much coverage your insurance company is providing before you close a deal.

HOW TO REVIEW A TITLE REPORT

Reviewing the title report is one of the most important steps potential buyers should take to be sure they are making an informed decision. Check the entire report for inaccuracies or inconsistencies. Any that you find must be discussed with your attorney and the title insurance company. Some of these issues may require you to work with the seller to resolve the problem with the title.

In order to play an active role in your real estate transaction, review each of the following items in your title report for accuracy:

• *Addresses:* Specifically check the addresses of the party who will close the deal, prepare the contract, or close the loan. Also make sure the addresses of the seller, buyer's real estate agent, lender, and attorney are correct so they will receive a copy.

• *Current Owner (Vested Owner):* Make sure the name of the seller of the property is accurate.

• *Description of the Property:* This must be the same description that appears on the real estate purchase agreement. If the description on the title report differs, the title company may not have performed a title search on the excluded property, thus leaving that part uninsured. You must make sure that all of the property you intend to purchase will be covered by the title insurance policy.

• *Plat Map:* This will describe the size of the lot and usually includes street names and the nearest intersection. Make sure that the plat map included in the title report matches the legal description of the property.

• *Interest or Type of Estate:* This will describe the type of interest in property you are buying from the seller. The most common type of property interest is the fee simple absolute. This and the other forms of interest are described in Chapter 17. If a type of ownership other than the fee simple absolute appears on the title, you must be knowledgeable of the type of interest you are acquiring and the limitations it involves.

• *Effective Date:* When the title insurance company prepares title reports, they generally get their information from a collection of public records called a title plant. The effective date will tell you the date through which the title plant is current, and therefore the facts known through that date.

• *Type of Policy Requested:* This will describe the details of your relationship with the insurance company. It should include the limit of the liability assumed by the insurance company, the premium to be paid, etc. Make sure that these details match those you discussed with your title insurance agent.

• *Report Number and Contact Person:* This information must be correct—this is whom you will contact if you have questions regarding the report. Use the report number to direct questions you have to the agent in charge of your file.

Once you have checked the above points for accuracy, you must carefully inspect anything the insurance provider has chosen to not insure you against. This is where you will find any restrictions or limitations on the property. These can come in many forms and have different consequences for the buyer. The following are examples of what you might find on your title report:

• *Easements:* This is when another person or the public has certain rights to your land. Although easements may not necessarily have a negative effect on your real estate deal, you must first be aware if one exists, and then you must consider what type of impact it will have. These are common types of easements:

1. A right of way: a third party's right to use a path or road located on your property.
2. A utility easement or right to place or keep something on the land: This can also include a third party's right to use and maintain a sewer pipe, telephone line, garage, or anything else on or across your property.
3. Right of entry: allows a third party to enter your property for certain and clearly defined purposes.
4. A right to the support of land and buildings: This may be applicable if you are purchasing a lower-story apartment in an apartment complex.
5. A right of light and air: gives a third party a right that may limit your ability to use or build on your property if that use violates their rights.

6. Right to water: gives a third party a right to use a waterway or divert water from a waterway located on or adjacent to your property.

7. A right to do some act that would otherwise amount to a nuisance.

• *Covenants, Conditions, and Restrictions:* These are usually referred to as CC&Rs. They can limit your ability to use or sell the property and are enforceable by the seller or third parties. These can include building limitations, limitations on use for business, and even aesthetic requirements for the building. Be sure you are aware of the consequences of a violation of such a restriction. Sometimes they can result in financial liability or may cause ownership to revert back to a prior owner or third party. Although CC&Rs don't necessarily have an adverse effect on your property (and may actually serve to increase property values), it is important to carefully study them. After all, they do affect your ability to use and sell the property.

• *Mortgage or Deed of Trust:* These are the result of loans taken against the property. In some states, an existing mortgage or deed of trust can affect the title directly or can create the potential for a lien or foreclosure and sale of the property. You must determine if this will affect the nature of the property you may purchase.

• *Notice of Default:* This indicates that there is an existing foreclosure proceeding against the property. If this is the case, you should not independently purchase the property. Instead, you may want to purchase it as part of the foreclosure proceeding. Always consult with your attorney before buying a foreclosure.

• *Parties in Possession:* This exception means that any rights or claims of parties that currently possess the property and are not recorded in the public records will not be covered by the insurance policy. To protect yourself from this, especially from the rights of someone who is wrongfully in possession of the property, have the property surveyed. This can determine whether any part of the property is currently in the possession of a third party.

• *Survey Exception:* This can include any rights or claims of parties in possession; easements or claims of easements not shown by public records; boundary line disputes; overlaps or encroachments; and any matters not of record that could be exposed by a survey and inspection. Simply by having the land surveyed and inspected, you can protect yourself against such an exception.

• *Mechanics' Liens:* These can be tricky because they may not appear on the record even if they exist. Mechanics' liens take effect when construction or improvement work starts, but aren't recorded until the work is finished but not paid for by the owner. This type of exception means that the insurance will not cover any lien or right to a lien for services, labor, or materials for any prior or subsequent development. However, some insurance companies may provide coverage if the seller guarantees against mechanics' liens and if both buyer and seller have proper documentation in place.

• *State or Federal Tax Liens, Judgments, Bankruptcy:* Any taxes, assessments, and judicial proceedings not shown as existing liens in public records will not be covered by the title insurance. It is a good idea to get a warranty from the seller that no such proceedings exist. Notice of default is important. In bankruptcy proceedings, a title insurance company will usually hold insurance until a court order is filed that removes the property from the bankruptcy court's jurisdiction.

Analyzing and understanding the title report early in the due diligence process can save a great deal of time and energy later in the acquisition process.

Environmental Concerns

Another very important contingency to include in your offer is one regarding the property's environmental condition. This is a crucial part of your due diligence. If you don't become familiar with your building's entire environmental history, you could end up liable for any previous problems that still exist. The following story is an example of what can go wrong if you don't investigate a property thoroughly.

Case No. 26
Allison and Antonio
Allison had always wanted to own her own restaurant. She was finally in a position financially that allowed her to start realizing her dream. She began

looking for a unique space to house her gourmet restaurant and wine bar. Because she believed that a new building wouldn't have the character she desired, she started looking in an older section of town.

It was there that she fell in love with a charming brick building located right on the edge of the river. From the moment she saw the place, she knew its old charm would provide the perfect backdrop for her restaurant. To her surprise, the price was lower than she had imagined. The seller, Antonio, was motivated to sell because of a divorce.

Antonio was in such a hurry to sell that he offered Allison a discounted price if she could have her inspection performed within fifteen days. Allison was initially uncomfortable with this short time frame, but she didn't want to lose the building, or the great price. She agreed to Antonio's stipulation and made her offer.

A quick inspection was performed, and Allison was satisfied that no structural problems were found in the building. Although the inspection process was not as thorough as she would have hoped, Allison felt she could take care of any problems that might arise with the extra money she would be saving.

A few months later, as she was painting the bathroom for her restaurant's upcoming opening, she noticed a strange smell. She decided it was probably just because the building was so old, but she made arrangements to have someone come in to check out the pipes.

What they found was worse than Allison could have ever imagined. The sewage tank was as old as the building itself. It had never been replaced or updated, and now it was leaking. Sewage was seeping into the ground below the restaurant and out into the river. Worse yet, the previous tenant was a dry-cleaning business. Instead of properly disposing of their hazardous solvents, they had simply poured them down the drain into the sewage tank.

The rotting sewage tank had been breached and was now leaking into the river. Dozens of children who had spent the summer months swimming downstream from the restaurant became ill. When doctors discovered the pattern, the city began testing the water in the river. Sure enough, they found sewage in the water and traced it back to Allison's building and its disintegrating tank.

Even though Allison had been unaware of damage, the town's residents were outraged. Allison paid to have the tank replaced, but then she faced lawsuits that the insurance company would not cover. She was forced to sell the building, with its new sewage tank, just to pay the settlements. By the time the nightmare was over, she had lost so much that she was never able to realize her dream of owning a restaurant.

HOW TO PROTECT YOURSELF

Allison was held strictly liable because she was the responsible party. The fact that there was hazardous waste on her property was all that had to be proved. There is strict liability in such cases, meaning that guilt or innocence is not the issue, but rather ownership. If waste is found on property you own, you are liable.

Federal law recognizes four classes of parties responsible for cleanup of hazardous waste:

1. The current owner and operator of the property.
2. The owner and operator of the property at the time the waste was deposited.
3. Those who generated the waste and sent it to the site.
4. Those who transported the waste to the site.

In our example, Allison is a liable party because she is the current owner. She could sue the dry cleaner, but he had died suddenly with no money to his name.

So what could she have done differently to protect herself? She should have had state-licensed engineers perform a Phase I environmental report, a survey of the potential environmental problems on the property. In a Phase I report, the engineers will either find no problems and record that in writing or will find a problem and suggest a more detailed Phase II report.

If you are unable to get a clean Phase I report on a property, it is probably not something you want to get involved in anyway. Banks most likely won't loan money for a property that does not have a clean Phase I report.

The importance of having a clean Phase I report is that it can protect you if a problem should arise in the future. You have a good argument that because you had an engineer inspect the property and the property was found to be clean at that time, you had no notice of any problems. If Allison had

had her property inspected by engineers, either they would have found the problem and she could have backed out of the deal—or she would have had a clean Phase I report that would have proved she was unaware of the problem and it had occurred after the inspection.

Keep in mind that you will also be held liable for any environmental hazard caused by your tenants. This means if one of your renters runs a methamphetamine lab out of your apartment building, you will be responsible for a toxic cleanup. This is just one important reason why you should know exactly who your tenants are and what they are doing in your building.

Refer to Appendix C for a checklist of environmental documents you should review before you purchase any property. Also found in Appendix C are other checklists of items to be reviewed during your due diligence process. While these checklists are not comprehensive and are not intended to be the only resource you use to the exclusion of all others, they provide a guideline to begin the review of your property. Checklists can be used to remind you and your broker to deal with items you may have overlooked. The more investigation you conduct on your property, the more likely it is that you will be completely satisfied with your purchase.

Chapter 27

Real-Life
Selection Stories

In preparation for this book, we spoke with many people involved in all aspects of real estate investing. In this section, we have even included the personal experience of one of the authors, Garrett Sutton. We figured the best way for you to learn is to gain insight from the mistakes and successes of others.

Garrett's Story: Selecting Properties, Selecting Managers

My first foray into real estate investing began by accident. Although I was licensed as a California real estate broker for many years, I personally had never held property for investment purposes. I did own a small starter house in a pleasant Reno neighborhood, but soon after my marriage and the birth of our first child, we decided we would need something bigger. We realized that after all the broker's fees and transfer fees we were going to lose money if we sold the house. So we decided to rent the place out.

Our first tenant was the type that always had a creative excuse for why he was late with his rent payments. This came as a shock because whenever I had rented places, I never turned in a late payment. My parents had instilled in me the value of timeliness, and here I was, landlord to someone who could not care less about being on time. As a lawyer I had spent years listening to other people's problems and lack of follow-through on contracts. However, this situation was becoming personally annoying because I still had a mortgage to pay.

On top of it all, I realized I didn't have enough time to deal with any of it. I felt I would be better off hiring a management company to take care of the details while I spent my time working to earn my own money. I figured it would be worth the fee they charged to get rid of some of the hassle. After interviewing several companies, I chose one with a good reputation around town as well as a reasonable fee structure. The company charged 10 percent of the gross rental revenues, but would take care of the bills, arrange repairs, and line up new, and hopefully responsible, tenants. When I calculated the value of the time I spent managing the place on my own, I was paying twice the amount the management company charged. Everything became so much simpler. In fact, the only contact I have with the company is a monthly statement.

However, for some reason, when it came time to purchase my next property, I had forgotten my lesson about the value of property managers. I figured that with the bigger property, I could manage it myself and hold on to all of the gross rents.

So the bookkeeper and I now had the duties of lining up vendors and handling repairs, paying bills and collecting rents, handling the bookkeeping, setting up new leases, and doing everything else involved with managing such a property.

Now instead of just one excuse every month, I received many, including:

"I am an artist. I don't pay rent."

"The bartender took all my money."

"The Raiders lost again."

"My wife met my girlfriend."

Again, for someone who lives with a fairly strict view of timeliness and fulfillment of obligations, these casual, half-baked excuses were maddening. More than once I asked, "Am I a landlord or a life skills counselor?"

The last straw, when my lesson was finally learned for good, was when a tenant called my law office and insisted that I be pulled out of a meeting. As I got on the phone, she demanded that I come down to the building right away. When I asked what the problem was, she explained that someone had left laundry in the dryer, and since she didn't know whether the laundry was sanitary, she would not touch it. She wanted me to come remove the laundry from the dryer myself.

That afternoon I began interviewing management companies.

How to Select and Use Property Management Companies

The previous story was not included to advise that everyone use a property manager. Some people enjoy the one-on-one interaction and maintenance of a rental property and feel a sense of pride about doing it themselves. Certainly, some will save a great deal of money by managing their own real estate. But for others, for whom a management company will actually save money and headaches, there are some guidelines to follow when selecting a company. The following are key elements to consider when selecting a management company:

- *Local Reputation and References:* Since the company you choose will be handling your money, it is important that it be trustworthy and well respected around town.
- *Vendor and Service Contracts:* Many management companies have strong relationships with vendors and service providers. This may result in lower costs for maintenance and upkeep than you would be able to find on your own.
- *Market Knowledge:* You want your management company to know what the local market will bear in terms of rents.

With a field narrowed by using the recommendations above, now you can do more in-depth investigation into the company's management contracts. Items to consider include:

- *Compensation for Services:* Management companies usually charge a percentage of the gross rental receipts, ranging from 5 percent to 10 percent.

If they receive a percentage, this gives them extra incentive to keep all the units full.

• *Duties and Responsibilities:* Make sure the contract clearly defines who is responsible for what. What do you, as an owner, want to be involved in, and what do you want to leave to the managers exclusively?

• *The Term and Termination Clauses:* You will want the option to give thirty days' notice to the company and be able to move on if you are not satisfied with their management of your property.

• *Spending Issues:* This will define how much the managers can spend without consulting with the owner. You will want to approve any large repairs and improvements.

• *Special Contract Issues:* Read the contract for any catches or small print. If a management company asks for a percentage of the brokerage commission if you decide to sell the building, either get the clause removed or use a different company.

• *Reports:* As the owner you will want to receive regular reports detailing income, expenses, and reserves.

After contracting with a management company, give them a few months to get settled. Then you will need to craft a system to analyze their performance. You can measure their success by the following:

- A lower vacancy rate
- Greater return to the owner
- Better collections
- Lower turnover
- Fewer complaints
- Better condition

If you take the time to choose the management company that works best for you and your property, it can benefit everyone involved.

Landbanking

Landbanking is an area of real estate that can yield impressive profits for the patient, prudent investor. As its hybrid name suggests, landbanking means banking land. It is the process of buying and holding land for future sale or development.

When it comes to the small investor, landbanking almost always means finding a parcel of pre-development land and holding on to it until its market value has reached the point at which the parcel will yield a handsome profit by selling it to a builder. The objective, therefore, isn't cash flow, but appreciation. Overhead for the investment is largely limited to the basic upkeep of the property and payment of taxes. Managing the investment mainly involves keeping tabs on the market and, when the time is right, advertising the property and fielding offers.

The parcel typically suited for landbanking meets three primary criteria:

1. It has no construction on it—as with agricultural or raw unimproved land.
2. It is in the direct path of urban growth and stands to attract a buyer within three to ten years.
3. It is zoned for residential, commercial, or industrial development, or is a candidate for such zoning.

There are many other factors for the landbanker to consider before purchasing a parcel. But the strategy is straightforward: buying land in an area where the population growth is pushing out with steady pressure from the metropolitan and suburbs; holding the land until builders are eager to construct houses, shopping centers, warehouses, or the like.

The returns on a parcel of land purchased when the market is cool, and sold when the market turns hot, typically exceed returns in the stock market. This is because good land is finite. Even in the large United States, there is only so much empty land fit to build on, and more of it can't be created. Yet the need for land on which to build remains constant because the population is increasing steadily. That means more demand for homes and everything that comes with residential subdivisions: retail stores and other businesses, office buildings, schools, parks, houses of worship, governmental services. Savvy investors who buy raw land fit for construction on the outskirts of booming urban areas position themselves to reap large profits.

As well, the savvy investor of moderate means can't afford land in the center of an urban area. But the outskirts are fair territory for speculation.

What's more, those who study American demographics predict that by 2040, ten "megapolitan" areas will hold most of the nation's population. These "megalopolises" will result from major cities and towns growing together—with the undeveloped spaces between them filling up with population.

Still, there are a number of pitfalls to avoid when searching for land to bank. Promotional ads for underdeveloped real estate have lured naive or overly optimistic investors for ages. Many buy land sight unseen, charmed by promotional advertisements and fast-talking hucksters. This game is constant, and parcels set in woods, prairie or sunbaked desert wastes, or even (as the cliché goes) swampland, where no city, suburb, or vacation resort will ever sprout, are churned on the market daily.

The biggest key to successful landbanking is performing thorough due diligence before buying a parcel. This means researching the area and its growth pattern, influx of businesses (such as Wal-Mart), and the city or county master plan. As we have discussed, when it comes to the specific parcel, due diligence means reviewing a preliminary title report on the property. The research can even involve having soil samples analyzed to ensure the property can be built on. Experienced landbankers often engage brokers to perform much of this work.

As with other real estate investments, location and timing are key. So is leverage. Three sources of financing for landbankers are bank loans, seller financing, and partnering with other investors. Land is a less liquid asset than structures, so banks typically lend 30 percent to 50 percent of the value of a parcel. For parcels several years away from development, sellers may carry 80 percent to 90 percent of the buyer's financing. A landbanker also can recruit investment partners, organized under a limited partnership or limited liability company.

One excellent guide for landbankers is the book *Pay Dirt: How the Individual Investor Can Bank Land for Great Profit and Avoid Shams, Scams and Worthless Real Estate,* by veteran landbanker Darren K. Proulx (SuccessDNA, 2006).

Tips from Experienced Real Estate Brokers

George and Gayle are real estate brokers who specialize in Lake Tahoe properties and invest for themselves around the western United States. Over the

years, they have developed their own set of guidelines they have found useful in helping their clients.

The first thing they believe every potential investor should clarify is the
stage of real estate investing they are in as well as what they'd like to accomplish with their real estate. For example, George and Gayle advise their older
clients to buy property that will bring them cash flow. However, they work
with younger clients differently. If they are just starting out in real estate,
they have time to reap the rewards of long-term appreciation. These clients
are also more likely than older, more established ones to buy a place that
needs lots of improvements or sweat equity.

Once you have decided where you and your investment goals fit into this
picture, here are some other pointers from George and Gayle:

• When you are considering purchasing a property, a rule of thumb is
to see if the monthly rents equal 1 percent of the purchase price. Following this rule, a property on the market for $330,000 must be able to gener-
ate monthly rents of about $3,300 for this to be a sound investment for
you.

• Talk to everyone you know about real estate. It is always a good topic
for discussion, and you can actually learn a lot and even find deals simply
from talking to others.

• If you have a choice between investing in an older, established neighborhood or a brand-new suburban development, choose the older neighborhood. The homes there will have more character and charm that cannot
be replicated. Homes in the suburbs are a dime a dozen.

• Buy into the best neighborhood that you can reasonably afford.

• Even if you hear that Miami Beach is *the* place to invest, if you can't
get there easily and regularly and you aren't familiar with the market, you will
be more successful investing close to your home base.

• Look at every potential property like you were going to resell it.
What type of improvements would you have to make? If you were to purchase it, would it be economical to make these improvements in order to
sell it later?

• Also look at every property from the perspective of a tenant. Is it close
to shopping, transportation, etc.? Would the type of tenants you want to rent
to find the property suitable for their needs? If not, could you improve it so it

would attract your ideal tenant? Also keep in mind that the lower the rent, the larger the pool of potential tenants you will attract.

- Get started in real estate investing as early as possible.

- Hold on to a property that is appreciating—don't sell. If you can, refinance the property and use the loan proceeds to buy your next property.

- Be careful when considering condominium units. Don't buy if 70 percent or more are not owner-occupied. In these situations, there may be little pride of ownership in the area.

- Also remember that with condominiums, you will have to pay association fees. Consider whether this money would be better spent on a larger mortgage payment.

- Invest near colleges or universities. Although there inherently will be some damage done to the property with this group, you can be assured you won't have much trouble finding tenants.

- If you are trying to choose between a two-bedroom, one-bathroom home and one with three bedrooms and two bathrooms, choose the latter. Two-bedroom, one-bathroom homes are always harder to sell.

In addition to these guidelines that can be put to use anywhere, become knowledgeable about your city's own regulations regarding rent, such as the existence of rent control measures. When looking for a real estate broker, it can be helpful if the broker owns investment properties of his or her own. This way, they have an especially clear understanding of what is involved and can even share some of the lessons they have learned in their own experiences.

George and Gayle like to share one of their personal experiences with their clients. Several years ago they were considering buying a home in Truckee, California, for $150,000. Although they knew it was a great deal, the property also needed $5,000 of plumbing work done on it. While they liked the location and look of the property, the couple was apprehensive about paying the plumbing expense right after the purchase. So instead, they bought a house in a nearby, albeit lesser, neighborhood for $125,000. Years later their investment was a sound one—they recently sold the house for $250,000, doubling their money. However, the house they passed up sold soon after their own—for $550,000. From this experience, they learned to look at the bigger overall picture when investing. Had they not overanalyzed their purchase years ago, they would have made a phenomenal return, even after paying for that plumbing work. Learn to respect your own judgment and intuition about a property.

Conclusion

You now have the foundation you need to start investing in real estate. We have shared the tax, legal, and selection strategies that successful investors use to select, protect, and maximize their real estate. Put these to use to build your own portfolio of real estate that can help secure financial freedom for you and your family.

As a real estate investor, your learning never ends. You should always strive for more knowledge, especially since many laws that affect you are constantly changing. For this reason, we have included a resource section in Appendix A with links to up-to-date content on the most current real estate information.

Remember to build a great team around you and continue to update your real estate knowledge. We wish you the best of luck in your investing.

SHARON LECHTER
GARRETT SUTTON

Appendix A

Rich Dad's Real Estate Resources

BOOKS

OPM—Other People's Money
  by Michael Lechter, Esq.
Own Your Own Corporation
  by Garrett Sutton, Esq.
Rich Dad's ABCs of Real Estate Investing
  by Ken McElroy
Rich Dad's ABCs of Writing Winning Business Plans
  by Garrett Sutton, Esq.
*Pay Dirt: How the Individual Investor Can Bank Land for Great Profit
  and Avoid Shams, Scams, and Worthless Real Estate*
  by Darren K. Proulx
*Exchanging Up: How to Build a Real Estate Empire Without Paying
  Taxes . . . Using 1031 Exchanges*
  by Gary Gorman, 1031 Exchange Expert
How To Use Limited Liability Companies & Limited Partnerships
  by Garrett Sutton, Esq.
Rich Dad's ABCs of Getting Out of Debt
  by Garrett Sutton, Esq.

GAMES

Rich Dad's CASHFLOW 101 Board Game and electronic game
Rich Dad's CASHFLOW 202 Board Game and electronic game

PROGRAMS

How to Increase the Income from Your Investments
6 Steps to Becoming a Successful Real Estate Investor
Rich Dad's Teach to Be Rich
Rich Dad's You Can Choose to Be Rich
How to Get Your Banker to Say "Yes!"
  CD: Robert Kiyosaki with Scott McPherson
How to Find—and Keep—Great Tenants
  CD: Robert Kiyosaki with Ken McElroy
How to Find Great Investments
  CD: Robert Kiyosaki with Sharon Lechter and Kim Kiyosaki
Rich Dad's INSIDERS

ON-LINE RESOURCES:

www.sutlaw.com	Sutton Law Center
www.expert1031.com	The 1031 Exchange Experts
www.creonline.com	Creative Real Estate Online
www.corporatedirect.com	Corporate Direct
www.nmhc.org	National Multi Housing Council
www.realtor.org	National Assn of Realtors
www.narpm.org	National Apartment Managers Assn
www.american-apartment-owners-association.org	American Apartment Owners Assn
http://www.richdad.com/community/join_insiders/insidersgetmore.asp	Rich Dad's INSIDERS

Appendix B

Frequently Asked Questions

Should my corporation hold real estate?

As a general rule, no. For tax reasons we don't recommend that you ever hold real estate in the name of a C corporation. Your C corporation will pay considerably more in capital gains when you try to sell that property than would a flow-through entity, such as an S corporation or an LLC (limited liability company). If your S corporation is holding the property and you are sued personally, a judgment creditor may be able to reach your shares in the S corporation and effectively take control of those shares and, through them, control of the S corporation and its assets. As well, the debt of an S corporation is not part of a shareholder's basis, thus reducing write-offs. Futhermore, transferring property out of an S corporation is a taxable event whereas it is not taxable in an LLC or LP. For these reasons we recommend that real estate be held in either an LLC or a limited partnership (LP).

Even if it doesn't own it, can I use my corporation to buy real estate?

Yes. One method is to have your corporation pay rent for an office building that you own, held in an LLC. The rent paid by the corporation is a tax deduction for the business and the income from the rent is offset by operating expenses as well as the phantom expense of depreciation. This strategy is discussed in Chapter 14.

What type of entity should I hold property in?

We recommend using either an LLC or an LP. Both offer flow-through income and taxation opportunities, and both offer excellent asset protection. In

Wyoming and Nevada, for example, legislation prohibits creditors of an LLC or LP from directly seizing assets of either type of entity. Instead, judgment creditors must secure their judgment against the LLC or limited partnership by way of the charging order procedure.

What is a charging order?

A charging order is, in essence, a lien filed against the LLC or limited partnership's earnings. When profit allocations are made by either entity to their members or partners, a portion would be paid to the judgment creditor to pay down the judgment. Having a charging order placed against an LLC or a limited partnership in many states does not convey voting rights, so creditors cannot take control of the entity and, through that control, reach the assets. It is important to organize in a state such as Nevada or Wyoming which has strong charging order protections instead of a state such as California which has virtually no protection. In addition, in a situation where the entity is profitable but management decides that the profit needs to be reinvested into the entity, no distributions of profit will be made at all. However, the IRS will consider each member of the LLC (or limited partner, in a limited partnership) to have received their share of the profits and will tax them on those phantom profits accordingly. So for a creditor, not receiving a cash distribution and being taxed on the distribution it did not receive is doubly annoying. Holding real property in either of these entities can be a great deterrent against nuisance litigation and claims.

What is a family limited partnership?

There is no such entity as a family limited partnership; there are limited partnerships that hold family assets. Beware of promoters touting the benefits of "FLPs." There is no such entity under state law. A limited partnership is all you need. (And it's all that really exists anyway.)

Should I set up an LLC for each piece of property?

That depends on your comfort level. Remember, the more properties you hold in a single entity, the more risk your income being affected in the event of a lawsuit. For example, if you hold five rental properties in a single LLC and that LLC is sued by the tenant in property number 3, all of the assets of the LLC could become negatively affected. Many people will prefer to have just one property, not all five, in each LLC, thus limiting the exposure of other assets to any one claim.

At the very least be careful about putting properties from different states into the same LLC. Because the properties are earning income, you will have to register them to do business in each state where the property is located, and adhere to local state taxation laws. So, if you have property in a very tax-aggressive state, you may find yourself in a situation where that state attempts to tax your earnings from all of your properties, not just the property located in that state.

Will a land trust give me the asset protection I need?

Not necessarily. A land trust is a great vehicle for privacy because it allows you to name another individual, company, or entity as the trustee, keeping your name off the public records and keeping the ownership of the land private. However, a land trust is not a corporate entity—it does not have a separate and distinct court-recognized existence—and so you remain personally liable for any injuries, problems, environmental issues, hazardous waste, or other problems related to the property held in the land trust. Even worse, a creditor can reach through and take your interest in a land trust, effectively taking it from you to satisfy a judgment against you. Neither can you claim at trial that you don't own the property held by a land trust. Because you are the beneficial owner of the land trust you are the beneficial owner of the land. However, a land trust owned by an LLC offers both privacy and asset protection, and can be a good strategy.

What are the benefits of holding property in a trust as opposed to an LLC?

There are many types of trusts. A living trust is a common estate planning vehicle that offers probate avoidance but no asset protection. In such a case, the real estate is best titled in the name of the LLC with the member interests owned by the living trust. When one party passes away, the LLC membership interests are transferred according to the terms of the trust but the property does not have to be retitled, since the LLC continues to own it.

Another trust is the spendthrift trust, an irrevocable vehicle set up by parents for their children. The assets of the trust may not be reached by later creditors, thus protecting immature and free-spending kids from themselves. Because an independent trustee administers the property until it is distributed, a greater measure of control is achieved. However, overall, such trusts pay higher taxes than LLCs and may not be advisable for strong income properties.

Should I put my family home into an LLC?

Yes. The IRS in recent years has liberalized its rules to make single member LLCs an excellent means for receiving both asset protection and the tax benefits of home ownership. Before using an LLC you will analyze whether your state's homestead laws offer acceptable asset protection. In Texas and Florida the protection is unlimited, thus minimizing the need for a primary residence LLC. In California the homestead exemption is only $75,000, thus increasing the attractiveness of a primary residence LLC.

Can I write off repairs done to my own house?

You cannot deduct the repair costs for your personal residence. But the costs of repairs or improvements for your home office are a deduction.

What can I do with my home office in the basement?

Consider renting that portion of your home to the business as a home office. There needs to be exclusive business purpose on that part of your home (in other words, that space is not merely a part of the dining room) and the space needs to be used in your business. It should be noted that you would only rent and not sell a part of the house to the business. Selling would involve complicated and burdensome title issues.

When a rental property is not rented, can I take that as a loss of income?

The expenses of operating the rental property including the advertising costs are still expenses. You cannot take a loss for lost revenue. You do not pay tax or receive a loss on something you don't receive.

Can I set up a management company to manage my own properties?

Yes. While you cannot be a limited partner or nonmanaging member in an LP or an LLC, respectively, and receive management fees, a separate C corporation, S corporation, or LLC may be established to assume management duties.

Can we use our vacation home as a corporate retreat for our corporation?

Your corporation can pay a fair market value of rent for the time used as a legitimate meeting place. For more on vacation home taxation see Chapter 12.

I bought an apartment complex yesterday but don't have an LLC set up yet. The loan is in my name. Is it difficult to transfer title after the fact?

The transfer itself is fairly easy, and may be done by way of a warranty deed or quit claim deed, which is prepared and filed at the local county recorder's office where the property is located. The lender's acceptance of this may be an issue. Many mortgages have a triggering clause (called a due on sale clause) that requires the entire mortgage to be repaid if title to the property changes hands. Although you are still ultimately the owner of the property, as you own the entity and you have not sold the property but merely transferred it, as far as your bank or lender may be concerned, the property has be retitled and the mortgage repayment clause triggered.

Some banks will work with you on this—they still have your personal guarantee and a security interest in the property—while others will not, as they mistakenly think you are trying to hide assets. If your lender fits into the second category consider finding a new lender. There are companies, such as llcloan.com, that specialize in asset protection loans for real estate investors.

What is the best way to protect myself against liability for my rental properties?

We believe that a comprehensive insurance package, combined with holding the entity in an asset-protecting entity such as an LLC or a limited partnership, is the best way to go. By holding your rental properties in a good entity, such as an LLC or limited partnership, you can protect yourself personally from claims of tenants or creditors. And, with a good comprehensive insurance package, you can protect your entity from the claims of others, or from certain disasters such as fire or flooding, and ensure that you will have the money to rebuild, if necessary.

If I live in California but own property in Nevada, can I set up a Nevada company?

Absolutely. Nevada has no residency requirements for people or entities who want to use Nevada entities to operate their real estate businesses. However, bear in mind that as a California resident, and assuming you hold your property in a flow-through entity such as an LLC or limited partnership, the income flowing back to you in California will be subject to California state tax.

Assuming my investment property is held in an LLC, can this be given to my spouse upon my death?

Yes. It can be done in many ways, from passing through in your will, being transferred pursuant to a living trust, or by holding your LLC interests as joint tenants with right of survivorship (JTROS). If you choose the JTROS or living trust route, upon your passing away the investment property will automatically be transferred to your spouse or other named beneficiary, saving the problem of having your estate probated before title can be transferred.

What type of repairs are deductible for a rental unit?

Expenses that are incurred to repair an item like fixing a leaky faucet or repairing a handrail on a stairway are deductible in the year paid. Expenses that are incurred that extend the life or improve the property must be capitalized and then depreciated. Examples of capitalizable items would be a complete new roof (as opposed to fixing a hole in the roof) or a room addition.

What are the benefits of an LLC compared to an LP for holding real estate?

The LLC provides for limited liability for all owners (members) whereas an LP only has limited liability for the limited partner. The general partner of an LP would have full liability. This can be easily overcome by forming a second corporation or LLC to serve as the general partner. In states with extra taxes on LLCs, such as California and Texas, the use of LPs (even though two entities are required for complete protection) is common.

Do I have to have a real estate license to be considered a real estate professional?

No, you do not need to be a licensed real estate agent in order to be considered a real estate professional. The test for real estate professional status relates to the hours you work in the real estate capacity in proportion to other work you do. If you work more hours in real estate activities, and a minimum of 750 hours per year, then you likely qualify as a real estate professional.

Can I write real estate losses off from one piece of property against the income of another?

As long as both properties are similar, such as both are rental properties in which you actively participate, then the loss against one can offset the income from another. If they are dissimilar, such as in the case of a motel operation (which is considered an active trade business) and a piece of property held for future development, they cannot offset.

I have heard of phantom deductions and paper losses related to real estate investing. What are they?

The term phantom deductions relates to the deductions for depreciation or amortization. The government allows you to write off your cost basis for certain assets over an established useful life for those assets. For instance, if you purchase an apartment house for an investment, the tax laws allow you to write off your cost ratably over 27.5 years (39 years for commercial property). This recognizes that as a building ages it will need repair and you will have to spend money to keep it functional. Depreciation is a non-cash deduction.

The term paper losses means the loss you show on a real estate property after deducting the depreciation. For instance you may have positive cash flow from your apartment building of $15,000, this is your net income before depreciation. After you deduct your depreciation of $25,000, you have a paper loss of $10,000. Your phantom deduction is $25,000 resulting in a paper loss of $10,000.

What does depreciation recapture mean?

When you sell certain property, whether personal or real estate, that you have depreciated, and received a benefit from that depreciation, the tax law may require you to report part of your income (equal to the depreciation you have taken and benefited from) as ordinary income taxed at a higher level than the capital gains tax rate. This is called the recapture of depreciation. Consult your tax advisor as to the possibility of depreciation recapture because it may make a big impact on your after-tax income. In certain circumstances, you may be able to "roll over" your gain on real estate through a 1031 exchange which can defer your gain further into the future. See Chapter 10 on Tax-Free Exchanges.

In other Rich Dad products you don't include the tax effect of a particular real estate investment when you analyze them. Why not?

In reviewing a particular real estate investment, we want to make sure that the property will generate a positive cash flow for you before you consider the tax effect. If it gives you a positive cash flow each month, then the added benefit of the tax impact is a bonus! It will also increase your already positive cash-on-cash return. If the property has a negative cash flow each month and is only positive after you factor in the tax impact, you will have to find a way to fund that negative cash flow each month until you can realize the delayed cash flow from the tax impact.

I have heard I can pay my kids and get a tax benefit. Is it true?

Yes, there is a provision that allows you to hire your children and receive a tax benefit. They are most likely in a lower tax bracket and will therefore be taxed at a lower tax rate. However, there are specific requirements that you must meet, to qualify for this benefit. For example, the amount of pay must be reasonable, your children must actually perform the specified duties, and your business must not be incorporated. Please consult your tax advisor to make sure you comply with these requirements.

If I form all of these entities, one for each property, aren't my expenses for the tax returns going to be high?

If you hold your property in a single owner LLC (in most states married couples or their living trust owning an LLC together qualify as a single owner LLC) then the income and expenses of the LLC can be reported on your personal tax return. You have the benefit of asset protection provided by the LLC and the benefit of filing a single tax return, instead of separate returns for each entity.

Can I write off all my future vacations if I am a real estate investor?

You must follow certain guidelines that your tax professional can explain to you. What is the primary purpose for the trip? What are the facts and circumstances of each trip? Are you really looking at potential real estate investments? Keep accurate records of your activities.

Several of the Rich Dad products say that the income from real estate is taxed at 0 percent, how can that be true?

As in the example above, you can often reduce your taxes on real estate income to zero through the ability to deduct depreciation against your real estate income. This is actually a deferral of income tax as you may have to recapture the depreciation when you sell the property. However, you may be able to defer this tax for a very long time through exchanging your properties for larger properties utilizing the 1031 exchange.

You refer to a capital gain tax of 15 percent, I thought it was higher.

The Jobs and Growth Tax Relief Reconciliation Act of 2003 lower the tax rate on capital gains to 15 percent through 2010. You must pay attention to the tax laws in your tax planning as to what tax rates will be effective when you plan on selling. Plus you must consider the state capital gains tax rates in addition to the Federal rates.

Rich Dad seems to be against flipping. Is it true?

The Rich Dad philosophy favors cash flow investing for real estate investors and this is primarily due to the difference in the income tax treatment between flippers and cash flow investors. Some people use flipping as a strategy

to raise capital with the intent to invest for cash flow. Just be sure to understand the tax implications of your strategy.

At what point should I consider forming an LLC or LP to hold my properties?

Preferably before acquiring the real estate, since you will want title to be held
in the name of the LLC or LP. If you already own real estate you should take
the steps to form an LLC or LP posthaste. Information on this process can be
obtained at www.sutlaw.com.

Appendix C
Useful Real Estate Checklists

A review of the information on these checklists as it relates to your transaction will provide you with the background necessary to either walk away or purchase with confidence. Please note that these checklists are not intended to be comprehensive, nor applicable to every transaction; rather, they should serve as starting points for your own due diligence review.

Buyer Disclosure Checklist
Owner Information

- ☐ Name, address, phone number, business number
- ☐ Reason for selling
- ☐ Occupation
- ☐ If owner broker/agent

Loan Information

- ☐ Name/address of lender
- ☐ Is current loan assumable? If yes, with or without qualification?
- ☐ Name title vested in
- ☐ Loan number
- ☐ Asking price
- ☐ Assessed value of property
- ☐ Interest rate
- ☐ Closing costs
- ☐ Current loan amount/dates

- ☐ Balance of current loan
- ☐ Is loan assumable?
- ☐ Discounts available for loan prepayment?
- ☐ If second can be discounted, if any
- ☐ If balloon payment/amount due/when

- ☐ If prepayment penalty
- ☐ Will seller help finance/pay points?
- ☐ Yearly tax amount
- ☐ New loan amount
- ☐ Length of loan
- ☐ Monthly payment amount
- ☐ Insurance costs/requirements
- ☐ Home guarantee?
- ☐ CC&Rs (covenants, conditions, restrictions)
- ☐ Move-in date
- ☐ How long on market
- ☐ If previously listed/length of time

Fees

- ☐ Application
- ☐ Appraisal
- ☐ Loan fee
- ☐ Inspections/pest, structure
- ☐ Recording fee

- ☐ Credit report
- ☐ Escrow fee
- ☐ Points
- ☐ Title report/insurance
- ☐ Insurance

Property

- ☐ Legal description of property
- ☐ Zoning of property
- ☐ Proximity of schools
- ☐ Extent of landscaping
- ☐ Sprinkler system/type
- ☐ Inspection report/environmental concerns

- ☐ Square footage of lot
- ☐ Location of property
- ☐ Easy access to shopping
- ☐ Size of yards/front and back
- ☐ Fences/condition of

Building

- ☐ Age of structure
- ☐ Number of stories

- ☐ Type and condition of roof

- ☐ Number of rooms
- ☐ Square footage of structure
- ☐ Condition of wiring
- ☐ Gas or electric heating/condition of
- ☐ Alarm system? Owned or leased? If leased, will it remain in home after sale?
- ☐ Kitchen amenities/condition of
- ☐ Utility costs/heating costs
- ☐ Condition of carpeting
- ☐ Number of bathrooms
- ☐ Inventory of what included/ draperies, etc.
- ☐ Garage/size/condition

- ☐ What kind of view

- ☐ Builder
- ☐ Condition and type of construction inside and outside
- ☐ Inspection report of structure/ termites, etc.
- ☐ Number of bedrooms
- ☐ Condition of plumbing
- ☐ Condition of foundation
- ☐ Air conditioning/condition of
- ☐ If fireplace/condition of? Has the chimney been cleaned recently?

- ☐ Gas or electric appliances/water heater
- ☐ What kind of flooring
- ☐ Number of bedrooms/square footage
- ☐ Other rooms/description/condition of
- ☐ Number of windows/condition of

- ☐ Insulation up to code/storm windows, doors
- ☐ Any needed repairs

Seller Disclosure Checklist
General/Legal

☐ Home insurance
☐ Previous pest inspection reports
☐ Any additions to building made by current and past owners? Were additions properly permitted?
☐ Restrictions on property
☐ Easements on property
☐ Anyone having right of first refusal or option to buy
☐ Known future problems affecting property
☐ Property owned near this property

☐ Previous inspection reports
☐ Year structure built
☐ Pending legal actions

☐ Liens against property/explain
☐ Is property leased?/when expire
☐ Known conditions affecting property

☐ Pending expansion/real estate development of area
☐ Problems with stability of ground beneath property, settling, cracks in cement/describe

☐ Property in designated zone/flood, hazard, etc., area

Roof

☐ Condition
☐ How old
☐ Any problems/leakage/date

☐ Composition
☐ Any repair/resurfacing/date

Heating/Electrical

☐ Date heating system installed

☐ Condition of heating system
☐ Manner of ventilation/describe
☐ Insulation up to code?
☐ Available voltage
☐ Date of last inspection/service

☐ Kind of heating system/make—gas or electric
☐ Previous heating inspections/date
☐ Acceptable ventilation
☐ Condition of electrical equipment
☐ Known defects/describe

Water/Sewer

☐ Water supply source/city, septic tank
☐ Condition of water supply
☐ Known prior plumbing leaks/rust problems
☐ Any flooding/date, how repaired
☐ Drainage problems/describe

☐ Type of water pipes
☐ Any water pressure problems
☐ Known standing water areas

☐ Adequate drainage/roof, ground
☐ Water heater/condition/age

☐ Capacity of water heater

☐ Location of water heater

☐ What company did inspection
☐ Condition of landscape
sprinklers/describe

☐ Water heater/safety/pressure
release valve
☐ Water heater last date inspected
and/or serviced
☐ Safety device for water heater

Commercial Property Due Diligence Checklist
Objective

☐ Estate building
☐ Tax shelter
☐ Other/description

☐ Equity return
☐ Spendable income/amount

Background Search

☐ Better Business Bureau
☐ Lending institution

☐ Chamber of Commerce
☐ Utility companies

Owner Information

☐ Name, address
☐ Bank reference
☐ Owner occupying property
☐ Attorney/legal status
☐ Amount of capital
☐ Date business was started

☐ Reason for selling
☐ Previously listed/price/time
on market

☐ Business phone/residence phone
☐ Occupation tax bracket
☐ Tax accountant
☐ Broker or real estate agent
☐ Annual gross income
☐ Operating statements for years in
business
☐ How long on market

Lease

☐ Lessee's name
☐ Time left on original lease/option
to renew/rent increased
☐ Rent based on percentage/
how computed
☐ Paid monthly/yearly
☐ Tax clause in lease

☐ Get copies of lease/agreements

☐ Type of lease/original or sublease
☐ Method of computing rent

☐ Rent based on square footage/
building only or frontage included
☐ Option to buy/renew/first refusal
☐ Who performs maintenance/interior,
exterior, landscaping
☐ Copies of contracts/management

Loan

- ☐ Type of loan/loan number
- ☐ Name title vested in
- ☐ Assessed value of property
- ☐ Assumable loan/transferable

- ☐ Will seller help finance?
- ☐ Balance of original loan/ date reported
- ☐ Any liens on property
- ☐ Prepayment penalty

- ☐ Interest rate
- ☐ Lender name and address
- ☐ Type of new loan/dates
- ☐ Can second loan be bought at discount? Amount of discount?
- ☐ Original amount loaned/date
- ☐ Balloon payment?/amount due/when

- ☐ Interest rate locked in?/time
- ☐ Preliminary title report

Building

- ☐ Age of building
- ☐ Condition of basement/foundations
- ☐ How building constructed

- ☐ Square footage

- ☐ Architectural design
- ☐ Exterior finish and condition
- ☐ Adequately view from street or parking lot

Building Interior

- ☐ Number of floors in building
- ☐ Efficient design of space
- ☐ Number of windows
- ☐ Adequate lighting
- ☐ Condition of floors
- ☐ Condition/age of wiring
- ☐ Condition/age of air-conditioning

- ☐ Security patrol/burglar alarms installed
- ☐ Inventory included/description, estimate of value

- ☐ Condition of space
- ☐ Ceiling height
- ☐ Condition of windows
- ☐ Toilet location and number
- ☐ Adequate wiring
- ☐ Condition/age of heating system
- ☐ Fire protection/overhead sprinklers/ number and location

- ☐ Number and condition of locks

Service Costs

- ☐ Services provided by shopping center
- ☐ Water/garbage
- ☐ Security
- ☐ Equipment cost/rental cost, depreciation
- ☐ Accounting/legal fees

- ☐ Heating/air conditioning

- ☐ Electric/gas
- ☐ Insurance
- ☐ Advertising costs

Property

- ☐ Legal description
- ☐ Restrictions
- ☐ Covenants/conditions/restrictions
- ☐ Square footage of property lot
- ☐ Room to expand
- ☐ List of repairs needed
- ☐ Adequate parking
- ☐ Condition of parking lot

- ☐ Survey report
- ☐ Zoning restrictions
- ☐ Map of area showing property plot
- ☐ Storefront footage
- ☐ Inspection report of property
- ☐ Landscaping/condition of
- ☐ Adequate loading area

Location of Property

- ☐ Easy access to building

- ☐ Foot traffic in front of building
- ☐ Population within range of business
- ☐ Condition of streets/neighborhood
- ☐ Nearest closely related business

- ☐ Closeness to main roads/freeway/ bus line
- ☐ Area traffic patterns
- ☐ Estimated income/size of area families
- ☐ Estimated area population growth
- ☐ Category of shopping center

Environmental Due Diligence Checklist
Documents to Review

- ☐ Lot description/square footage
- ☐ Primary use description
- ☐ Regulations/requirements—local, state, federal
- ☐ Complaints by citizens

- ☐ Contracts with disposal services, waste transport
- ☐ Insurance coverage/claims for environmental loss with resolution
- ☐ Pending litigation
- ☐ Judgments, settlement agreements

- ☐ Building description
- ☐ Operating permits
- ☐ Maps, aerial photos, diagrams, technical reports
- ☐ Environmental assessments, Phase I and Phase II reports
- ☐ Reports on produced pollutants

- ☐ Description of noncompliance penalties
- ☐ Environmental violations

Environmental Information with Descriptions

- ☐ Standard Industrial Classification number
- ☐ Manner disposed of
- ☐ Spillage of waste
- ☐ Underground tanks
- ☐ Records of spills/accidents

- ☐ Hazardous waste on property

- ☐ Recycling done
- ☐ Stored materials
- ☐ Known leaks
- ☐ Known contamination to water or ground on this property

☐ Claims against company for shipping waste

☐ Water pollution history

☐ Last site check

☐ Prior claims against owner

☐ All permits

Reports/Permits/Citations

☐ Ownership history/detail

☐ Geotechnical

☐ Water quality

☐ Sanitation Department

☐ Hazardous Material Site characterization

☐ Air quality

☐ Department of Health Services

☐ Environmental Protection Agency

Setting

☐ Type of soil

☐ Soil stains

☐ Destination of surface water runoff

☐ Vegetation—healthy?

☐ Ground water depth

On-Site Facilities Used for/Description and Storage of Chemicals Used

Businesses of:

☐ Dry cleaning

☐ Plant nursery

☐ Gas station

☐ Paint/repair of automobiles

Manufacturing, storing, etc. of:

☐ Copiers

☐ Glue/rubber products

☐ Pesticides/fertilizer

☐ Furniture/wood preservatives

☐ Plastics/foams

☐ Chemicals/explosives

☐ Glass

☐ Semiconductors/electrical devices

☐ Detergent/soap

☐ Paper products/pulp

☐ Jewelry/metal plating or products

☐ Petroleum products

☐ Paint

☐ Auto parts

Sharon Lechter

A life-long education advocate, Sharon Lechter is co-author of the international best-selling book *Rich Dad Poor Dad* and the Rich Dad series of books as well as one of the founders of The Rich Dad Company. She is a CPA, entrepreneur, philanthropist, educator, international speaker and Mom.

She graduated with Magna Cum Laude honors from Florida State University with a degree in accounting, then joined the ranks of a Big Eight accounting firm.Sharon held various management positions with computer, insurance, and publishing companies while maintaining her professional credentials as a CPA.

She has been a pioneer in developing new technologies to bring education into children's lives in ways that are innovative, challenging and fun and remains committed to education – most especially, financial literacy.

"Our current educational system has not been able to keep pace with the global and technological changes in the world today," Sharon states. "We must teach our young people the skills – both scholastic and financial – that they need to not only survive but to flourish in the world."

The Rich Dad Company has grown into an international powerhouse with over 20 books, board games, website, CDs, audio cassettes, seminars, and coaching services. *Rich Dad Poor Dad* has been on *The New York Times* Bestseller List for over 5 years and is available in 45 languages and sold in more than 90 countries.

Sharon's speaking topics range from educating children and adults on taking control of their personal finances to the entrepreneurial business strategies she used in building Rich Dad's international success. She shares the spectacular history of this mega-hit and how *Rich Dad Poor Dad* was originally designed to be only a brochure for their CASHFLOW board game.

A committed philanthropist, Sharon also gives back to the world communities as both a volunteer and a benefactor. She directs the Foundation for Financial Literacy, is an active member of Women's Presidents Organization, and serves on the national board of Childhelp USA, a national organization founded to eradicate child abuse in the United States. In 2002, Childhelp honored Sharon and her husband, Michael, as recipients of that organization's "Spirit of the Children" Award. In 2004, Sharon and Michael were recognized as an Arizona "Power Couple". Sharon was just named as a 2005 Woman of Distinction by the Crohn's & Colitis Foundation of America.

Robert Kiyosaki, her business partner and friend, says "Sharon is one of the few natural entrepreneurs I have ever met. In The Rich Dad Company, I am the horn and Sharon is the engine. My respect for her continues to grow every day that we work together."

About the Authors

Garrett Sutton

Garrett Sutton, Esq., author of *Own Your Own Corporation, The ABC's of Getting Out of Debt, The ABC's of Writing Winning Business Plans,* and *How to Buy and Sell a Business* in the Rich Dad's Advisors series, is an attorney with over twenty-five years experience in assisting individuals and business to determine their appropriate corporate structure, limit their liability, protect their assets and advance their financial, personal and credit success goals.

Garrett and his law firm, Sutton Law Center, have offices in Reno, Nevada, Jackson Hole, Wyoming and Sacramento, California. The firm represents hundreds of corporations, limited liability companies, limited partnerships and individuals in their real estate and business-related law matters, including incorporations, contracts, and ongoing business-related legal advice and accepts new clients. The firm also assists its clients to find and analyze appropriate real estate projects.

Garrett attended Colorado College and the University of California at Berkeley, where he received a B.S. in Business Administration in 1975. He graduated with a J.D. in 1978 from Hastings College of Law, the University of California's law school in San Francisco. He has appeared in the *Wall Street Journal* and other publications. He is the radio host of the nationally syndicated *Entrepreneur Magazine Law & Money Show,* which is archived at www.successdna.com.

Garrett is a member of the State Bar of Nevada, the State Bar of California, and the American Bar Association. He has written numerous professional articles and has served on the Publication Committee of the State Bar of Nevada.

Garrett enjoys speaking with entrepreneurs and real estate investors on the advantages of forming business entities. He is a frequent lecturer for small business groups as well as the Rich Dad's Advisors series.

Garrett serves on the boards of the American Baseball Foundations, located in Birmingham, Alabama, and the Reno, Nevada-based Sierra Kids Foundation.

For more information on Garrett Sutton and Sutton Law Center, please visit his Web site at www.sutlaw.com.

How Can I Protect My Real Estate and Business Assets?

Corporate direct↗

Creating Your Financial Future.®

For information on forming corporations, LLCs and LPs to protect your personal, real estate, and business holdings in all 50 states, visit: www.corporatedirect.com or call toll free 1.800.600.1760. Mention this book for a 5% discount on formation fees.

Where Can I Receive More Legal Information?

SUTTON
LAW CENTER
A PROFESSIONAL CORPORATION

For free information on a variety of legal topics, visit the Sutton Law Center Web site at: www.sutlaw.com.

Join the Rich Dad Revolution...
Raise a Rich Family!

Rich Kid Smart Kid.com

Money is a life skill---but we don't teach our children about money in school. We are asking for your help in getting financial education into the hands of interested teachers and school administrators.

RichKidSmartKid.com was created by The Rich Dad Company as a free innovative and interactive Web site designed to convey key concepts about money and finance in ways that are fun and challenging... and educational for young people in grades K through 12.

Schools around the world may also register at www.richkidsmartkid.com to receive a FREE download of our electronic version of CASHFLOW for Kids at School™.

Join Us

Play CASHFLOW® for KIDS™ and CASHFLOW 101 with family and friends and share the richkidsmartkid.com Web site with your local teachers and school administrators.

By taking financial education to our schools, together we can better prepare our children for the financial world they will face.

Thank you!

Rich Dad's Road to Riches
6 Steps to Becoming a Successful Real Estate Investor

How do succcessful investors find great real estate investments? How do they know good investments from bad investments? The answer is simple – there are six steps that every successful real estate investor follows.

Rich Dad's Roads to Riches is a comprehensive, step-by-step guide that will give you the six steps to becoming a successful real estate investor. This program includes five CDs, a 104-page hands-on workbook, and a bonus gift – Rich Dad's Real Estate Evaluator.

Rich Dad's How to Increase the Income
from Your Real Estate Investments (4 CDs and Checklist)

Are your properties returning you as much money as possible? Would you like to increase your income and reduce your expenses?

The secret to successful real estate investing is property management. This program gives you the secrets of professional property manager Ken McElroy.

This program includes one of the most valuable tools a professional real estate investor needs...

a comprehensive due diligence checklist. Every professional investor must have one of these.